C 13/A

The Case for Mental Imagery

The Case
for Mental Imagery

Stephen M. Kosslyn,
William L. Thompson,
and Giorgio Ganis

OXFORD
UNIVERSITY PRESS

2006

OXFORD
UNIVERSITY PRESS

Oxford University Press, Inc., publishes works that further
Oxford University's objective of excellence
in research, scholarship, and education.

Oxford   New York
Auckland   Cape Town   Dar es Salaam   Hong Kong   Karachi
Kuala Lumpur   Madrid   Melbourne   Mexico City   Nairobi
New Delhi   Shanghai   Taipei   Toronto

With offices in
Argentina   Austria   Brazil   Chile   Czech Republic   France   Greece
Guatemala   Hungary   Italy   Japan   Poland   Portugal   Singapore
South Korea   Switzerland   Thailand   Turkey   Ukraine   Vietnam

Published by Oxford University Press, Inc.
198 Madison Avenue, New York, New York 10016

www.oup.com

Oxford is a registered trademark of Oxford University Press.

Library of Congress Cataloging-in-Publication Data
Kosslyn, Stephen Michael, 1948–
The case for mental imagery / by Stephen M. Kosslyn, William L. Thompson, and Giorgio Ganis.
     p.   cm.—(Oxford psychology series; no. 39)
Includes bibliographical references and index.
ISBN-13: 978-0-19-517908-8
ISBN 0-19-517908-0
1. Imagery (Psychology)   I. Thompson, William L. (William Ladd), 1965–
II. Ganis, Giorgio.   III. Title.   IV. Series.
BF367.K655 2006
153.3'2—dc22   2005014885

9 8 7 6 5 4 3 2 1

Printed in the United States of America
on acid-free paper

Preface

In this book we make the case that mental images depict information and that these depictions play a functional role in human cognition. We have not only tried to summarize the conceptual grounds for positing this species of internal representations but also appealed to many and varied sorts of empirical discoveries. In addition, we have outlined a specific theory of how depictive representations are used in information processing and how they arise from neural processing. We have summarized this theory not to defend our specific formulation but rather to provide an existence proof that such a class of theory can be developed and supported.

This book required us to review the arguments that no "images" of any sort are used in mental processing (e.g., in problem solving, memory, and creativity). We have done our best to present these arguments as clearly and forcefully as possible, making the strongest case we could against depictive images before presenting our refutations. If this book succeeds, it will do so in part because we profited from the labors of many critics and were able to use their writings to guide our defense. Although it may appear awkward to thank those who have caused us so much work over so many years, we recognize that science depends on a dialectic in which only when thesis and antithesis are developed can there be an ultimate synthesis—and thus we wish to express our appreciation to the critics whom we cite in the following pages.

We also wish to thank the people and organizations who made this book possible: Catherine Carlin of the Oxford University Press supported this project in the strongest possible terms; her confidence was (and is) much appreciated. We also thank Laurie Scott for helping us assemble the references and for checking the manuscript with diligence and care; her close reading has improved the coherence and clarity of what we produced. We also thank Massimo Piatelli-Palmarini, Pascal Wallisch, Jonathan Weiss, Daniel Willingham, and an anonymous reviewer, who gave us copious and wise feedback. Andrew Shtulman helped ensure that we responded appropriately to the reviews. We also appreciate the assistance of Danny Bellet and Michael Hoffman. Conversations with Ned Block always proved useful, and we thank him for his time and efforts to set us straight. We also thank Alan Dershowitz for inspiring the title. We also must acknowledge the contributions of all of those who have collaborated with us on work cited and discussed herein; their contributions should not be underestimated.

Next, we must thank the institutions that have made this project possible. This material is based on work supported by the National Science Foundation (Grants REC-0106761 and REC-0411725), the National Institutes of Health (Grants 2 R01 MH060734-05A1 and R21 MH068610A-01A1), the National Space and Biological Research Institute (Grant NCC 9-58-193), the National Geospatial-Intelligence Agency, and the John Simon Guggenheim Memorial Fellowship program. Any opinions, findings, and conclusions or recommendations expressed in this material are those of the authors and do not necessarily reflect the views of the supporting agencies listed here. We also thank the American Psychological Association, Nature Publishing Group, Harvard University Press, and MIT Press for permission to adapt material from earlier publications (as is specifically noted when appropriate).

Finally, we wish to thank our friends and families for the time they allowed us to steal from them in order to invest the effort required to complete this work.

Contents

The Case for Mental Imagery

1

Mental Images and Mental Representations

Do you know which is darker green, a frozen pea or a pine tree? Or what shape are Mickey Mouse's ears? Or the hand in which the Statue of Liberty holds the torch? Most people report that they answer these questions by visualizing the named objects, which allows them to recall the information. Similarly, people report that they use mental imagery to reason about a wide variety of problems. For example, when deciding whether a car can fit into a specific parking space or a jar could squeeze into a gap on the top shelf of a pantry, many people report "projecting" a mental image to discover whether a specific solution would work. As a simple example of such reasoning, please decide whether the uppercase letter *N* would form another letter if it were rotated ninety degrees clockwise. In all of these cases, people report the experience of perceiving, but in the absence of the immediate appropriate sensory input. We take such experiences as a hallmark of the presence of a specific type of mental representation—and in this book we focus on the nature of that species of representation.

At this point, some readers may be puzzled. They may have had no experience of imagery, or they may have had such an experience but wonder how it is relevant to the issue of internal representation. As we shall see, there are many reasons to be uncomfortable with the idea that mental processes make use of any sort of images. In fact, mental imagery was a controversial topic in psychology well before the field split off from philosophy and has remained controversial ever since. First, let us be clear on what we mean by the term *mental image*: in our usage, a mental image occurs when a representation of the type created during the initial phases of perception is present but the stimulus is not actually being perceived; such representations preserve the perceptible properties of the stimulus and ultimately give rise to the subjective experience of perception. As this characterizing makes clear, we are not limiting mental imagery to the visual modality. Although visual imagery is accompanied by the experience of "seeing with the mind's eye," auditory mental imagery is accompanied by the experience of "hearing with the mind's ear," and tactile imagery is accompanied by the experience of "feeling with the mind's skin," and so forth. Unlike afterimages, the modality-specific representations that underlie mental imagery are relatively prolonged and can be called up voluntarily.

Mental images were at the heart of early theories of mental activity, dating at least as far back as the classic Greek philosophers and figuring predominantly in both philosophy (until the nineteenth century) and early scientific psychology (see Boring, 1950; for a more detailed historical review of the role of imagery in theories of mental events, see Kosslyn, 1980). Scholars accorded imagery a special role in thought on the basis of introspection—the process of "looking within" (as we invited you to do at the outset of this chapter). Introspection suggested that imagery is important in memory, problem solving, creativity, emotion, and language comprehension. For example, Sir Francis Galton (cousin of Charles Darwin and the founder of the scientific study of individual differences in psychology, as well as the inventor of fingerprint identification and the dog whistle) asked people to recall what was on their breakfast tables—and found that most people visualized the table in order to recall the items. Similarly, if you need to purchase new window shades and must recall the number of windows in each room of your home, you will probably visualize each wall and scan along, counting the windows. Moreover, such worthies as Albert Einstein and Marcel Proust reported that imagery played a central role in their creative processes (see Miller, 2000; Shepard & Cooper, 1982). Imagery has even been placed at center stage in theories of how mental events can affect the body, such as can occur during hypnosis (Kosslyn, Thompson, Costantini-Ferrando, Alpert, & Spiegel, 2000; Oakley, Whitman, & Halligan, 2002; Shenefelt, 2003; Williamson, 2002).

Many of the claims about imagery appear plausible on their faces, but others are less obvious. And even the claims that seem plausible to some people may seem implausible to others. How can we sort the wheat from the chaff? This has proven a thorny issue. A major problem in theorizing about the nature of mental images has been their inherently private nature, which long prevented objective assessment of their structure or function.

This problem led some behaviorists to reject the very idea of mental imagery, and to banish it from scientific discussion (Watson, 1913, 1928). Watson believed that "thinking" is actually a very subtle talking-to-oneself, which is accompanied by faint throat twitches. He did not see mental imagery as a different sort of event:

> What does a person mean when he closes his eyes or ears (figuratively speaking) and says, "I see the house where I was born, the trundle bed in my mother's room where I used to sleep—I can even see my mother as she comes to tuck me in and I can even hear her voice as she softly says good night"? Touching, of course, but sheer bunk. We are merely dramatizing. The behaviorist finds no proof of imagery in all this. *We have put all these things in words, long, long ago.* (Watson, 1928, pp. 76–77)

The radical behaviorist B. F. Skinner took a different tack. He did not deny the existence of mental imagery as a phenomenology, but rather denied the utility of studying images as mental representations, arguing that that imagery was better viewed as a behavior that is subject to the same reinforcement contingencies as any other behavior. In his book *About Behaviorism*, he states:

> Behaviorism has been accused of "relegating one of the paramount concerns of the earlier psychologists—the study of the image—to a position of not just neglect, but disgrace." I believe, on the contrary, that it offers the only way in which the subjects of imaging or imagining can be put in good order.... Seeing in the absence of the thing seen is familiar to almost everyone, but the traditional formulation is a metaphor. We tend to act to produce stimuli which are reinforcing when seen.... A person is changed by the contingencies of reinforcement under which he behaves; he does not store the contingencies. In particular, he does not store copies of the stimuli which have played a part in the contingencies. There are no "iconic representations" in his mind; there are no "data structures stored in his memory"; he has no "cognitive map" of the world in which he has lived. He has simply been changed in such a way that stimuli now control particular kinds of perceptual behavior. (Skinner, 1974, p. 82–84)

Like views predominated until methods developed in cognitive psychology offered a way to begin to assess properties of internal representations, which opened the door to studying mental imagery objectively (e.g., Kosslyn, 1980; Paivio, 1971; Shepard & Cooper, 1982). At about the same time that the methods of cognitive psychology began to be employed to study imagery, advances in computer science offered new ways to conceptualize human information processing in general (e.g., Newell, Shaw, & Simon, 1957) and imagery in particular (e.g., Baylor, 1971; Moran, 1973). Although imagery researchers had assumed that mental images are in fact images and hence often compared visual mental images to pictures, the initial computer science–based approaches relied on language-like internal representations of the sort that are easy to implement in programming languages such as LISP.

Squarely within this emerging new computer science–inspired perspective, Zenon Pylyshyn (1973) argued that "the picture metaphor underlying recent theoretical discussions [of visual mental imagery] is seriously misleading—especially as it suggests that an image is an entity to be perceived" (p. 1). Moreover, he claimed that

> an adequate characterization of "what we know" requires that we posit abstract mental structures to which we do not have conscious access and which are essentially *conceptual* and *propositional*, rather than sensory or pictorial, in nature. Such representations are more accurately referred to as symbolic descriptions than as images in the usual sense. (p. 1)

Kosslyn and Pomerantz (1977) responded to these claims, marshalling both logic and empirical results to argue that the idea that mental images depict (as opposed to describe) is not only defensible but also most consistent with the emerging body of data about imagery. So began what is now commonly called "the imagery debate" (e.g., Tye, 1991).

In this book, we revisit the debate some thirty years later. Why now? The debate has evolved through three distinct phases and is now in a fourth phase. (We are tempted to predict that this is the final phase—but experience has taught us the folly of such optimism!) In the first phase, initiated by Pylyshyn (1973), the issue focused on the adequacy of different forms of internal representations for imagery (see Anderson, 1978; Kosslyn & Pomerantz, 1977). Specifically, researchers asked whether the pictorial properties of imagery that are evident to introspection reflect functional characteristics of the representations involved in information processing or are epiphenomenal, like the heat thrown off by a light bulb when one reads (which plays no role in the reading process). Pylyshyn (1973), Anderson and Bower (1973), and others pressed a kind of "propositional imperialism," in which they argued that all representations used in thinking are like those that underlie language. Many experiments were conducted to pit alternative theories against each other (for a review, see Kosslyn, 1980).

The second phase focused on how best to interpret the data from such experiments. Pylyshyn (1981) claimed that tacit knowledge (for example, our unconscious knowledge of how a ball will bounce on grass versus concrete) could explain those results. The key idea was that imagery tasks are defined (had implicit "task demands," in Pylyshyn's terms) such that participants use tacit knowledge to mimic what they think would occur in perception. We explore further the idea of tacit knowledge in chapter 3.

The third phase relied on neuroscientific data to counter many of the criticisms levied against the early experiments, which relied solely on measures of behavior to infer the nature of internal representations. One virtue of neuroscientific data is that they are not susceptible to task demands and cannot be explained in terms of tacit knowledge (Kosslyn, 1994). Another virtue of such data is that they are closer to the mechanisms in the brain that actually implement the functions; they provide a more fine-grained look at the way information is actually processed in the human brain.[1]

In the fourth, newest phase, Pylyshyn (2002, 2003) has published critiques of the use of neuroscientific data in imagery research and in cognitive science more generally. The debate has thus evolved to bear on a much more general issue, namely the relation between mental phenomena and their underlying neural substrate. Although Pylyshyn asserts that neuroscientific data cannot contribute to resolving the debate, we will argue that the debate has in fact moved forward, and rather dramatically so, because of the introduction of neuroscientific data.[2]

In spite of the fact that many researchers have made up their minds, one way or another, about the status of mental imagery as a distinct type of internal representation (Reisberg, Pearson, & Kosslyn, 2003), the issues are still hotly debated (e.g., see the commentaries of Pylyshyn, 2002). Three major questions are still in play. First, can we discover whether imagery is a distinct type of representation? If the brain is to be understood mechanistically, this question should have a definite answer; either the brain uses more than one type of representation or it does not. And if psychology is a science, we should be able to discover the answer. Second, can turning to the brain inform us about the nature of mental function? It is possible that psychology really is a "special science" and relies on a distinct, relatively abstract, level of analysis (e.g., Fodor, 1968). Many researchers have argued that understanding mental function is like understanding a computer program. If so, then one might argue that facts about the brain are marginally relevant, if at all. And third, taking the opposite perspective, are computational concepts useful for understanding how the brain gives rise to mental function? Researchers in computer science and cognitive science developed a rich set of theoretical tools, but almost none of them have been applied to interpreting results from neuroimaging studies. In fact, the current generation of cognitive neuroscientists seems to have lost this conceptual infrastructure. In this book we explore the utility of computational ideas for understanding what the brain does. In short, it is timely and useful to consider closely the issues and positions in the imagery debate and to put them in context.

Format versus Content

To begin, let us be clear what the "imagery debate" is a debate about. The debate focuses on the *format* of internal representations. A format is a type of code. The same information typically can be conveyed (albeit more or less efficiently) by different formats. For instance, the information in this sentence can be conveyed in a written English format, in spoken French, as Morse code, and, presumably, by smoke signals. A crucial point, which will be articulated in the rest of this book, is that different formats make different information *explicit and accessible* (to use Marr's [1982] terminology).

A simple example may help illustrate this fundamental point. One can represent the location of points on a surface using many formats. One could use a Cartesian coordinates format (each coordinate represents the distance of the point from the origin along one of two orthogonal axes). One could also use a polar coordinates format (one coordinate represents the distance of the point from the origin and the other represents the angle between the line passing through the point and the origin and a reference axis). For example, the three points (3, 2), (3, 5), and (3, 7) in Cartesian format have coordinates (3.6, 33.7), (5.8, 59), and (7.6, 66.8), respectively, in polar format. Figure 1.1 illustrates these points. The Cartesian format makes explicit and accessible the fact that the three points are on a vertical line, whereas the polar format does not. Conversely, the three points (2.6, 1.5), (5.2, 3.0), and (7.8, 4.5) in Cartesian format have coordinates (3, 30), (6, 30), and (9, 30) in polar format (see figure 1.1). In this case, the polar format makes explicit and accessible that the points lie along the same diagonal line, passing through the origin, whereas the Cartesian format does not make this information explicit and accessible. And if we plot the points in a two-dimensional space, both patterns are evident to our eyes. Although the same information is represented, the format of the representation determines what information is made explicit and is easily accessible.

Much effort has been expended in recent years to understand the nature of the format used in mental imagery. Mental images are fleeting, ethereal entities; how should we conceptualize them in a way that explains not only how they can represent information about the world but also how "mental"

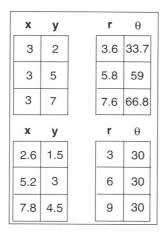
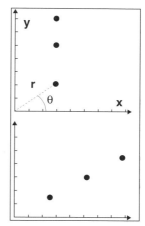

Figure 1.1. How different representational formats make explicit and accessible different types of information. It is easy to decide that a set of points lies on a vertical (or horizontal) line by looking at a list of Cartesian coordinates (top left panel), whereas this is difficult to do with a list of polar coordinates (top middle panel). Conversely, it is easy to decide that a set of points lies on a line passing through the origin by inspecting a list of polar coordinates (bottom middle panel), but it is difficult to do so with a list of Cartesian coordinates (bottom left panel). And if we plot the points in a two-dimensional space, both patterns are evident to our eyes (right panels). Although the same information is represented, the format of the representation determines what information is made explicit and is easily accessible.

images relate to the physical brain itself? This issue has plagued theorists at least since the time of Plato, who in his *Theaetetus* likened images to patterns etched on a block of wax (individual differences in imagery ability were explained by differences in the hardness and purity of the wax). The brain is an organ of the body, and like other organs of the body, it can be described at numerous levels of analysis. We can divide these levels into two general classes, the physical and the functional.[3] For example, stomachs can be described either in terms of cell types, enzymes, and so on, or in terms of their role in digestion. Similarly, brains can be described in terms of their physical composition—cells, anatomical connections, neurotransmitters, and so on—or in terms of their functions. The primary function of brains is to store and process information. A "mental representation" is a description at the functional level of analysis of how the brain stores information, whereas a "mental process" is a description at the functional level of analysis of how the brain interprets or transforms existing mental representations into new mental representations.[4]

The debate has focused on two means of representation that have been proposed for mental images, one that confers a special status on images and one that treats them as no different in kind from linguistic representations. These two alternatives are called *depictive* and *propositional* representations. These types of representations correspond to two different formats, different types of codes. Every type of code is defined in part by a specific syntax. The syntax is characterized by (1) the elementary, or "primitive," symbols and (2) a set of rules for combining the symbols. Symbols usually belong to different "form classes" (e.g., "noun," "verb," "determiner," and so on), and the rules of combination are defined in terms of these classes—which allows the rules to be applied to an infinite number of distinct symbols. A format is also defined in part by the semantics of a code. The semantics is determined by how meaning is conveyed by individual symbols and combinations of symbols. For example, the symbol "A" can be interpreted as a part of speech if read as a word, or as a configuration of birds in flight (as seen from above) if interpreted as a picture. The same marks are used in both formats, but what differs is how they are interpreted (i.e., how they are taken to convey meaning). The rules of semantics assign a meaning (or sometimes more than one, if the symbol is ambiguous) to a specific symbol.

Palmer (1978) offers a more elaborate treatment of these distinctions, but this overview is sufficient for present purposes. In order to see how the results from experiments can distinguish between the two formats that figure centrally in the imagery debate—propositional and depictive representations—we need to characterize these representational types in more detail.

Propositional Format

Consider a propositional representation of a simple scene containing a ball sitting on a box. We can write the representation using the notation "ON (BALL, BOX)." This kind of notation is close to the way propositions are represented in formal logic and in computers and serves to make it clear that we are not talking about sentences in a natural language (such as English). A propositional format can be characterized as follows:

The syntax: (1) The symbols belong to a variety of form classes, corresponding to conceptual relations (e.g., ON), entities (e.g., BALL, BOX), properties (e.g., RED, NEW), and logical relations (e.g., OR, NOT, SOME). (2) The rules of symbol combination require that all propositional representations have at least one relation ("BALL, BOX," in and of itself, does not assert anything). (3) Specific relations have specific requirements concerning the number and types of symbols that must be used (ON(BOX) is unacceptable because ON relates one object to another, and hence at least two symbols must be used).

The semantics: (1) The meaning of individual symbols is arbitrarily assigned, requiring the existence of a lexicon (as is true for words in natural languages, whose meanings must be looked up in such a mental dictionary). (2) A propositional representation is defined to be unambiguous, unlike words or sentences in natural languages. A different propositional symbol is used for each of the senses of ambiguous words (such as for the *port* that is a wine and the *port* that is a destination of ships). (3) A propositional representation is abstract. That is, (a) it can refer to non-picturable entities, such as "sentimentality"; (b) it can refer to classes of objects, not simply individual ones (such as boxes in general); and (c) it is not tied to any specific modality (a propositional representation can store information acquired via language, sight, touch, and so on). (4) Some theorists add another characteristic to the semantics of propositions: the assertion expressed by a proposition is either true or false (see, for example, Anderson & Bower 1973). However, this appears to be not a property solely of the representation per se, but rather a relation between the representation and a specific state of the world (see Palmer, 1978).

Depictive Format

Now consider a drawing of the same scene, of a ball on a box. The drawing is an example of a depictive representation. Depictive representations differ from propositional ones on almost every count. There is no explicit symbol that stands for the relation ("ON" is not represented separately, but only emerges from the juxtaposition of the symbols standing for the ball and the box). The rules of combination are not defined over form classes (indeed, the rules are very lax; any dot can be placed in any relationship to any other dot). The semantics is not arbitrarily assigned, and depictions can be ambiguous because they are interpreted as resembling an object (and a picture can be seen as resembling more than one object). Depictions are not abstract: they cannot directly refer to nonpicturable concepts (although they can do so indirectly, by forming a separate association); they represent individual instances (not classes), and they are specific to a particular sensory modality (we have focused here on visual depictions, but auditory and motoric depictions are also possible; see Kosslyn, in preparation).

Thus, depictions are not propositions. But what are they? We can characterize depictive representations as follows:

The syntax: (1) The symbols belong to two form classes: points and empty space. (2) The points can vary in size, intensity, and color. (3) The points can be arranged so tightly as to produce continuous variation, or so sparsely as to be distinct (like the dots in a comic strip). (4) The rules for combining symbols require only that points be placed in spatial relation to one another.

The semantics: (1) The association between a representation and what it stands for is not arbitrary; rather, depictions "resemble" the represented object or objects. That is, (a) each portion of the representation must correspond to a visible portion of the actual object or objects, and (b) the represented "distances" among the portions of the representation must correspond to the distances among the corresponding portions of the actual object (as they appear from a particular point of view). Table 1.1 summarizes the key characteristics of propositional and depictive formats.

An actual picture (a literal depiction) is not the only form of depictive representation. Rather, a pattern in an N-dimensional array in a computer can be a *functional depiction*; it can operate to depict objects because the points can correspond to points on the surface of an object, with the corresponding distances on the object being preserved by the number of cells (filled or empty) between the points in the array. A functional space, such as an array in a computer, depicts geometrical relations among points. In this case, the patterns of ones (representing points) and zeroes (representing empty space) in the computer's memory are interpreted as if they were arranged in a matrix, such that some points are adjacent, others are arranged along a diagonal, some are nearer than others, and so forth. Even though there is no actual corresponding spatial layout in the computer's memory, the array functions as if it were such a space because processes operate on the information stored in memory in a particular way.

What the Two Formats Make Explicit and Accessible

The two sorts of representations—descriptions and depictions—make different sorts of information explicit and accessible. For example, consider the depiction of the pattern A and the description "two diagonal lines that meet at the top, joined halfway down by a short horizontal segment." In the depictive representation, the shape of the empty space, the triangle, is both explicit and accessible, whereas in the descriptive representation the shape of the empty space is not explicit and is accessible only with difficulty; it must be computed in a multistep logical process. Of course, a description could be created that simply notes the shape of the empty space, but that is not the only emergent property of the depictive representation. The depictive representation makes explicit and accessible a near-infinite number of spatial relations among portions of the shape. For instance, this representation indicates that the top of the A is above the center bar, is above the terminus of

Table 1.1
Summary of Properties of Propositional versus Depictive Formats

	Propositional	Depictive
Example:		
	ON(BALL, BOX)	
Syntax:		
Symbols		
	Belong to form classes:	Are points, which can vary in:
	Relations (e.g., ON)	Size
	Entities (e.g., BALL)	Intensity
	Properties (e.g., RED)	Color
	Logical relations (e.g., NOT, ALL)	
Rules of Combination		
	Must have at least one relation; must have symbols for entities that satisfy requirements of relation	Points are placed in relative locations in a space
Semantics:		
Symbols		
	Meaning arbitrarily assigned	Meaning assigned via "resemblance": Any portion of the representation must represent a portion of the object; represented distances among representations of portions of the object must correspond to the distances among the corresponding portions of the object
	Are unambiguous	Can be ambiguous

(*continued*)

Table 1.1
(*Continued*)

	Propositional	Depictive
	Abstract: Can refer to non-picturable entities	Cannot be abstract in any sense: Refers to picturable entities
	Can refer to classes of objects	Refers to exemplars
	Not tied to any specific sensory modality	Specific to a particular sensory modality
Rules of Combination		
	Arrangement of symbols can assert a true or false state of affairs	As spatial relations among points are distorted, the depiction becomes increasingly less accurate

the right leg, and so on. Such spatial relations are immediately accessible in a depictive representation, and thus depictive representations may be more efficient in representing the spatial layout of objects. On the other hand, the fact that there are three "lines" (i.e., strokes) is explicit in the descriptive representation but not in the depictive one. In the depiction, all portions of the pattern are both explicit and accessible, but they are not semantically interpreted; thus, to access the concept of "line," a process must interpret the pattern. In contrast, the propositional representation makes this interpretation of the pattern explicit and accessible.

In sum, depictive representations make explicit and accessible all aspects of shape and the relations between shape and other perceptual qualities (such as color and texture), as well as the spatial relations among each point. In contrast, propositional representations make explicit and accessible semantic interpretations, which can include aspects of shape and other perceptual qualities. Depictive representations of shape must also incidentally specify size and orientation; propositional representations only specify what was explicitly included when the representation was created. Depending on the precise task at hand, one or the other format may be most useful.

Depictions in the Brain

As we saw in the computer analogy described above, there need be no actual picture in the brain to have a depiction: all that is needed is a "functional space" in which distance can be defined vis-à-vis how information is processed. (However, as we discuss in chapter 2, a functional space is sufficient as a depictive form of representation only if the geometric properties of the representation emerge because there are fixed, hard-wired processes that interpret the representation as if it were a space; if the processes are not fixed, then the representation is not necessarily a depiction.)

Nevertheless, even though all that is required in order to have a depiction is a functional space, there is good evidence that the brain depicts representations literally, using space on the cortex to represent space in the world. To be specific, we will argue in the following chapters that images rely in part on areas in the brain that are specifically designed to depict patterns. These areas are *topographically organized*—they preserve (roughly) the geometric structure of the retina. Such areas use space on the cortex to represent space in the world (e.g., see Felleman & Van Essen, 1991; Fox et al., 1986; Heeger, 1999; Sengpiel & Huebener, 1999; Sereno et al., 1995; Tootell, Hadjikani, Mendola, Marrett, & Dale, 1998; Tootell, Silverman, Switkes, & De Valois, 1982; Van Essen, 1985). For example, figure 1.2 illustrates the results of an experiment reported by Tootell, Silverman, Switkes, and De Valois in 1982. They trained a monkey to stare at the pattern shown on the left, which consisted of a set of blinking lights arranged as shown. The animal was injected with a radioactive form of sugar, which was taken up into brain cells in proportion to how active the cells were while the animal observed the pattern; the more active the brain cell, the more sugar it took up. This particular isotope gets lodged in the neurons and is not quickly broken down by metabolic processes. The animal was then sacrificed, and its brain was removed. Figure 1.2 illustrates the first cortical area to receive input from the eyes, known variously (but synonymously) as area V1, area 17, area OC, the striate cortex, and the primary visual cortex. The dark bands in the right part of figure 1.2 label brain cells that took up a lot of the radioactively tagged sugar. As is clear, the geometric structure of the stimulus is physically laid out on the cortex!

These areas do not simply have a topographically organized physical structure; they *function* to depict information. If a patch of cortex in one of these areas is damaged (for example, because a tumor had to be removed), this damage will produce a scotoma (i.e., a "blind spot") in the corresponding part of the visual field. The scotomas that arise when the topographically organized visual cortex is damaged demonstrate conclusively that these areas function to depict information; crucially, the closer two damaged regions of the topographically organized visual cortex are, the closer in the visual field the corresponding scotomas will be. And this result is not simply about the effects of chronic damage: transcranial magnetic

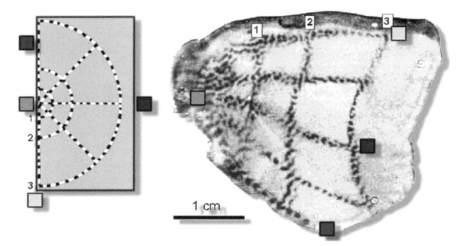

Figure 1.2. A geometric pattern of flashing lights (*left*) shown to a monkey after it was injected with a radioactive sugar, which is taken up into the brain cells in proportion to their level of activity. The animal was trained to stare at the stimulus, and then was sacrificed so that its brain could be examined. The occipital cortex of the monkey (*right*) is shown with dark bands revealing the neurons that were most activated while the animal viewed the pattern. A pattern of activation corresponding to the geometric structure of the stimulus can be seen clearly. This result demonstrates that visual stimuli are represented topographically in the occipital cortex of the monkey brain. Shaded squares are used to demarcate the points on the visual stimulus that are represented in corresponding space on the visual cortex. The numbers 1, 2, and 3 indicate the inner, middle, and outer bands of flashing lights that are clearly represented on the cortex. Note that for simplicity, only half the circular light stimulus is shown here, along with a section of V1 from a single hemisphere of the brain. (Adapted with permission from Tootell et al. [1982]. *Science, 218,* 902–904; and Tootell et al. [1988]. *Journal of Neuroscience, 8*[5], 1531–1568.)

stimulation has been used to stimulate occipital cortical sites transiently to produce phosphenes (i.e., bright flashes of light that are not produced by sensory input); when nearby sites are stimulated, phosphenes appear in nearby locations in space, and when far apart sites are stimulated, phosphenes appear in far apart locations in space (e.g., Kastner, Demmer, & Ziemann, 1998).

The appearance of figure 1.2 notwithstanding, the pattern of activation is not literally a picture of what the animal is seeing. From the point of view of an outside observer (such as the reader, observing that illustration), metric information on the cortex is distorted. However, as we discuss at length in the following pages, the key is how processes that receive outputs from this cortex interpret distance on the cortex—not how a human observer armed with a ruler would interpret such distances. If we were to treat the cortex like a piece of paper, we would conclude that the depiction is distorted, with the central part amplified—but the brain processes that access this representation correct for such distortions. Within the context of the brain as a whole, these topographically organized areas truly depict information.

Why does the brain use space on the cortex to represent space in the world? Although the ease of genetic coding or other factors may play a role, the best current guess is that this structure has been retained through evolution for a simple reason: this trick makes explicit and accessible information needed for the tasks at hand.[5] For example, the first cortical visual areas to receive input from the eyes are confronted with the task of organizing figure from ground. In order to do so, they must delineate edges. This task is facilitated by the fact that many (perhaps most) of the connections among neurons in a topographically organized area are both very short and inhibitory. This means that if one neuron is stimulated, it attempts to inhibit its neighbors—which represent adjacent points in space. The effect of this is to exaggerate differences in neural activation across the boundaries of edges. For instance, if an object reflects a lot of light and the background does not, then neurons that are near the edges of objects will inhibit those that register the background, which will amplify the difference in their activation—thereby helping to identify edges of objects.

For mental imagery, purely functional depictions may have been sufficient; there is no obvious reason why physical depictions are required. However, because the imagery system draws on mechanisms used in like-modality perception (as we demonstrate throughout the remainder of this book), it relies on such physically topographically organized structures. As we argue, many of the properties of imagery arise because of this simple fact. For instance, because the input to early topographically organized areas changes every time the eyes move, the patterns of activation within them cannot linger for long; if they did, the world would seem smeared as we moved our eyes. But what is a virtue for perception is a drawback for imagery: as we argue in chapter 5, it is difficult to maintain images for long, in part because they rely on neural machinery also used in perception.

In short, each location on the topographically organized cortex corresponds to a specific location in space, and distance between the locations on cortex corresponds to distance between the corresponding locations in space. The brain has numerous such representations, but we shall emphasize two classes of them in this book. First, many of these depictive representations are involved in processing shapes, particularly in the occipital lobe. We group the topographically organized areas in the occipital lobe into a single functional structure, which we refer to as the *visual buffer*. Patterns of activation within the visual buffer depict shapes, according to the definition of *depiction* offered here. The visual buffer, in essence, is the canvas upon which images are painted; it is the medium that supports depictive representations. In later chapters we provide strong evidence that topographically organized brain areas are in fact used in visual mental imagery, but first we will use the idea that imagery relies on patterns of activation within such areas to show that the arguments levied against depictive representations do not hold water.

Second, the brain also uses depictive representations to specify information about the locations of objects in space. These representations are primarily in the posterior parietal lobes (e.g., Sereno, Pitzalis, & Martinez, 2001). Although a depictive format is used both to represent shape and location, we shall see that the contents of these representations differ markedly. As we discuss in later chapters, because of the differences in content, we will distinguish between *object images,* which represent shape (and shape-related properties, such as color and texture), versus *spatial images,* which represent relative locations in space.

In the most recent round of the debate, at stake is the very idea that turning to the brain can inform theories of cognition. We will argue that the function of the brain—which is, after all, the organ of thought—has evolved in tandem with its structure, and vice versa: the brain is not a "general purpose computer," like a von Neumann machine (such as your personal computer), which acts very differently depending on the program it has in memory. Instead, the brain is largely a special-purpose machine, which is tailored to function in specific ways. Because different formats make different information explicit and accessible, different formats are more or less useful for performing different tasks. Thus, an efficient strategy for the brain is to use different formats in different situations, and animals that could do this may have had an adaptive advantage over their less specialized brethren.

Hybrid Depictive Representations

Consider again the gripping illustration in figure 1.2. Those dark lines indicate where neurons were particularly active while the monkey was observing the pattern. If we take this finding to indicate that a depictive representation is being used (as we should, given our characterization of such representation), we are led to conclude that mental images are not like points in an array in a computer in at least one fundamental respect: each neuron in this visual area does not simply register the presence or absence of a point of light. Rather, the neurons also code for specific properties such as the orientation of the line segments, hue, and binocular disparity (which is a cue for depth). Thus, although the representation has a depictive component (because the information-bearing elements are arranged in a functional space such that the properties of depictions summarized in table 1.1 apply), it is in fact a hybrid representation. Each point is interpreted in part in terms of its role in the depiction, but also in part in terms of the additional information it codes abstractly.

In spite of their coding nondepictive information, these hybrid representations cannot be reduced to propositional representations. Crucially, they use space (literally, on the cortex) to represent space in the world. The fact that each point codes additional information does not obviate its role in depicting the shape.

Representational Imperialism?

The issue is not whether propositional representations are used in imagery; in some processes, they probably do play a role. For example, stored descriptions may well be used to compose images of objects into scenes (see Kosslyn, 1980, 1994); moreover, propositions are probably used to interpret images, which will disambiguate otherwise ambiguous forms. In fact, each point in the depiction may be accompanied by a set of propositions that codes additional information (such as color; cf. Tye, 1991). Rather, the issue is whether *only* propositional representations are used in imagery, or whether depictive representations also play a role. If all information processing relies solely on propositional representations, then the depictive properties of imagery evident to introspection are epiphenomenal, that is, they play no functional role in processing the information. Let us illustrate the force of this claim with an example, the results reported by Shepard and Cooper (1992). They asked congenitally blind, color-blind, and sighted people to rate the similarity of named colors and then performed multidimensional scaling on the ratings. This technique produces a diagram in which items that are more similar are placed closer in a space (and it is often possible to discern specific dimensions running through the space). The obtained solutions for the color names were remarkably similar for the color-blind and normal participants, in spite of the fact that the solutions differed markedly when the participants judged actual patches of color.

Even more striking, some of the congenitally blind participants (three of the six) produced solutions that were similar to the classic "color wheel" (see also Marmor, 1978). These blind participants may have based their ratings on associations among propositional representations (such as "red is hot" and "blue is cool"). Pylyshyn argues, essentially, that in imagery sighted people use the same type of propositional representations apparently used by the more successful blind people in this study. In this case, the phenomenological experience of imagery is irrelevant; all of the cognitive work is accomplished by propositional representations.[6]

Why have we chosen to focus on these two formats? For example, one can also posit motoric and procedural formats. We pit propositional formats against depictive formats for two reasons: First, many computer scientists—perhaps because of their familiarity with list-processing languages such as LISP—have the strong intuition that language-like formats are sufficient for representing all knowledge. At the core of the imagery debate is the claim that there is a single "language of thought" (Pylyshyn, 1973), as opposed to the idea that cognition relies on multiple representational systems. Second, historically, from the time of Plato at least up to William James (1892/1962), philosophers and psychologists have relied on their introspections to argue that depictive images play a functional role in psychology. If this view is correct, we will gain important insight into the nature of consciousness—given the striking correspondences between some aspects of the phenomenology and the underlying representational format. There is no logical reason why introspection had to reflect aspects of the underlying information processing. If it turns out that introspection does reveal some aspects of the machinery of the brain, this will open the way to asking additional questions about the nature of consciousness itself.

It would be a sad commentary on the state of scientific psychology if this issue could not be resolved. If psychology is a science, we should be able to characterize the alternatives crisply and agree on what sorts of data would distinguish among them. Do cognitive processes rely on a single representational format, or are there at least two? When one visualizes the letter *A*, specific representations are present. We should be able to identify them, to determine the fact of the matter.

In this book we argue that the imagery debate should now be settled, as much as any debate in science is ever settled. Even today, there are those who argue that the world is flat—that photographs to the contrary taken from space rely on trick photography, that atmospheric quirks account for the existence of a horizon, and so on (see http://www.flat-earth.org). Lest you dismiss these claims out of hand, consider the following quotation from the Web site of the Flat Earth Society (which we found in May 2005):

There exist some genuine photographs from high altitudes, which appear to the untrained eye to show a spherical Earth. The reason for this effect is that the Earth's atmosphere becomes denser the further one ascends, after thinning out at about 5 miles. This causes light to be refracted more at high altitudes, giving the appearance of a spherical Earth.

Similarly, although individual arguments against the existence of depictive representations may appear plausible in isolation, we show that the sum total does not provide a compelling case.

The plan of this book is as follows:

In chapter 2, we begin with a concrete example of an empirical phenomenon—mental image scanning—and compare propositional and depictive accounts. We then review the propositional arguments against depictive theories and consider whether propositional accounts do in fact undermine the depictive ones in principle.

Chapter 3 turns to an entirely different class of criticisms of the claim that visual mental images depict information. These broadsides against depictive theories hinge on attempts to explain away the data. One set of critiques rests on the idea that participants in imagery experiments use "tacit knowledge" about perception when they are asked to visualize (such as the unconscious belief that it would take longer to scan greater distances over a surface when searching for an object); according to this argument, the participants use such knowledge to mimic the behavior they think they would exhibit in perception. We analyze such claims carefully and rebut them.

In chapter 4, we explain why neural data bear on the debate and summarize evidence that supports our theory that topographically organized visual areas are used during visual mental imagery. In this chapter we also discuss neuroimaging evidence that at first blush might appear to contradict the claim that the topographically organized visual cortex depicts information during mental imagery. We show that what appear to be mixed findings can, in fact, be explained easily, and we show how these findings do not undermine our claims. We summarize this literature in detail in the appendix, and in this chapter report a meta-analysis that documents the conditions in which such depictive representations of an object's shape are used.

Chapter 5 pulls together our theorizing and illustrates how an information processing system that uses depictive representations can be instantiated in the brain. In this chapter we summarize our brain-based theory of visual mental imagery and provide an overview of how it accounts for major facts about imagery.

Finally, in chapter 6 we consider why the debate has persisted so long and not only discuss differences in the conception of what theories should accomplish in cognitive science but also consider sociological factors. We conclude with a discussion of how new methodologies have allowed us to gain traction on what appeared to be an intractable problem—mental imagery.

Notes

1. As is discussed at length in chapter 3, task demands are implicit requirements built into a task. For example, the instruction to "scan" a visualized object might implicitly imply that one should move one's eyes over it. Tacit knowledge is the knowledge *or belief* regarding how one would behave in the corresponding actual situation. For example, one might believe that one would take substantially more time to scan longer distances (not knowing about saccades). We distinguish such accounts from "cheating" or the like; cheating would occur when one intentionally attempts to circumvent the instructions or intentionally attempts to produce specific results. Neither the effects of tacit knowledge (in response to task demands) or outright cheating can explain specific patterns of brain activation unless (a) participants know which brain areas are predicted to be activated (and, more specifically, the distribution of activation in those areas) and (b) have voluntary control over such activation. Neither assumption is warranted in the sorts of studies that we describe in the following pages.

2. We focus many of our arguments on Zenon Pylyshyn's critiques because he has provided the most detailed criticisms of our views and because his criticisms have been widely read.

3. This distinction is only an initial cut through the space of alternatives. For example, we could more finely distinguish between various sorts of physical representations (e.g., at the level of individual neurons or the biochemical events that occur within and between them). Nevertheless, for present purposes this initial distinction is sufficient.

4. After the invention of "neural network" models (e.g., Rumelhart, McClellan, & the PDP Research Group, 1986) one might question whether the distinction between structure and process can be maintained. In a neural network model, information is stored as a pattern of weights that is distributed over the links that connect elements. These same weights modulate how activation is propagated through the network, leading a given input to produce a given output. Thus in neural networks, the structure and process are conflated. In our view, such networks are best viewed as models of "implicit processes" (Schacter, 1987), where there is a consistent and direct mapping from input to output. In contrast, when working memory is required, the same information can be interpreted and transformed in many ways (Baddeley, 1986). Mental imagery is a good example of the kind of representation used in working memory. For such representations, it makes sense to distinguish

between the structure and process: many different types of processes can be applied to the same representation (e.g., an imaged pattern can be scanned, added to, or rotated), and the same types of processes can be applied to numerous different representations.

5. There is good evidence that the organization of cortical maps is determined primarily by neural connectivity in local circuits (e.g., Chklovskii & Koulakov, 2004). However, because creating connections among neurons that are distant in space is expensive metabolically (because of the long axons and dendrites), it is also likely that evolutionary pressure favored configurations in which connected neurons are close to each other. In fact, maps such as those in early visual cortex may represent near-optimal solutions for the minimization of wiring length.

6. To avoid confusion, it is important to note explicitly from the outset that this debate is orthogonal to the one about "dual code theory" formulated by Allan Paivio in the 1970s: Paivio's dual code theory refers to the *content* of memory representations (verbal and nonverbal), whereas the imagery debate deals with the *format* of the representations used in mental imagery. It is possible that propositional representations can be used both to name an object (producing a verbal code) and to describe its shape and structure (producing a code that specifies visual content).

2

Evaluating Propositional Accounts

What researchers usually mean when they talk of visual mental imagery is that one has retrieved or generated representations from memory like those that underlie the experience of seeing. That is, when we see something, some characteristic internal representations must be formed; some of these representations may underlie emotional reactions, some may be formed as one describes an object or scene, and so on. As we noted in chapter 1, image representations are like those that underlie the experience of seeing something, but in the case of mental imagery these representations are based on information retrieved or formed from memory, not on immediate sensory stimulation.[1]

This characterization of imagery does not implicate any specific form of representation, and in this chapter we consider the virtues of depictive versus propositional formats for representing visual mental images. In the first part of this chapter we provide a concrete example of depictive versus propositional theories and show how theorists have accounted for one well-documented imagery phenomenon by appeal to depictive representations or by appeal to propositional representations. We illustrate how both types of theories can account for the findings.

In the second part of this chapter, we consider arguments that might tip the scales in favor of propositional formats. We summarize two general categories of such arguments, which assert (1) that depictive imagery as a theoretical construct is incoherent and logically flawed and thus should not be treated as a bona fide psychological entity and (2) that imagery phenomena are best explained using more general cognitive principles. Taken together, these arguments assert that the functional component of imagery is just an aspect of and no different in kind from the propositional system used in other domains (such as language); hence, the experience of imagery is relegated to the status of an "epiphenomenon," if it is discussed at all. Thus, one purpose of this chapter is to pull together and summarize, in one place, the arguments against a depictive format as opposed to a propositional format.[2]

In the third part of this chapter, we lay out the corresponding counterarguments in favor of depictive representation, addressing each aspect of the propositional critique in turn. These counterarguments undermine the purported problems with the idea that imagery relies on depictive representations and provide support for the view that imagery is not simply a result of propositional processing but instead may sensibly and usefully be regarded as a distinct class of cognitive phenomena.[3]

Scanning Visual Mental Images: A Case Study

In this section we focus on a single imagery phenomenon and provide a concrete example of how the two sorts of theories—depictive and propositional—characterize the mental representations and processes used in the task.[4] This phenomenon is image scanning, which consists of shifting one's attention over a visualized object. The first such experiment was reported by Kosslyn (1973), who tried to use scanning as a way to characterize the format of the underlying representation. His reasoning was as follows: By their very nature, depictions embody space (recall that "distance" is an intrinsic part of the representation). Thus, if depictive representations underlie the experience of "having an image," then the spatial nature of the representation should affect how images are processed. Kosslyn (1973) reasoned that one way to discover whether image representations embody space is to determine whether it takes more time to shift attention greater distances across an imaged object. If participants take more time to scan a longer distance across an imaged object, this would be evidence that distance is indeed embodied in the representation of the object.

The first experiment began by asking participants to memorize a set of drawings. Half of these drawings were vertical and half were horizontal, as illustrated in figure 2.1. After the participants had memorized the drawings, they closed their eyes, heard the name of one (say, "speedboat"), and visualized it. Once it was visualized, the participants were asked to mentally

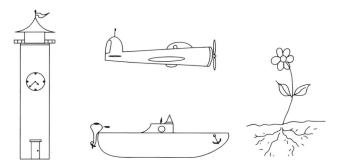

Figure 2.1. Examples of vertically and horizontally oriented objects that participants were asked to visualize in Kosslyn's (1973) scanning study. (From Kosslyn, S. M. [1973]. Scanning visual images: Some structural implications. *Perception & Psychophysics, 14,* 90–94.)

focus ("stare" with the "mind's eye") at one end of the object in the image (for the speedboat, either the left side or right side). Then the name of a possible part of the object (e.g., *motor*) was presented on tape. On half the trials the name labeled a part of the drawing, and on the other half it did not. The participants were asked to "look for" the named component of the object in their image. An important aspect of this experiment was that the "true" probed parts (i.e., parts that were in fact included in the drawing) were at either one end or the other of the object or in the middle. The participants were told that the investigator was interested in how long it took to "see" a feature on an imaged object (the word "scan" was never mentioned in the instructions), and they pressed the "true" button only after "seeing" the named component and the "false" button only after "looking" but failing to find it. If image representations depict information and scanning images requires shifting the focus of attention over a representation, then it ought to take more time to locate the parts located farther from the point of focus. And, in fact, this is exactly what occurred.

At first glance, the results from this experiment seemed to show that depictive representations are used in imagery. But it soon became clear that a propositional explanation could easily be formulated. D. Bobrow (personal communication, April 1973) suggested that the visual appearance of an object is stored in a propositional structure like that illustrated in figure 2.2. This representation is a series of linked propositions, with each part of the structure describing a part of the object. Note that we could rewrite the propositions illustrated here as BOTTOM-OF(PROPELLER, MOTOR), REAR-OF(MOTOR, REAR DECK), and so on—a set of distinct propositional representations. In the diagram, each link is a relation that combines the

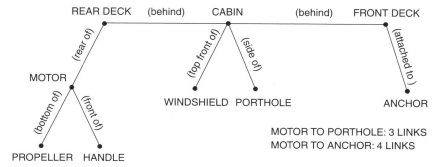

Figure 2.2. The structure of a propositional representation of the motorboat illustrated in figure 2.1. (From Kosslyn, S. M. [1983]. *Ghosts in the mind's machine.* New York: Norton.)

symbols at the connected nodes (which represent the related entities in the proposition) into a proposition. According to Bobrow's theory, people automatically (and unconsciously) construct these sorts of propositional descriptions when asked to memorize the appearance of drawings. When the participants later were asked to visualize and then to focus on one end of the drawing, they would then activate one part of the representation (for instance, for speedboat, the node for motor). When subsequently asked about a part, they then searched the network for its name. The more links they had to traverse through the network before locating the name, the more time it took to respond. For example, for "speedboat" it took more time to find "anchor" than "porthole" after the participant focused on the motor because four links had to be traversed from motor to anchor but only three from motor to porthole. Thus, the effect of "distance" on scanning time may have nothing to do with distance's being embodied in an underlying depictive representation but may instead simply reflect the number of intervening items that need to be traversed in a propositional network (see also Lea, 1975). According to such theories, the conscious experience of scanning a pictorial mental image is somehow produced by processing this network, and the depictive aspects of images available to introspection are epiphenomenal.

It should now be clear why it was necessary to go into so much detail in characterizing the differences between the types of representations: we need a reasonably precise characterization of the two formats if we are to perform experiments to discriminate between them. According to the characterization provided in chapter 1, although propositional structures can be formulated to capture the spatial arrangement of the drawings, they are not depictions. Recall that in depictions, in contrast to this sort of propositional representation, space in the representation is used in such a way that it embodies space in the real world and thus, the shape of empty space is represented as clearly as the shape of filled space. Moreover, there is no explicit representation of relations (such as REAR-OF).

The next experiment in this series was designed to eliminate a critical problem with the first one. In this experiment, Kosslyn, Ball, and Reiser (1978) independently varied the metric distance scanned across and the number of items scanned over. The results of this experiment were straightforward: scanning times increased when participants shifted their mental attention over greater distances, even when the amount of material was held constant. In addition, participants required an increment of time for each additional item they scanned over—which is as expected if each item was checked to ensure that it was not the target. These results are consistent with the claim that images rely on depictive representations.

The notion of depiction leads us to expect that image representations embody distance in at least two dimensions. To test this hypothesis, Kosslyn, Ball, and Reiser (1978) asked participants to memorize the map illustrated in figure 2.3. Seven objects were carefully positioned on the map, which could be related by twos to form twenty-one pairs—and each pair was separated by a different distance. The participants learned to draw the locations of each of the seven objects on the map. After memorizing the map, the participants closed their eyes and heard the name of one of the seven objects; they mentally focused on that object and then heard the name of another object (e.g., "bench"). Half the time the second object was on the map, and half the time it was not. The participants' job was to imagine a small black dot flying from the object being focused on to the second object, moving as quickly as possible— and to push a button when the dot arrived at the second object. Alternatively, if the second named object was not on the map, they pressed another button. As is evident in figure 2.4, the time to scan the image increased linearly with increasing distance scanned across. This result is exactly as predicted if image representations depict information in two dimensions.

However, it is possible to create a propositional counterexplanation even here. The network contains "dummy nodes" that mark off units of metric distance. That is, these nodes convey no information other than the fact that an increment of distance (say, 5 centimeters) exists between one object and another; hence, there would be more nodes between representations of objects separated by greater distances on the map. By putting enough dummy nodes into a network, the propositional theory developed for the original results can be extended to these results as well.

To attempt to rule out this propositional counterexplanation, Kosslyn, Ball, and Reiser (1978) conducted a control experiment that involved a

Figure 2.3. The island map used in Kosslyn, Ball, and Reiser's (1978) study of mental scanning. Seven locations were depicted, with varying distances between them. (From Kosslyn, S. M., Ball, T. M., & Reiser, B. J. [1978]. Visual images preserve metric spatial information: Evidence from studies of image scanning. *Journal of Experimental Psychology: Human Perception and Performance, 4*[1], 47–60.)

variation on the map scanning task. In this experiment, participants again visualized the map and focused their attention on a particular point, but now they were told simply to decide as quickly as possible whether the probe named an object on the map. The investigators reasoned that the participants had memorized the map so well that they had encoded not only a depictive image but also the names of the locations into a propositional list; if so, they would not need to visualize the map to respond and instead could respond simply on the basis of the stored list of names. (We stress that the depictive theory does not deny that propositional representations are sometimes used; instead, the claim is that depictions can also be used, in addition to propositional representations.) However, if the propositional theory is correct, and propositions are always used (and the effects of distance have nothing to do with depictions), then we should find effects of distance here, too; after all, the participants were asked to form the image (which purportedly corresponds to accessing the appropriate propositional network) and to focus on a given location (which purportedly corresponds to activating a specific node or region of the network). The results were

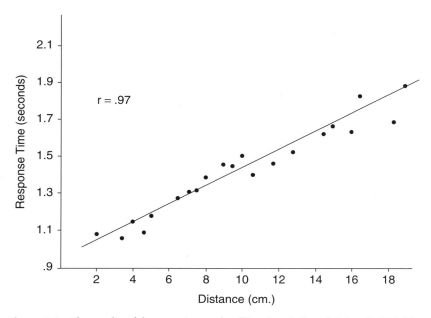

Figure 2.4. The results of the scanning study of Kosslyn, Ball, and Reiser (1978). The time to scan between pairs of objects on the map increased linearly with distance between the objects. (From Kosslyn, S. M., Ball, T. M., & Reiser, B. J. [1978]. Visual images preserve metric spatial information: Evidence from studies of image scanning. *Journal of Experimental Psychology: Human Perception and Performance, 4*[*1*], 47–60.)

clear cut: There were absolutely no effects of the distance from the focus to target objects on response times. The depictive theory did not predict effects of distance because a depictive image was not actually used; instead, the relevant information could simply be looked up in a list.

However, a propositional theorist could argue that there is no guarantee that participants activated the same propositional structure when asked to use an image as they did when asked simply to respond as quickly as possible. There is no reason why people could not have encoded two propositional structures, one that included the spatial structure of a display and one that simply listed the objects that were present in the display. If so, then when given a free hand in how to respond, we would expect them to use whichever list was most efficient to search—which would probably be the simpler list. And the ease of searching this list would not reflect the distances among objects.

In short, this is a slippery business. In fact, Anderson (1978) proved mathematically that as long as behavioral data—such as response times—were the only means of distinguishing the theories, propositional accounts can *always* be generated to mimic depictive accounts. This proof rests on the possibility of structure-process tradeoffs: when characteristics of the representation (the structure) differ from one theory to another, these differences can be compensated by changing the processes that operate on the representation. Anderson showed that such trade-offs can always allow one class of theories to mimic the other.

The Propositionalist Case against Depictive Representation in Imagery

The claim that a single format is used in all cognition appeals to many theorists, who have mustered many arguments against depictive theories of imagery. Many of the anti-imagery arguments consist of attacks on the idea that visual images are stored in memory much as a snapshot is stored in a photograph album.[5] It is important to realize that the "images" being attacked are likened to "mental photographs" that are treated as replicas of previous patterns of sensory activity at or near the receptor level. These patterns purportedly are stored in a relatively undifferentiated, unorganized form. According to this view (clearly expressed by Pylyshyn—the most outspoken and widely cited antidepictivist), experiencing an image consists of retrieving and examining one of these mental photographs. For example:

> Recently there have been claims that neuroscience evidence supports what would otherwise have been a grotesque proposal; that to have a mental image is to project two-dimensional moving pictures onto the surface of your visual cortex. (Pylyshyn, 2003, p. 114)

> For example, some of the psychophysical evidence that is cited in support of a picture theory of mental imagery suggests a similarity between the mind's eye and the real eye that is so remarkable that it ought to be an embarrassment to picture-theories. It not only suggests that the visual system is involved in imagery and that it examines a pictorial display, but it appears to attribute to the "mind's eye" many of the properties of our own eyes. (Pylyshyn, 2002, p. 178)

Misleading Properties of the Metaphor

The critique against depictive representation hinges in part on arguments that the metaphor of actual images (such as pictures) is misleading. One line of argument focuses on the claim that the "picture metaphor," as it has been called, introduces a host of inappropriate analogies between seeing and imaging. For example, a "mind's eye" is often said to "see" images internally. This notion seems to require a second processing system, or "mind's eye's brain," to interpret information from the mind's eye, which in turn would require another eye to interpret the images projected onto this internal brain, and so on in an infinite regress. This is the classic "problem of the homunculus" (the "ever-present danger of a homunculus regress," Pylyshyn, 2002, p. 220) where the theory requires a "little man" who actually does all of the work (and hence positing the little man explains nothing).

This critique also notes that when asked to image something like a tiger and count its stripes, most people report having difficulty. The critics observe that it is not as if a picture is present and merely waiting to be viewed. Mental images can be noncommittal in a way that visual percepts are not; for instance, visual mental images need not have a particular color, texture, or shading, and may not even be three-dimensional.

> If you actually saw a token of a B you would see either a lower or an upper case letter, but not both and not neither. If someone claimed to have an image of a B that was noncommittal with respect to its case, you would surely be entitled to say that the person did not have a visual image at all. In terms of other contents of an image, the situation gets murkier because it becomes less clear what exactly the task of imagining entails. For example, does your image of the letter "B" have to have a color or texture or shading? Must you represent the background against which you are viewing it, the direction of lighting and the shadows it casts? Must you represent it as viewed from a particular point of view? What about its stereoscopic properties; do you represent the changing parallax of its parts as you imagine moving in relation to it? Could you choose to represent any or none of these things? Most of our visual representations, at least in memory, are noncommittal in various respects (for examples see Pylyshyn 1978). In particular, they can be noncommittal in ways that no picture can be noncommittal. (Pylyshyn, 2002, p. 166)

Moreover, critics view it as problematic that the picture metaphor leads us to speak of perceptual events such as scanning and focusing in relation to image processing and claim that these analogies are difficult to reconcile with the fact that no mind's eyeballs exist to do the scanning or focusing. Furthermore, the critics note that information access from visual images is different from that from a perceived scene. For example, one may examine a 3×3 matrix and read the values in it over and over in a different order, but it is not as easy with imagery. Scanning the matrix diagonally is particularly difficult, as Pylyshyn (2002) points out:

> Try writing down a 3×3 matrix of random letters and read them in various orders. Now imagine the matrix and try doing the same with it. Or, for that matter, try spelling a familiar word backwards by imagining it written. Unlike the 2D matrix, some orders (e.g., the diagonal from the bottom left to the top right cell) are extremely difficult to scan on the image. (Pylyshyn, 2002, p. 177)

Why is it so difficult to scan the matrix smoothly if people can scan imaged patterns as if they were pictures?

In addition, the picture metaphor wrongly implies that images are perceived much as pictures are perceived. Unlike pictures, images are pre-organized into objects and properties of objects—which explains why when we forget part of an image, it is not a random part. It is not as if a corner is torn from a photographic picture in the head. For example, if our image of a room is incomplete, it is not missing half a sofa or half a lampshade. Rather, images seem to be organized into meaningful parts, which in turn are remembered in terms of spatial relations among them (see Reed, 1974).

Another problem with conceiving of images as akin to pictures is that one is led to assume that images convey information because they resemble (in the same way that pictures resemble) the objects they depict. However, resemblance is neither necessary nor sufficient to serve as a basis for reference or meaning. For example, a depiction of an Elvis look-alike does not refer to Elvis, though it resembles him, and an image of Elvis in a distortion mirror may still refer to Elvis even if it does not resemble him very much.

Continuing along this line, critics of the idea that mental images depict information claim that much of the appeal of this idea comes from mistaken identification of internal representations with physical objects. Consider the classic results of Shepard and Metzler (1971), in which they found that the further an object had to be "rotated" in an image, the more time participants required. (To get a sense of the phenomenon, decide whether the uppercase version of the letter P would be another letter if rotated 180 degrees clockwise. In order to "see" the second letter, you need to rotate the first.) The critics assert that it is incoherent to say that an image rotates, because mental images are not physical objects. Unlike a picture, an image cannot be dropped, carried under one's arm, and so on. Images do not automatically obey the laws of physics or assume physical properties, such as rigidity and spatial extent. If images pass through intermediate orientations when they seem to rotate, for example, critics claim that they do not do so for the same reasons that a rotating physical object passes through intermediate states. Instead, researchers in the field have purportedly erred in acting as if physical properties came "free" with the imagery format.

Finally, some researchers have actually questioned whether the very goal of trying to characterize pictorial properties of images is an error; some researchers (e.g., Raab & Boschker, 2002) have claimed that "mental imagery is intrinsically dynamic and that the very nature of mental imagery will not be uncovered by studying static pictures. Understanding mental imagery of motor actions reveals that any theory of mental imagery should start off with the temporal nature of real-life experiences" (p. 208).

Inefficiency

Those who have espoused the antidepictive view have raised two points that hinge on assumptions about processing efficiency (e.g., see Pylyshyn, 1973). First, Pylyshyn argues that processing and storing of information in a depictive format would be cumbersome, if not totally unworkable, because a huge storage capacity would be necessary to preserve all the information transmitted by the retina. He asserts that the amount of stored information would soon exceed the capacity of the brain if people did indeed store the wealth of images they commonly claim to remember using a depictive format.

Second, even if all the unanalyzed images could be stored depictively, critics of depictive theories have argued that it would be virtually impossible to search for one particular image among them, since uninterpreted images could not be organized into a format facilitating their retrieval. But people who experience imagery report no awareness of such searching: the desired image seems to come to mind directly and quickly. Thus, it seems necessary to assume that some sort of "interpretation" is stored in memory along with each image. If this is granted, critics have argued, it would seem more economical to store only the interpretations and dispense with the images entirely.

Flawed Evidence

Much of the appeal of depictions stems from our introspections, but we should be wary of taking those introspections too seriously. As compelling as the depictive aspects of imagery may be to some of us through our introspections, this does not justify the use of the concept of depictive representation in an explanatory way. The mere experience of depictive imagery, as vivid and undeniable as it may be, does not imply that such imagery plays any causal (as opposed to merely epiphenomenal) role in cognition. Moreover, not everyone reports experiencing depictive images, and those who do cannot always agree on the nature of their experience.

In addition and perhaps more fundamentally, depictive theorists have been accused of confusing the properties of a representation (as an object in its own right) with the properties of what is being represented. This is known among philosophers as the *intentional fallacy*. For example, Edelman (1998) notes that no researcher thinks that the representation of a cat is itself fuzzy, and—following this line of thought—Gold (2002) argues (based in part on Harman, 1990) that depictive theorists confuse the properties of the represented object with the representation itself (see also Pylyshyn, 2002; Slezak, 2002). According to this view, in imagery "we are not in fact examining an inner state, but rather are contemplating what the inner state is about" (Pylyshyn, 2002, p. 158). And because this state specifies properties of visible objects and events, we must be careful not to confuse the properties of the events that are being represented with the properties of the representations themselves. The depictive theorists have mistakenly displaced the object onto the mental state. Although introspectively it seems that we are re-perceiving a picture, the experience is misleading; the representation does not have the properties of what is being represented. Pylyshyn (2002) stresses repeatedly that we are "deeply deceived by our subjective experience of mental imagery" (p. 158).[6]

Problems of Definition

Some scholars have claimed that the very notion of "imagery" (which rests on the idea of depictive representation) is hopelessly muddled. One view is that the "depictive image" is an ill-defined construct that is in need of further explication. Theorizing about imagery has involved much vagueness and many glosses, and the actual operational definitions used in experiments have not followed explicitly, or always even implicitly, from theory. Furthermore, some critics have claimed that the operational definitions of imagery vary so widely from experiment to experiment as to obscure the common construct being addressed.[7]

In addition, critics claim that if one examines the definition of depiction carefully, they will find that any system that is compositional and that adequately represents what it is meant to represent will be functionally depictive (Pylyshyn, 2002). Fodor and Pylyshyn (1988) have argued that any adequate form of representation will be compositional, given that the content of all representations arises from their parts and the rules that govern how the parts are combined (see also Pylyshyn, 1984, 1991a, b). For example, in propositional representations parts of expressions can be mapped recursively onto parts of physical states, and syntactic relations can be mapped onto physical relations. As a result, the argument goes, the characterization of "depiction" offered earlier applies to *any* adequately expressive symbol system, not just one in which space is used to represent space.

According to Pylyshyn (2002), only the strongest sort of depictive representation, in which images are laid out in real physical space on the brain, is clearly distinct from a description. But, he claims, it makes no sense to talk about actual pictures in the brain, for the reasons noted earlier (e.g., such pictures would require a homunculus to look at them).

Lack of a Distinct Domain

On this view, talking about "imagery" as a distinct entity reflects an incorrect way of dividing up the cognitive system into component subsystems. Certainly, all subsystems, such as the language and perceptual systems, are to some extent interactive. But genuine subsystems have separate operating principles that distinguish them from one another. The propositionalists argue that this is not so with imagery. To the contrary, they claim that imagery is simply a facet of a more general cognitive faculty that is best characterized as using only propositional representation. Thus, in this view, imagery is not properly treated as a distinct domain worthy of a special theory.

Propositional representations, as discussed in chapter 1, are abstract language-like representations that assert facts about the world. Numerous theorists have claimed that this sort of representation is required to store information because what we know about the world is a set of facts or assertions that are necessarily either true or false (but see Barsalou, 1999, for an interesting dissenting view). Part of what it means to say a "proposition" is "abstract" is to say that it is amodal and hence can be used with equal facility in representing information encoded via the senses or via language. For example, the representation of a red ball on a box next to a tree might be a set of elementary descriptions, such as "ON(BALL, BOX)," "IS(BALL, RED)," and so on. Mental pictures, on the other hand, do not assert anything and hence are neither true nor false; they merely exist, with no truth value (although propositions about a picture's correspondence to an object or scene do have truth value). Thus, the argument goes, if image representations are considered to be mental pictures, they are inadequate for representing knowledge of the world.

Moreover, critics have also claimed that even if there were a consistent operational definition of depictive imagery, such imagery could not serve in an explanatory role because it is not a "primitive construct." According to this view, images derive from more basic aspects of a computational system, which specify how syntactically defined units are combined, and a proper explanation relies on these aspects of the system. By analogy, to understand the structural properties of a wall, one needs to know the nature of bricks and mortar and how they function together to produce a rigid object. These critics want explanations of mental phenomena to involve only the most primitive, atomistic, and mechanistic elements possible. Imagery, however defined, is not a primitive construct and ought to be further reduced.

A related argument against imagery's being treated as a separate domain is that one must specify images in the context of a processing system. And because properties of representations can be understood only with respect to the processes that operate on them, one must always specify representation/process pairs when proposing an explicit account of some data. Critics have claimed that if imagery is viewed as a set of representations that is processed in specifiable ways, it is not any different from other representations in kind—and hence is not to be treated within a distinct theory.

Conceptualizing imagery in the context of a broader processing system has led some scholars to posit a fundamental weakness in the idea that imagery requires a distinct type of representations and processes. The argument goes like this: First, it is clear that verbal formats must exist at some level, simply because we can transmit and receive verbally encoded messages; similarly, it is clear that perceptual (for example, visual) formats are necessary to account for our perceptual capacities. But how do the two types of representations, verbal and perceptual, link to each other? A third coding system must also be postulated; this coding system is abstract (amodal), propositional, and not externalizable. According to Pylyshyn and others (for example, Clark & Chase, 1972; Moscovitch, 1973), our ability to translate or exchange information between verbal and visual formats (as when we describe a picture) requires the existence of a third "interlingual" format because the structural differences between visual and verbal representations preclude direct translation:

> But the need to postulate a more abstract representation—one that resembles neither pictures nor words and is not accessible to subjective experience—is unavoidable. As long as we recognize that people can go from mental pictures to mental words or vice versa, we are forced to conclude that there must be a representation (which is more abstract and not available to conscious experience), which encompasses both. There must, in other words, be some common format or interlingua. (Pylyshyn, 1973, p. 5)

Because images will necessarily be reduced to a third format during processing, the argument goes, and hence are inextricably bound to the general processing system, it makes no sense to construct a separate imagery theory, distinct from theories of other forms of representation.

Moreover, because eventual translation into a third format is thus necessary, it would be more efficient simply to encode all information into the common format to begin with. The critics of depictive theories claim that use of a single amodal representational format would result in a considerable simplification of the mental machinery needed for retrieving information. The need for a pictorial interpretive process (a "mind's eye"), in addition to processes needed to retrieve nonpictorial information, would be eliminated if information were represented in a single format. This suggests to these theorists that all knowledge is coded in an abstract propositional format, from which translation into verbal or perceptual structures can be made as needed. If so, then there is no cause for a distinct theory of imagery.

Finally, some scholars feel that it is more aesthetic and parsimonious to posit only a single form of internal representation for all knowledge. They say that we should try to posit only a single format if at all possible, not only because such a system is parsimonious, but also because it is elegant.

These arguments are summarized in table 2.1. In the following section, we return to each of them and consider counter-arguments.

Critique of Arguments against Depictive Imagery

The major attacks against depictive representation, such as Pylyshyn's, are based on a particular conception of imagery, namely, the "picture in the head" hypothesis. Clearly, this approach is untenable. But this is not at issue: No researcher in the field would seriously argue that visual mental images are pictures; pictures are concrete objects that exist in the world, whereas mental images are internal representations (and, as we shall see later, are accompanied by specific neural events). We refer to the properties of images as "quasi-pictorial" because images lack some of the properties of pictures: obviously, people do not have computer-like screens in their heads (no matter how hard you hit someone's head, you won't hear the tinkle of breaking glass). Nor do we have any other kind of actual picture in our heads: pictures are objects that can be hung on walls, dropped on toes, and so on. To have a picture in one's head would be very uncomfortable. We now return to each of the points summarized in table 2.1.

Table 2.1
Summary of Arguments against Depictive Representations

General Class of Argument	Key Idea
Misleading properties of the metaphor	There is no homunculus
	Mental images can be noncommittal
	Images are preinterpreted and organized
	Resemblance does not determine meaning
	Physical properties are not "free" (they do not automatically apply to representations)
Inefficiency	A huge storage capacity is necessary for depictions
	Uninterpreted images cannot easily be retrieved
Flawed evidence	Introspection is unreliable and potentially misleading
	Representations do not have properties of represented objects
Problems of definition	"Depictive imagery" is an ill-defined construct
	Properties of "depiction" apply to any adequately expressive symbol system
	Only literal depictions are truly depictive
Lack of distinct domain	Propositional representations are required to express facts
	Depictions are not explanatory because they are not a primitive construct
	Depictions are no different from propositions because they must be processed
	A third "interlingual" format is required to link images and words
	Storing all information in a propositional format is most efficient
	A single form of internal representation is elegant

Misleading Properties of the Metaphor

Although at first glance the arguments against depictive representation may seem compelling, they do not stand up well to careful scrutiny.

The Mind's Eye and the Missing Homunculus

Many of the visual metaphors used in theorizing about imagery are not as ill conceived as some have argued. The fact that mobile eyeballs are not available for viewing images does not pose insurmountable problems. For example, in Sperling's (1960) famous experiments on scanning afterimages (or "icons"), eye movements were clearly irrelevant—and yet participants could scan afterimages without difficulty. Similarly, Posner and his colleagues (e.g., Posner, Snyder, & Davidson, 1980) have long shown that one can fixate straight ahead but shift attention to the left or right field voluntarily, without moving one's eyes. Furthermore, Kaufman and Richards (1969) showed that where one's eyes are directed and where one thinks one is looking are not necessarily the same. What is required for scanning an image is a shift of attention from one part of the image to another. This no more requires physical motion through a trajectory than does the shift of a "pointer" within a data structure in a computer's memory.

It is important to realize that there is nothing paradoxical or incoherent in the notion of a "mind's eye." We can think of the mind's eye as a processor that interprets depictive representations (which in turn—somehow—ultimately give rise to visual perceptual experiences). When these interpretive processes are applied to remembered perceptual information instead of information that is provided online via the senses, an image rather than a percept will be experienced.

And what about that homunculus? In the following chapters we present strong evidence that visual mental imagery draws on very much the same neural system as visual perception. Nevertheless, nobody worries that a homunculus is required to explain perception; rather, its putative functions are understood in terms of processes that create and interpret a series of representations (e.g., Marr, 1982). And the same is true of imagery. If we do not need to posit a little man to explain perception, we do not need to posit one to explain imagery.

Indeed, early computer programs (such as those described by Boden, 1977; Winston, 1975) demonstrated conclusively that a homunculus is not required for a perceptual system (see Neisser, 1967). The procedures used in these programs can operate just as well on information being fed in from the computer's memory (imagery) as from a TV camera (perception). Later computational models have underlined this point by postulating recurrent connections between memory structures and structures close to the input (e.g., Grossberg, 1999a; Mumford, 1991; Ullman, 1995). More sophisticated versions of these programs have even been embedded in real robots that learn to see and act by exploring the environment without any supervision (see, for example, the program "Darwin," which constitutes the brain of NOMAD— the Neurally Organized Mobile Adaptive Device; Edelman et al., 1992).

However, according to Slezak (2002), having a running computer simulation of a theory does not allow one to reject the possibility that the theory relies on a homunculus. This is an interesting claim, but we would love to see where the little man actually sits in the computer simulations of imagery (e.g., those of Kosslyn, 1980, 1994; Kosslyn, Flynn, Amsterdam, & Wang, 1990; and Kosslyn & Shwartz, 1977). Turn the situation on its ear: Let's say that we, not a philosopher, actually wanted to claim that the operation of our computer simulations depends on a homunculus. One might point out that there is no such thing in either the hardware or software of the machine, at which point we might assert that our little man is very, very small and hence invisible. One might then ask how this microman affects the operation of the machine, and we could reply by appeal to paranormal powers. The reasonable critic could then point out that we need none of these extra assumptions to explain how our simulation operates—and that critic would of course be absolutely correct.

Rorty (1979, p. 235) claims that replacing a "little man in the head" with a "little machine in the head" is not an advance. If the little man, or little machine, makes intelligent decisions, a theory that relied on it would not be explanatory (one would only have to appeal to the little man or machine, which would still necessitate the question of how the process operated). But this objection cannot be levied if clear principles govern the behavior of this "little machine in the head" such that its internal workings are themselves transparently mechanistic. Contemporary theories of depictive imagery, such as the one summarized in chapter 5, do not posit a magical machine-within-the-machine, and hence a homunculus (even a very, very small one) has no place in such theories.

Mental Pictures

In addition, we agree that mental images are fundamentally different from pictures in some ways, but this does not undermine the claim that mental images depict information. The way geometric properties are specified is key to determining whether images depict. For example, unlike descriptions, images must—by the way they convey information—specify a relative size and orientation whenever they specify a shape. Because the geometric properties are stored separately in the brain from other qualities, such as color and texture, these additional properties may be omitted (or combined with shape incorrectly; in fact, illusory conjunctions among values of the different dimensions can occur when some are specified perceptually and some in mental images; Craver-Lemley, Arterberry, & Reeves, 1999). The presence or absence of color, texture, and other details is irrelevant to the issue of whether images depict the shape of an object; the fact that all details of an imaged object are not present or perceptible (for example, the number of stripes on a tiger) is beside the point. Even an actual painting, such as an Impressionist work, need not have distinct, countable details.

Moreover, even if images were perfectly photographic, one might not have encoded this information in the first place. If information is not encoded and stored in memory, it cannot appear later in a mental image. In fact, perception itself need not register all of the details of objects; when we actually see a tiger, for example, we may not individuate each and every stripe but instead perceive a textured pattern. In addition, we often may fail to notice many details. For example, research on "change blindness" indicates that people often fail to be aware of even major changes in a display if they are not paying close attention to precisely the relevant portion of the stimulus (Levin & Simons, 1997; O'Regan, Rensink, & Clark, 1999; Rensink, 2002; Rensink, O'Regan, & Clark, 1997, 2000; Simons & Levin, 1997). It is also worth noting that the simple introspection that images seem indeterminate cannot tell us whether such indeterminacy reflects properties of the representation or properties of the processes that operate on it. For example, people sometimes have trouble counting the precise number of parts (such as a tiger's stripes) even if each part is in fact included in a picture of an object; try counting the number of dots on an acoustic tile of a ceiling sometime (for data, see Kowler, Benson, & Steinman, 1975). In this case, even though the number of stripes or dots is fixed, we may have the impression—due entirely to our processing limitations—that the number is indeterminate.

In addition, by considering how images may be produced we can gain insight into the reasons why imaged patterns may be difficult to process. For example, if parts of images fade in and out, this can explain why it is difficult to scan diagonally across an image of a matrix of numbers. As modeled originally by Kosslyn and Shwartz (1977), because parts are added individually when an image is generated and each begins to fade as soon as it is added, images can only depict a fixed number of parts simultaneously. Imagery is like a juggling act in which only a small number of balls can be kept aloft at once. Thus, if the task requires holding too much information in mind for too long, people will find it difficult. For example, if a task requires scanning over material organized in separate units, one will need to regenerate multiple units in order to perform it. Scanning will be easier if one scans along a perceptual unit that was encoded initially (such as the top row of a matrix) or one that is relatively easy to reorganize because relatively little of the image needs to be maintained at the same time in order to do so—as is required to organize the first letters of each row of a matrix into a column. In contrast, if one needs to retain the entire image for a long period of time to reorganize it, as required to organize entries along the diagonals into units, the task will be difficult indeed.

This account raises another issue. Do we need to know the limits of the numbers of elements that can be generated and time limits before decay in order to generate predictions? Empirical results exist that allow us to predict the relative difficulty of retaining images in different tasks. For example, studies have shown that parts are added one-by-one when an image is generated (Kosslyn, Cave, Provost, & Von Gierke, 1988; Kosslyn, Reiser, Farah, & Fliegel, 1983). If so, then the more parts in the image, the more time the initial ones have to fade before the image is complete. In addition, other studies have shown that mental images generated from long-term memory do not activate the topographically organized visual cortex (which, as we discussed in the previous chapter, implements depictive representations in the brain) as strongly as do external percepts (e.g., Ganis, Thompson, & Kosslyn, 2004; Ishai, Haxby, & Ungerleider, 2002; O'Craven & Kanwisher, 2000), and hence we would expect them to fade more quickly—they were "faded" to begin with. The precise fading rate is irrelevant if the only question to be answered is why some tasks (such as scanning a matrix diagonally) are more difficult than others.

What about the claim that we are misguided even in trying to characterize depictive properties of images (e.g., Raab & Boschker, 2002)? Did the visual system really evolve just to process dynamic information? This objection is off the mark: on the one hand, people can in fact identify and reach for perfectly static objects. The human visual system is not designed simply to process motion. Indeed, object properties and spatial properties—including motion—are processed by separate neural systems (see chapter 3). On the other hand, people can visualize not only static but also dynamic information, as shown by studies of motion imagery, as we will discuss later. Given that the imagery debate focuses on the nature of the format for representing shape, it seems most appropriate in this context to focus on the representation of shape per se.

Interpretation and Organization

We are not uncomfortable with the observation that mental images are not simply re-embodiments of stored sensations. Although storage of primitive sensations is possible (as in afterimages), the products of higher perceptual activity can be stored as well. Perception is a process of information reduction whereby a welter of sensations is reduced into a simpler and more organized form. These organizational processes cause our percepts to be structured into units that correspond to objects and properties of objects. It is these larger units that can be stored and later assembled into mental images. Just as it is incorrect to consider the representation of an object during perception as photographic, by the same token it is erroneous to equate image representations with mental photographs; this view would overlook the fact that images are composed from highly processed perceptual encodings. Indeed, Reed (1974) long ago showed that people can "see" parts of imaged forms that correspond to perceptual units more easily than parts that cross perceptual units; for example, if you visualize a Star of David, you will "see" the two large overlapping triangles more easily than the three parallelograms that are embedded in the form.

Resemblance

Depictions convey meaning via resemblance, which raises thorny issues. We agree that resemblance is not a necessary or sufficient condition for conveying meaning. But because of the way in which depictions represent, there is a correspondence between parts and spatial relations of the representation and those of the object; this structural mapping, which confers a type of resemblance, underlies the way images convey specific content. In this respect images *are* like pictures. Unlike words and symbols, depictions are not arbitrarily paired with what they represent.

Physical Properties

What about the critique that images are mistakenly taken to be copies of the represented objects? According to the critique, this error misleads us into assuming that properties of the physical world are inherent in imagery. However, one system need not be a copy of another in order to mimic it. In principle, patterns of activation on cortex could literally be rotated (and, in fact, we shall see that there is some evidence for just this), but this is not necessary: if images are represented by functional depictions (again, think of the analogy to points in an array in a computer), then all that is necessary is that the pattern be rotated within that functional system. In other words, vis-à-vis the processes that interpret the pattern, all that is necessary is that the represented orientation be altered incrementally (so that the object passes through a trajectory along an arc). This is demonstrably possible in computers, and there is in principle no reason why it is not possible in brains. We concur that researchers should not be satisfied with using an unanalyzed term such as "rotation" as an explanation, but in our view the task is to discover the ways in which certain image transformations are like physical rotations—and there is no reason in principle why representations cannot be processed in ways that can appropriately be described in such terms.

Inefficiency

We also are not persuaded by arguments based on processing efficiency, which hinge on assumptions about capacity limitations and accessibility. Our reasons for rejecting these arguments are as follows.

Capacity Limitations

First, consider the claim that image representations would strain the limited capacity of the brain. This point remains moot because (1) we do not know what the capacity limitation of the brain is, or even if—for all practical purposes—it has one,[8] and (2) we have no good measure of the amount of information contained in an image or a percept of a scene. Furthermore, the capacity-limit argument would be effective only against the most primitive picture theory, in which the image is thought to consist of relatively unprocessed sensations. If most images are composed of relatively large, interpreted, perceptual "chunks," corresponding, for example, to the arms, legs, head, and trunk in an image of a person, the number of informational units to be encoded need not be so great—even if details, such as the shape of a person's eyebrows, are sometimes encoded. In addition, we ask whether propositional accounts of imagery suffer from even greater capacity limitations. Consider the amount of processing that would be required to describe a complex scene in terms of propositions and language-like symbols— and the storage space needed if the shapes and all spatial relations among them were stored. If anything, depictive representations would appear to be more efficient at representing information, which, perhaps, is one reason for their existence.

Accessibility

Pylyshyn's claim that an enormous amount of time would be necessary to retrieve a particular depictive image rests on a key assumption. Specifically, this claim rests on a very narrow view of how information can be searched. Namely, the underlying idea is that images are examined one at a time, in order, as if one were paging through a photo album, examining each snapshot in turn. Counter to this assumption, it is possible that images themselves can be searched in parallel whenever a particular one is sought, just as Pylyshyn suggests. Indeed, this is just how holographic memory systems work (Grawert et al., 2000; Hong, McMichael, Chang, Christian, & Paek, 1995; Psaltis & Mok, 1995). Briefly: Here's an easy way to think about such systems, as illustrated in figure 2.5. A laser is bounced off one object

CREATING AN ASSOCIATIVE HOLOGRAM

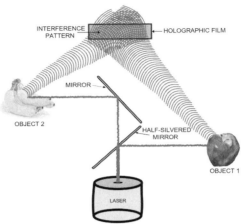

HOLOGRAPHIC FILM ENCODED WITH
INTERFERENCE PATTERN

USING HOLOGRAPHIC MEMORY

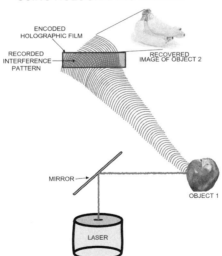

Figure 2.5. Associative holographic memory. (*Top*) An associative hologram is created by shining a laser through a half-silvered mirror, so that part of it bounces off one object and part of it continues through the mirror, and then is reflected onto a second object by a second mirror. Light bouncing off the two objects interacts on

and the light passes through a half-silvered mirror. This mirror allows half the light to pass through, which then falls on a photographic plate. The mirror also deflects half the light, so that it in turn bounces off a second object, and that light then falls on the photographic plate. The light bounced off both objects forms interference patterns on the plate, which is then fixed and developed. Subsequently, when a laser is bounced off only one of the objects and this light passes through the developed photographic plate, that light is modulated—the plate acts like a filter. This modulation process results in an image of the second object's being reconstructed; if you stood behind the plate, you would see an image of that second object. The same plate can retain images of many pairs of objects—all of which are "searched" in parallel when light is shined through it. One can easily conceive of such a memory integrated with an automated image recognition system, so that when the second image is produced it can be named and otherwise processed. We have no way of knowing what the speed of such a search might be and need not assume that the search would be apparent to consciousness.

Flawed Evidence

Critics of depictive representation have also raised questions about the status and role of introspections about imagery.

Introspective Evidence

The following two points should be made concerning introspective data. First, introspections are not adequate in and of themselves to attest to the functional role of depictive representations (i.e., mental images) in cognition. However, they are one source of evidence that, when taken together with behavioral performance data (such as the time necessary to make certain introspections) and neurological data (such as the effects of brain damage on performance and observations of the brain areas that are activated during specific tasks), can assist in demonstrating that depictive

---

the film, and the film is developed. (*Center*) A close-up of the interference pattern recorded on the holographic film. (*Bottom*) After the film is developed, laser light shined off either object will be modulated by the film, so that an image of the second object is reconstructed. Images of many pairs of objects can be associated in the same film, and these images are searched in parallel whenever laser light from one object is passed through the film.

images have distinct functions in cognition. Certainly, much progress has been made in the study of perception and psychophysics by considering "objective" data in conjunction with participants' introspections about the qualities of their experiences.

Second, the experience of depictive imagery is undeniable, even as its functional role can be debated. This experience must arise as a consequence of some underlying processes; simply labeling it as epiphenomenal will not make it go away. The study of phenomenology is a legitimate enterprise in its own right, and any theory that serves to illuminate phenomenological issues achieves added value. We note that propositional theories lend absolutely no insight into the phenomenology of imagery. Depictive theories, on the other hand, provide the basis for understanding why our experiences have specific characteristics (i.e., they are a direct reflection of the underlying representation used in information processing)—and lead us then to ask why some aspects of the underlying representation make themselves known in our phenomenology whereas other aspects do not.

The Intentional Fallacy

Critics have claimed that proponents of the depictive theory confuse properties of the content with properties of the format; they mistakenly believe that because the content specifies characteristics of perceptual images, the format also must be an image. However, it is an error to believe that people cannot attend to properties of a representation itself as well as to its content. Indeed, the weight of the empirical data indicates that people can attend to images, not just the contents of the images—as evident, for example, by the fact that people can assign vividness ratings reliably (they are not rating the object, but rather the image itself).[9] According to the present view, this should not be surprising. By analogy, consider the fact that we can regard a painting in two ways. On the one hand, we can attend to its content, admire its composition, and reflect on the painter's mood and message. On the other hand, we can attend to the painting itself as an object, noting the texture of the canvas, the way the frame encroaches on the borders of the tableau, and so on. And we argue that the same is true for imagery: we can ask about the contents of a depiction as well as the properties of the depiction itself. When speaking of imagery, the depictive theorists want to turn the "intentional fallacy" exactly on its ear: when one says that an image of a cat's head is blurry, or has a certain size, this doesn't mean that the cat is in fact blurry, or that the cat has a certain size. The concept of "visual angle" makes sense when applied to an image for exactly this reason: independent of the particular content of the image, the image itself appears to occupy a certain proportion of the visual field (Kosslyn, 1978).

Problems of Definition

Is the very notion of "imagery" (which rests on the idea of depictive representation) hopelessly muddled? We think not, for the following reasons.

Fuzziness of Concept

The absence of a truly formal definition of *image* at present hardly constitutes grounds for deciding on the ultimate ontological status of imagery or its role as a theoretical construct. Pylyshyn expresses concern that different theorists and experimenters operationalize imagery in different ways and that there is no single operation that can uniquely define the existence or functioning of the image. This situation is common in science and far from being undesirable (e.g., see Kuhn, 1962). Most psychologists have become comfortable with the use of "converging operations" in attempts to define entities that are not subject to direct observation. Garner, Hake, and Eriksen (1956) argue that unitary operational definitions should be avoided when dealing with inferred constructs, because such definitions confound the entity being measured with the instrument used in making the measurement, as has sometimes happened with the construct of hypnosis. Rather, a number of independent operations should be devised to "converge" on the construct. In fact, there is no greater problem with imagery in this regard than with any other unobservable construct in science. The construct of an electron can be critiqued in the same way, but it has long held a place in physical theories.

We further note that operational definitions—no matter how many or how cast—should not be equated with the actual psychological entities of interest. The meaning of *electron* did not change with the advent of new measuring instruments (although the description of it did change as new information was gathered). Operational definitions may be necessary precursors of more precise formulations of hidden internal structures and processes that are the actual objects of study.

Can Propositional Descriptions of Shape Be Functional Depictions?

In principle, propositional representations can convey the same content as depictive representations (Anderson, 1978). However, they would not necessarily make the same information explicit and accessible as depictive representations (see chapter 1). Using space—even functional space—to represent actual space affects information processing in distinctive ways, which are not shared by other kinds of representations. For example, by virtue of how depictions represent, the object *must* subtend a particular visual angle and have a specific orientation in an image—even if this information is not relevant for a specific task. Other representational formats do not have this requirement. Similarly, the ease of detecting parts of depicted objects *necessarily* depends on how perceptually discriminable they are, whereas the ease of accessing properties represented symbolically need not be affected by this characteristic (Kosslyn, 1975, 1976).

Literal versus Functional Depiction

The argument that functional depictions do not truly represent in a depictive format misses a central point about how representational systems operate: representations only "represent" in the context of a processing system. By analogy, the same physical pattern in a computer's memory can represent a sentence or an array—it depends on how the contents of memory are "read" by the CPU. In the brain, unless the appropriate connections exist between an area and later areas that receive input from it, even a veridical picture laid out on the cortex would not function to depict. Although the brain contains many topographically organized areas, which literally use space on cortex to represent space in the world, in fact it matters not a whit what a representation looks like to an outside observer; all that matters is how a representation is interpreted within the processing system at hand. By the same token, it would be possible to have a depictive format that relied on a set of spatially distributed parts of cortex, each of which represents a specific part of the visual field. If the physical representation were scrambled, appropriate connections could "unscramble" the arrangement for later levels. Provided that those connections are fixed, are "hardwired," the representation can be taken to depict *within the context of the system.* As it happens, depictive representations in the brain are in fact literally depictive from the point of view of external human observers (as noted in chapter 1; we discuss this further in chapters 3, 4, and 5), but this is not a necessary requirement.

Thus, in principle the brain could have had a functionally depictive visual buffer (i.e., structure that supports depictive representations, as discussed in chapter 1) that nevertheless did not appear (to an outside observer) to depict on the cortical surface. With the appropriate hardwired connections from the structure that represents imagery to the later ones that interpret patterns of activation within it, any physical pattern of activation can serve to depict a shape; the proper hardwired connections can unscramble an image, from the "point of view" of a later process. However, that is not the way the brain evolved. And as scientists, it's our good luck that the brain makes use of topographically organized cortex, because (as discussed in the following chapter) it makes it much easier to document that depictive representations are used in imagery.

Lack of a Distinct Domain

There is no dispute that virtually any information can be represented in terms of propositions. The invention of the "proposition" originally was motivated in part by a desire to capture the common "idea" underlying synonymous statements, even if they were expressed with different words. Consequently, the construct of the proposition was formulated to be as powerful and flexible as possible, with the goal of utilizing it to represent all knowledge. The issue here is not whether a system using only propositional representations can be formulated to account for imagery phenomena. That seems trivially true (see Anderson, 1978). But *sufficiency* does not imply *necessity*: the mere fact that it is possible to formulate a propositional theory, of the sort we discussed at the outset of this chapter, does not imply that such a theory is correct. We must test the theory. That is, the brain is a specific sort of machine, which operates in specific ways in particular circumstances; there is a fact of the matter—it either is capable of using depictive representations or it is not. At the present juncture, we want to know whether there are strong a priori concerns that should dissuade us from formulating a separate imagery theory that makes use of depictive representations, even if a separate imagery theory could in fact more parsimoniously account for the data and have greater value in leading us to predict new and interesting results. If there are no compelling reasons against the plausibility of such a distinct theory, then it makes sense to try to cast one and discover whether this is a useful way to proceed.

The Factual Nature of Knowledge

It is true that simply having an image does not imply that one has knowledge—but the same is true for propositional representations: mere possession of representations in propositional format does not constitute knowledge, any more than a page has knowledge because a sentence is written on it. It makes sense to speak of knowledge only in the context of processes that make use of internal representations. If not a mind's eye, some sort of "mind's frontal lobe" (i.e., an evaluation process) is necessary to interpret even abstract propositions (and yet we do not feel in danger of an "infinite regress" of propositions and "mind's frontal lobes"! We know that the frontal lobe can't do anything without the representation, and vice versa). If knowledge is viewed in terms of information processing systems that include active processes performed on representations, rather than in terms of the static structures themselves, then using propositions instead of images as the format for these structures does not necessarily gain us anything. In either case, processors must be postulated that operate on representations. The power of any representational format can be assessed only by considering its compatibility with the available processors.

Thus, a person does not have knowledge when he or she has a mental image any more than a camera has knowledge when it contains film after one takes a snapshot (see Wittgenstein, 1958). Nevertheless, images may contain information from which knowledge can be derived. If images are sensory patterns that have been organized and stored, the question of how knowledge can be derived from images is on the same footing as the question of how knowledge is derived from ongoing sensory activity during perception. Knowledge obviously is derived from perceptual representations, and there seems to be no reason why it should not also be gleaned in similar ways from mental images.

But what about the concern that images are inherently ambiguous and so cannot be used to represent knowledge independently (because they would not necessarily be interpreted the same way when recalled from time to time)? In the words of Wittgenstein:

> I see a picture; it represents an old man walking up a steep
> path leaning on a stick—How? Might it not have looked the
> same if he had been sliding downhill in that position? Perhaps
> a Martian would describe the picture so. I do not need to
> explain why we do not describe it so. (Wittgenstein, 1958,
> p. 54, n. 139 [b])

The point here is that we humans have default interpretive systems, which strongly bias us to interpret most patterns in specific ways. Just as we tend to interpret pictures consistently when revisiting them, we tend to interpret mental images consistently.

Reduction to Primitives and Levels of Analysis

The use of imagery in theories of psychological phenomena was also criticized because imagery can be described in terms of more elementary components. But will this exercise increase our understanding of mental phenomena, or merely cloud important distinctions? As Putnam (1973) points out, we must take care to distinguish explanations from "parents of explanations." Consider Putnam's example of the appropriate explanation for why a certain square peg will not fit into a certain round hole. The proper level of analysis would not entail discussion of subatomic particles, but would make use of emergent properties such as "rigidity" and "contour," properties that cannot necessarily be derived from knowledge of the molecular constitution of the objects involved. Similarly, one would not learn much about architecture simply by studying bricks, mortar, and other building materials. Thus, if images are functional internal representations different in format from other representations, it makes sense to study imagery per se, rather than to study only the most basic irreducible representations. In our view the issue is whether a depictive image—however derived—has distinctive characteristic properties and so can serve as a distinct form of representation. Do such images make accessible and explicit information that was inaccessible and only implicit in the representations that gave rise to them? If so, then images deserve a role in psychological explanations.

Representation and Process

Is the type of representation/process pair used in imagery different in kind from those underlying more general cognitive functions? A key idea is that if the representations are in a distinct format, then a different kind of processing system as a whole will be necessary. That is, given the existence of representations with particular functional properties, there are constraints on the possible nature of the processes in the system. The interpretive procedures that operate on depictive representations are very different from the procedures that interpret linguistic strings. For example, they do not have to enter a lexicon to identify the "form class" of a symbol. As discussed in chapter 1, depictive representations do not bear an arbitrary relation to the thing represented, unlike descriptive representations. Information about an object is inherent in the pattern of the representation itself, is worn on its sleeve, as it were. The issue then becomes an empirical one, whether this kind of distinct format is in fact used in human mental activity. If imagery makes use of a distinct kind of representation and accompanying processes, it is fallacious to claim that a single theory ought to subsume imagery and other forms of processing.

Necessity of a Third Code

Those who have claimed that translation between verbal and perceptual representations requires a separate propositional representation system have never specified how this translation would be accomplished. It appeared to Kosslyn and Pomerantz (1977) that this assumption simply pushes the problem back a step: How is translation to be accomplished between images and propositions? Between propositions and verbal codes? Translation problems exist if one stores images and verbal material or if one stores only propositions. In fact, having to translate from images to propositions and from verbal codes to propositions may be more difficult than simply translating directly from images to verbal codes (which requires only a single set of translational rules). Furthermore, as Anderson (1978) points out, if all translation requires an intervening code, then we are faced with an infinite regress: to translate between a visual code and a propositional one requires yet another code, but to translate to this code again requires another code, and so on. However translation between verbal and imagery codes is achieved, it is not clear that an intermediate propositional representation would aid in this process.

To solve the translation problem, one must have a set of transformational rules that specify how one format is represented in, or mapped into, another. Such rules would not represent information about the world, but only about the codes between which translation is required. These rules would take the form of processes or routines, which when applied to information codes in one format would produce a corresponding representation in another format. No intermediate third form of representation need be involved. For instance, there is no need for a third code to translate hexadecimal numbers to binary numbers in a computer. Thus, the translation problem does not imply that imagery is merely one aspect of a more general processing system, which itself is the only appropriate object of study.

Efficiency

Will processing really be easier if all knowledge is stored in a propositional format? Depending on the task, the different characteristics of representation systems can lead to differences in the nature, speed, and efficiency of the processing they support. Consider two formats for representing geographical information: a map and a chart of intercity distances. These two systems may be completely isomorphic to each other in all important respects, because either one can be generated from the other.[10] Nevertheless, these two sorts of representations have clearly different properties. The map is a depictive representation, which makes it suitable for rapid geometrical computations; the chart of intercity distances is digital, which makes it suitable for rapid arithmetic computations. If we want to know quickly whether there are any three cities in some region that fall on a straight line, we consult the map; if we want to know the total distance of an air flight from New York to Los Angeles to Miami, we consult the chart. Clearly, other forms of external representation besides these two are possible: lists of sentences expressing propositions such as "Miami is south of Atlanta," for example, or tree structures containing similar propositional information. It is likely that each of these formats would be well suited for some purposes but not for others. The "efficiency" of a representation, then, depends in part upon the purposes to which one puts that representation.

Given that different types of external representational formats lend themselves to performing different tasks, we can easily argue that the same is true for internal representations. By using different representations, tailored for the task at hand, the system *gains* in efficiency. The brain did not evolve to respect the philosopher's or scientist's views of parsimony. Rather, the brain evolved to perform its tasks as well as possible, given architectural constraints (Gould & Lewontin, 1979). Different sorts of information need to be made explicit and accessible for vision, audition, and motor control, and different sorts of representations would function more or less effectively for each type of content. As we shall argue in the following chapters, there is good evidence that information can be represented internally in at least two different formats, which differ in their suitability for different tasks. Thus, it is neither necessary nor clearly desirable to assume that information must always be recoded into a common, propositional format.

Furthermore, before we can compare the economy of representation systems including a distinct image representation subsystem with the economy of those relying solely on propositional representation, it is necessary to know how many propositions are necessary to represent an object, scene, or event. This question is difficult to answer because (1) we lack the means to measure the amount of information in a percept of an object, scene, or episode and (2) we do not know which of a (probably infinite) number of sets of propositions best represents an object, scene, or event. In any case, when one considers the propositional models of imagery proposed to date (for example, Baylor, 1971), one is impressed with the sheer number of propositions needed to represent even relatively simple objects. These numbers become even greater if one assumes, with Pylyshyn, that propositions are constructed to represent knowledge at several different levels of hierarchy at the same time. Thus, it might be much more wasteful to generate hordes of propositions at the time of encoding than to store a smaller number of perceptual units which could then be used at a later time for drawing inferences and making deductions. If limited encoding or memory capacity is an important factor in internal representation, then it is advantageous to encode and store as little as possible and to infer or deduce as much as possible when more detailed information is required. Although propositions could also be used for inferences and deduction, certain implicit relations may be derived much more easily from depictive images.

As noted earlier, because the storage capacity of the brain and its encoding systems is unknown, not much weight should be given to these considerations.[11] Nevertheless, it is clear that the capacity arguments levied against positing a distinct imagery representation system can be wielded with equal force against formulating a general propositional system.

Elegance

Finally, some critics have asserted that a separate theory of imagery is inelegant. We have two comments to make on this point. First, because a theory positing only one type of representation does seem simpler than a theory positing more than a single type of representation, the onus is on us to argue that depictive images are a distinct format and to provide data supporting this position. That said, we note that this metric of parsimony may be misguided. On the one hand, we must consider not just the number of formats but also the number of types of processes that are required to operate over them. Because propositional representations are intended to be used in all forms of cognition, a very large range of processes must be posited to create and interpret these representations appropriately. In contrast, when representations are tailored for a specific task (making explicit and accessible the relevant information), the accompanying processes will be relatively simple. On the other hand, reflecting this difference, propositional accounts are not particularly straightforward or simple for many imagery results. Essentially, then, we have a trade-off between the parsimony of the theory (determined in part by the number of different formats posited) and the parsimony of the accounts. Positing only one format at the expense of very unwieldy accounts may not really be more parsimonious than positing two formats if much simpler and more straightforward accounts of data are forthcoming.

Second, we again stress that sufficiency does not imply necessity: the simple fact that one might be able to formulate accounts of all data using a single representation does not eliminate the possibility of alternative mechanisms. It is not surprising that some propositional model (albeit ad hoc and post hoc) can usually be offered for any given result. Current propositional theories do not possess strong inherent constraints; thus, some variant of a propositional model usually can be formulated, with equal ease, it would seem, to "explain" any empirical finding or its converse. It could even be argued that propositional "theories" of this form fail to meet Popper's (1959) criterion of a scientific theory: they cannot be disproved (the same criticism has been leveled against psychoanalytic theories).

One consequence of this is that even though some kind of post hoc propositional account of imagery data is always possible, these accounts are virtually always sterile. Unlike the depictive imagery accounts, few (if any) new predictions or insights have followed from them. A theory must lead one to ask further questions if it is to play any real role in a research program.

Conclusions

In this chapter we examined the nature of propositional alternatives to depictive theories of imagery. We can conclude:

Depictive representation in imagery is not an inherently flawed concept; there are no compelling a priori reasons to reject the use of depictive imagery in psychological explanations. Only the most simplistic "picture metaphor" conception of imagery can be rejected outright. The essential claim that imagery is a distinct representation system, utilizing representations of a special depictive format, is neither internally inconsistent, incoherent, nor paradoxical.

Imagery is not necessarily only a special aspect of a more general propositional representation system. There is nothing inherently inconsistent or incoherent in the notion of a distinct imagery processing system, nothing that would demand that proposition-like representations in fact do most of human information processing.

Explicit theories are needed. The foregoing discussion underlines the need to specify exactly how particular sets of processes work over representations that have particular characteristics. Without such specification, we have great liberty in the sorts of properties that follow from a given form of representation, and we can continue to offer arguments and counterarguments on both sides indefinitely. What is needed are explicit theories of visual mental imagery that can be empirically tested and evaluated in terms of generality, parsimony, and so on. As it now stands, there are simply too many possible varieties of depictive and propositional theories, theories that have appreciably different properties, to allow any sort of evaluation of relative efficacy on purely rational grounds. In chapter 5 we present one example of such a theory.

Finally, we must confront Anderson's (1978) demonstration that one can always produce a new theory by changing the representation of one theory and then compensating for that change by altering the theory of processing. The problem is that nothing is nailed down in advance: there are no a priori constraints. Anderson also pointed out, however, that the brain can serve to constrain this wanton arbitrariness. A theorist *cannot* make up properties of the brain—such as functions of specific brain areas and the anatomical connectivity among areas—simply to account for data. Thus, cognitive theories can be *constrained* by such facts about the brain; the facts do not dictate the theories, but they limit the range of what can be posited. Facts about the brain anchor theories in such a way that theorists cannot invent alternative accounts for sets of data by changing theories of representations and processes at their convenience.

Notes

1. Most of the arguments against depictive representations are addressed to the topic of visual imagery. We will follow suit, although the reader should keep in mind that parallel arguments also may be levied for and against imagery in other modalities.

2. The anti-imagery arguments are gleaned primarily from Anderson and Bower (1973), Clark and Chase (1972), Dennett (1969, 2002), Pylyshyn (1973, 1975, 1981, 2002, 2003), and Reid (1974). Unless otherwise noted, the arguments against depictive representation are drawn from Pylyshyn's original paper (1973) and his follow-up paper in 1981.

3. Much of this chapter is built around chapter 2 of Kosslyn (1980), which in turn was based on the Kosslyn and Pomerantz (1977) paper. James Pomerantz deserves credit for helping develop the arguments offered here.

4. The following section is adapted from Kosslyn (1983), with permission of the publisher.

5. Unless otherwise specified, we will use the terms *image* and *imagery* to refer to depictive representations. After all, it is only such representations that are truly "images."

6. Millar (2002) notes that Pylyshyn's assertion is "odd in the context of evolutionary biology" (p. 202). We will not go down this path here, but it is likely to lead to yet another line of disagreement between the camps.

7. Most initial distinctions in science—especially in biology—are qualitative; the quantitative characterization of relations only comes later, after a phenomenon is relatively well understood. We acknowledge that there is much work left to be done, but this is not to say that the distinctions we have already drawn and supported cannot accomplish much explanatory work.

8. Note that even current measures of the amount of information contained in single neuron spike trains (e.g., Osborne, Bialek, & Lisberger, 2004) say very little about overall capacity limitations of the human brain as a collection of interacting neural networks.

9. The point being made here is simply that people can be aware of the phenomenology of the image itself, not simply the information being conveyed. However, the fact that imagery vividness ratings are reliable (Marks, 1973) does not imply that they necessarily reflect specific aspects of information processing—this is a separate issue.

10. Anderson (1978) claims that a map will have additional information indicating absolute orientation. Usually this is indicated explicitly by a compass or direction arrow; however, if a "north point" is placed top and center and this point is included in the intercity distances, a multidimensional scaling solution will then also recover this orientation information. In any event, it is not clear whether the absolute orientation information is a property of the map itself or of how the reader can process it.

11. Although it is possible that measurements derived from information theory (e.g., Osborne, Bialek, & Lisberger, 2004) may one day provide realistic estimates of brain storage and processing capacity, these measures would still address only the content, not the format, of representations. By analogy, one could characterize the processing capacity of a computer but not know which high-level programming language is running on that computer.

3

Evaluating Experimental Artifact Accounts

The imagery debate took a new turn in 1981 when Pylyshyn (see also 2002, 2003) rejected the idea that the results of imagery experiments reflect properties of underlying mechanisms. Instead, he claimed that these results are to be understood by appeal to three principles: (1) Imagery experiments necessarily incorporate *task demands* as part and parcel of the task itself; these task demands are aspects of the task that require the participants to try to mimic what they would do in the corresponding perceptual situation (such as shifting one's attention across a scene while scanning). (2) Participants have *tacit knowledge* of how their perceptual systems work (such as knowing that it takes more time to shift one's head through greater arcs when scanning a scene), and can access such knowledge (perhaps unconsciously). (3) Participants can use tacit knowledge to regulate their responses, so that they can in fact mimic what they believe they would have done in the corresponding perceptual situation. We will refer to these three principles working together as the *tacit knowledge account.*

Can one explain away all results from imagery experiments, claiming that they reflect nothing more than tacit knowledge working in conjunction with task demands? This may have been possible when the debate focused solely on behavioral data—but is wildly implausible when neural data are considered. To see why, we need to consider this class of counterexplanation in detail. Following this, we will consider two other accounts of imagery findings that do not appeal to the nature or functioning of mechanisms.

Tacit Knowledge as an Explanation

The force of this approach rests on numerous claims. In this section we summarize the core claims, and in the following section we consider how firmly grounded these claims are.

Intrinsic Properties of Imagery?

The tacit knowledge account rests on the idea that during imagery, one simply mimics what one has seen, and that results of imagery experiments reflect such mimicry—and not characteristics of mechanisms. For example, Farah, Soso, and Dasheiff (1992) showed that a patient who had the occipital lobe removed from one cerebral hemisphere (for medical reasons) developed a case of tunnel vision and also developed tunnel imagery. In fact, the visual angle subtended by objects in her images was reduced by half, in both perception and imagery—but only in horizontal extent; the vertical extent of her images was not affected. This finding makes sense from the point of view of our theory of the visual buffer, which corresponds to the topographically organized brain areas in which depictive images occur. As discussed in chapter 1, we hypothesize that the visual buffer is implemented in topographically organized cortex in the occipital lobe. If so, then Farah et al.'s finding follows because the left hemisphere's occipital lobe processes the right side of space and the right hemisphere's occipital lobe processes the left side of space—and thus, removing one hemisphere removes the neural underpinnings of half of the visual buffer. In contrast, both hemispheres process the same degree of vertical extent, and thus removing one occipital lobe should not reduce the vertical extent of the visual buffer.

According to the tacit knowledge account, however, the patient would have had sufficient time to come to know what things now looked like, after her operation, which would explain why she would describe imaged objects as appearing as if they were reduced by tunnel vision. According to its advocates, this account clearly should be preferred to the mechanistic theory we propose. For example, according to Pylyshyn, "The picture that we are being presented, of a mind's eye gazing upon a display projected onto the visual cortex, is one that should arouse our suspicion. It comes uncomfortably close to the idea that properties of the external world, as well as of the process of vision (including the resolution pattern of the retina and the necessity of moving one's eyes around the display to foveate features of interest), are internalized in the imagery system" (Pylyshyn, 2002, p. 178).

In addition, the tacit knowledge account suggests that many features of imagery that are taken by depictive theorists to be due to the intrinsic form of the cognitive architecture (specifically, the organization of the visual buffer) are in fact part of the definition of what an image is. For example, the idea that one cannot have an image without having a representation of size and orientation is simply part of what it *means* to have an image. Thus, according to the tacit knowledge account, many physical features of images are part of the definition of images, and have nothing at all to do with the mechanisms of the imagery system.

Failure of Mechanistic Accounts

There are several perceptual phenomena that do not occur in imagery, which must be explained. For example, Emmert's Law is not typically observed with visual images (the subjective size of visual images projected onto a perceived scene does not change as the background recedes, unlike the size of visual afterimages). Similarly, when we reach out to grasp an imaged object, we are essentially pantomiming a reaching movement rather than engaging the visuo-motor system, and people cannot smoothly track imagined objects (Kowler, 1990). Moreover, people are notoriously poor at imagining how colors will appear when they are mixed in novel ways. Such findings cast doubt on the idea that imagery outputs are directly fed into the subsequent visual processing systems, as they would be if there were a topographically organized cortical projection to the corresponding brain areas.

Cognitive Penetrability

Cognitive penetrability occurs when one's conscious or unconscious beliefs, attributions, or expectations about a cognitive phenomenon alter that phenomenon. According to this idea, intrinsic properties of images (i.e., that are based on the architecture of the imagery system) cannot be detected because these properties are masked by the possibility that one's knowledge or assumptions about the phenomena produce the observed effects. In fact, Pylyshyn takes this idea to an extreme. It's not just that beliefs, attributions, and expectations modify or alter processing, but that they form the basis of certain kinds of processing: "Kosslyn et al. believe that it is the spatial format, and not the content, that explains the data; but in this they are simply wrong for those cases (such as scanning) where tacit knowledge provides a better explanation" (Pylyshyn, 2002, p. 225).

A corollary of this idea is that images have no properties other than those that the imager assumes they have. If this view is correct, one should never be surprised by the content of one's images. A similar point was made by Sartre (1948), which has been developed further by others (e.g., Dalla Barba, Rosenthal, & Visetti, 2002). According to Sartre, imagery entails a specific relationship between an object and consciousness, which, he claimed, is fundamentally different from that between an object and the perception of it: because one forms an image of a specific object, one cannot then find something new in its contents. "I can keep looking at an image for as long as I wish: I will never find anything but what I put there" (Sartre, 1948, p. 11). According to Sartre, because we create mental images, our "disposition" toward them is fixed: the image can embody only what we expect.

The Null Hypothesis

In his most recent statements, Pylyshyn emphasizes that the content—not the format—of what is stored explains performance in imagery tasks (see the quotation above). And this claim leads him to assert that there is no evidence for a format different from the one used in linguistic thought. This is his "null hypothesis." However, when pressed to supply details, he claims that mental images are implemented by the same sorts of symbolic (i.e., propositional) representations that he assumes are used in other domains of cognition. Specifically, Pylyshyn prefers propositional representations because they are the class of representations that

> we know something about (since it includes all the various formal
> languages and symbolic calculi for which we have a formal
> semantics to tell us how the meanings of complex structures are
> composed from the meanings of their parts) and because it meets
> certain minimal requirements that must be met by any system
> adequate for the representation of knowledge and for reasoning.
> In particular, we know that a recursive system of symbols
> has properties such as productivity, compositionality, and
> systematicity, and that these are essential for reasoning and
> knowledge representation (for a detailed argument on this point,
> see Fodor & Pylyshyn 1988). (Pylyshyn, 2002, p. 219)

Nevertheless, the thrust of the null hypothesis is to avoid any mention of format and instead to rely on the content.

Assessing Tacit Knowledge

The extent to which participants will appear to have specific knowledge depends heavily on the way their knowledge is assessed. Thus, according to proponents of the tacit knowledge theory, a failure to find evidence that participants in studies have the appropriate tacit knowledge of their perceptual systems only shows that this knowledge was not assessed properly. Pylyshyn (2002) asserts that whether participants have tacit knowledge of a phenomenon cannot be ascertained by asking them and definitely not by testing their knowledge of psychology. Thus, attempts to evaluate this theory by interviewing participants in studies, or asking them to predict their results by "mentally simulating" their behavior, are misguided. Rather, one must focus on subtle aspects of how tasks are performed, relying on behavioral data, which will clearly document the contribution of tacit knowledge.

Accounting for Key Imagery Phenomena

According to the tacit knowledge approach, key imagery phenomena can be explained without recourse to mechanisms of any sort.

Image Generation

Probably the most basic facts about imagery are that: (a) we have images and (b) we do not have specific images all the time. A tacit knowledge account would dismiss the idea that an image representation is created during the act of image generation and instead would simply claim that participants mimic perception when they need to do so.

Scanning

As we discussed in chapter 2, more time generally is required to scan greater distances across imaged objects. According to a tacit knowledge account, this result is due to tacit knowledge about what it would be like actually to scan the object visually. Participants in these experiments presumably simulate what it would be like to see (or hear, in the case of auditory imagery) a certain scene or stimulus. For example, if one were to imagine a minute waltz and it did not take about a minute, then we can assume that the participant was not doing what he or she was supposed to do. Similarly, if one were asked to scan an image and it did not require more time to scan greater distances, he or she apparently did not understand the nature of the task.

In contrast, Pylyshyn (2002) notes that, just as would occur in perception, if you imagine a light going off at one location and another coming on at another location on a map, you do not need to scan (and the time to react to the turning on of the second light will not depend on the distance between the two points).

Zooming

Similarly, reporting details from smaller images (i.e., ones that seem to subtend a smaller visual angle) requires more time than reporting details from larger images (Kosslyn, 1980). According to the tacit knowledge account, this is because people know that objects in smaller images are typically of lower resolution and the details are thus more difficult to see—and as long as being blurrier is part of the definition of being smaller, the results must come out in the predicted way.

Rotating

According to the tacit knowledge account, the finding that more time is required to rotate objects in an image through larger arcs (Shepard & Cooper, 1982) only indicates that participants have perceived and remembered how actual objects rotate—and thereafter mimic this phenomenon in their imagery.

Image Organization

Imaged objects have an internal structure; for example, we can "see" the large triangles in figure 3.1 more easily than the parallelograms that are embedded in its shape (Reed, 1974). Proponents of the tacit knowledge account argue that such findings simply indicate that people are aware (unconsciously) that the corresponding object was perceptually organized. They may be aware of this because they stored a description of the object, which captures its internal organization. For example, figure 3.1 might be described as "a rectangle with the sides removed, containing two adjacent X marks," and one knows that the lines of X marks delineate sides of a triangle—and hence later it is easier to affirm that the figure contains a triangle than a parallelogram.

In addition, Reisberg and Chambers (1991) and Chambers and Reisberg (1992) report interesting experiments in which they show that people cannot easily reinterpret the patterns in their images—which they take to reflect the inherent organization of the image. For example, when shown an ambiguous figure that they interpret one way (e.g., the duck in the famous duck/rabbit figure—see figure 3.2), they then cannot "see" the alternative interpretation in their image. Similarly, they cannot mentally rotate a

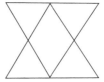

Figure 3.1. A pattern can be encoded as being composed of many small units or relatively few overlapping ones. (From Kosslyn, S. M., Reiser, B. J., Farah, M. J., & Fliegel, S. L. [1983]. Generating visual images: units and relations. *Journal of Experimental Psychology: General, 112,* 278–303.)

pattern, such as a map of the state of Texas, and "see" the new pattern it resembles. Reisberg and Chambers (1991) have drawn a number of conclusions from these findings, which are consistent with the propositionalist perspective. For example, they write: "Hence, in imagery, one cannot set one's understanding aside to reinterpret the (geometrically defined) form because there is no representation of the geometry standing free of specifications one has in mind" (p. 339). Reisberg (1998) infers that people cannot "return to some 'raw material' akin to the proximal stimulus" when using imagery (p. 101).

Countering Tacit Knowledge Accounts

We now allow the other shoe to drop and consider the force of these most recent critiques.

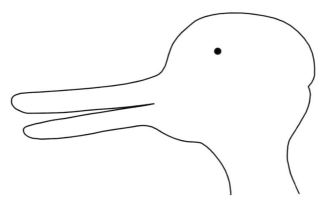

Figure 3.2. The ambiguous duck/rabbit figure. (From Wittgenstein, L. [1958]. *Philosophical investigations.* New York: Macmillan.)

Intrinsic Properties of Imagery?

The aim of tacit knowledge accounts is to displace mechanistic accounts of imagery phenomena that posit depictive representations. Let's return to one finding Pylyshyn (2002, p. 182) discussed, Farah et al.'s (1992) finding that removal of one occipital lobe reduced both the horizontal span of perception and the horizontal extent of visualized objects. Pylyshyn notes that a possible test of the explanation of the tunnel vision and imagery findings offered by depictive theorists would be to study patients whose loss of peripheral vision and delay in testing followed roughly the same pattern as Farah et al.'s patient but in whom the damage was purely retinal. His prediction is that under the same instructional conditions such patients would also exhibit tunnel imagery, even though there was presumably no relevant cortical damage involved.

As it happens, Kosslyn and Cave (1984) studied a patient very much like the hypothetical patient Pylyshyn described. Patient J. B. is a right-handed male who was diagnosed as having a left thalamic tumor at age six. The tumor encroached on his optic tract near the lateral geniculate nucleus and had become surrounded by a cyst. Two shunts were surgically inserted to drain the area. The tumor was not removed. Since then, he has had a highly restricted visual field. J. B. was 24 years old at the time of testing and was a junior at a private university in New England. He reported that reading was quite arduous because he could not see more than two letters at a time. To examine this claim, an upper-case printed letter was mounted on a 1.5 degree disk at the end of a wand (the letter subtended about 1 degree), and J. B. was asked to report when he could name the letter as the wand moved in from the periphery. He failed to name the letter until it was at the fixation point, regardless of whether it was presented in the left or right visual field—which documented that his vision was in fact highly restricted.

What about his imagery? In one test, he was asked a question about the size-ratio of different dimensions of various objects. A typical question had the form, "Is the following object higher than it is wide?" followed by the object's name (e.g., "coffee mug"). Such questions induce imagery (at least during the first time they are answered). Immediately after answering the question, J. B. used a pointer apparatus to indicate where the left and right sides of the object would have been if it had actually been seen as it appeared in the mental image used to answer the question. That is, he was asked, if the image had been an actual picture on a screen, where would its sides have been? (Note that although this paraphrase was intended primarily to clarify the task, it also had the result of potentially predisposing him to use tacit knowledge about how he typically viewed pictures.) By measuring how he positioned the pointer apparatus, it was possible to obtain an estimate of the visual angle subtended by objects in his images. The crucial finding was that J. B.'s average angle was thirty-five degrees, which was vastly larger than the angle at which he could see letters and objects clearly during perception. This result is strongly contrary to what is predicted by a tacit knowledge account.

In addition to noting the failure of the tacit knowledge account to predict these findings correctly, we also fail to see the force of arguments for replacing mechanistic accounts of imagery with tacit knowledge accounts. As we hope was clear in chapters 1 and 2, a theory that posits depictive representations does not need to incorporate a vague notion of a "mind's eye," nor does it need to incorporate the idea of a picture's literally being projected on visual cortex. Instead, representations are patterns of neural activation that in turn affect other patterns of activation in the processing system. If the visual system relied solely on bottom-up processing, then Pylyshyn's claim that imagery is too malleable to arise from the visual system would have force. However, as discussed in chapter 5, the visual system also relies on top-down processing, during which one's knowledge and beliefs can alter the course of processing during perception. The possibility of top-down processing is different from the idea of cognitive penetrability, which refers specifically to the way a phenomenon can purportedly be altered by one's knowledge, beliefs, or expectations about that phenomenon. Top-down processing need not alter a phenomenon to bring it into accord with one's knowledge, beliefs, and expectations.

If knowledge of what things would look like in the real world is the crucial variable for explaining the results of imagery experiments, then one way to distinguish between the two classes of theory, tacit knowledge accounts versus depictive theories, is by finding a perceptual phenomenon that relies on depictive properties but that is completely unknown to participants. And here is a crucial point: all it takes is *one* example where the tacit knowledge account cannot explain findings that otherwise implicate depictive representation. If even one such case is found, the debate is settled: depictive representations are used in at least some circumstances. The focus would then shift to when, precisely, depictive representations are used.

We have thus studied the "oblique effect," which is the fact that a field of narrow black-and-white stripes is more difficult to resolve visually when the lines are oriented diagonally than when they are oriented either horizontally or vertically (Appelle, 1972). Two studies, using entirely different methods, have demonstrated this effect in imagery (Kosslyn & Pennington, summarized in Kosslyn, 1983, and Kosslyn, Sukel, & Bly, 1999). For example,

Kosslyn, Sukel, and Bly (1999) asked participants to memorize sets of black-and-white stripes, which were either horizontal, vertical, or diagonal. The same stripes were used in different conditions for different people. After memorizing the stimuli, the participants then were asked to close their eyes and visualize a pair of these patterns and compare the two along a named dimension (e.g., deciding which set of stripes was wider). As predicted, this task was more difficult when oblique stripes were visualized than when horizontal or vertical stripes were visualized.

Given that participants had no experience with the oblique effect and thus no knowledge about it (tacit or otherwise), a tacit knowledge account cannot explain the result. In contrast, if the result emerges from the neurophysiology of the visual buffer, it is easily explained by depictive theories. In fact, neurons in topographically organized areas are known to have orientation tuning (e.g., Koulakov & Chklovskii, 2001) and to be less sensitive to distinctions along the diagonal. In addition, at least in area V1 in the cat brain, so-called simple cells (which fire when the animal sees edges and not to complex combinations of features) not only fire more vigorously when horizontal and vertical lines are shown than when diagonal lines are shown but also have sharper tuning for horizontal and vertical lines (Li, Peterson, & Freeman, 2003). These results underscore the fact that the oblique effect reflects properties of the neurons that populate early visual cortex.

The depictive properties of mental imagery also affect processing in other nonintuitive ways. For example, mental imagery may affect one's perception of the subjective visual vertical (SVV), which is determined when one judges the orientation of a line as being vertical. Mast, Kosslyn, and Berthoz (1999) asked participants to judge the SVV as they were lying on their sides in a dark room. The participants rotated a bar with two light-emitting diodes (LEDs), one on each end, to indicate their SVV. The experimental paradigm is illustrated in figure 3.3. In one condition, they were shown a background set of stripes, which was oriented either 67.5 degrees clockwise or counterclockwise with respect to the participant's baseline SVV judgment. When viewing the stripes tilted clockwise at the same time they adjusted the LEDs to indicate their SVV, the participants shifted the SVV to the left; when viewing the stripes tilted counterclockwise, they shifted the SVV to the right. In another condition, the participants did not actually see the stripes, but merely visualized them. Crucially, the same effect was found here—induced by the geometrical properties of their images! There were no task demands built into this study, and because this laboratory phenomenon does not occur in daily life, the participants could not have tacit knowledge of it. In fact, debriefing after the study revealed that the participants were not aware of the influence their images had on their assessment of the SVV.

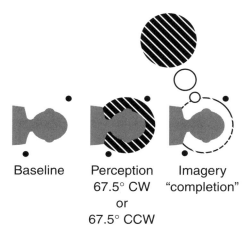

Baseline   Perception   Imagery
              67.5° CW   "completion"
                 or
              67.5° CCW

Figure 3.3. An illustration of a key aspect of the paradigm used in the Mast, Kosslyn, and Berthoz (1999) study. Participants, lying on one side, were asked to estimate their subjective visual vertical (SVV) by rotating a bar equipped with light-emitting diodes. Sets of stripes were presented at either 67.5 degrees clockwise or counterclockwise (as shown here). Baseline SVV measurements were recorded before each condition and the SVV was recorded again during each condition, while they were viewing or visualizing the stripes. (From Mast, F., Kosslyn, S. M., & Berthoz, A. [1999]. Visual mental imagery interferes with allocentric orientation judgments. *NeuroReport, 10,* 3549–3553.)

Another study along these lines was reported by Mast, Berthoz, and Kosslyn (2001), who compared the influence of perception and imagery on roll-vection. Vection is the subjective impression that one is moving even though it is in fact one's surroundings that are in motion. If you've ever been in a parked car when the one next to you starts to move backwards, you may have experienced this phenomenon. Roll vection occurs when one views a rotating display in the absence of other visual cues (for example, in total darkness). Mast, Berthoz, and Kosslyn (2001) asked participants to indicate the subjective visual horizontal (SVH) in much the way that they measured the SVV in their previous study. In this study, they presented participants with rotating displays of dots in one condition and asked them to visualize the rotating dots vividly in another. Analogous to the results in the first study, when participants visualized rotating dots, the SVH was modified comparably to what occurred when they actually viewed the dots. Again, the geometric properties of an image affected performance, even in the context of a subtle laboratory phenomenon of which the participants had no knowledge, implicit or otherwise.

Many other results conclusively demonstrate that tacit knowledge cannot account for all imagery results. If a phenomenon is evoked only in a laboratory, then by definition naive participants cannot have knowledge of it (tacit or otherwise). As yet another example, D'Angiulli (2002) has shown that some aspects of the imagery contrast sensitivity function closely resemble those found in perception. In this study, the author exploited the fact that the contrast sensitivity function is different in dark-adapted (scotopic) and light-adapted (photopic) conditions. One of the differences is that the scotopic contrast sensitivity function peaks at a lower spatial frequency (about two cycles/degree) than the photopic one (about four cycles/degree). Therefore, the relative sensitivity at a pair of appropriately chosen spatial frequencies (e.g., two versus six cycles/degree) is reversed under scotopic and photopic conditions. Participants were asked to visualize small and large images in scotopic and photopic viewing conditions. The results showed the expected relative reversal in the two viewing conditions: in scotopic conditions, small images were generated faster than large images, but vice versa in photopic conditions. Even though the participants had no knowledge of the relative effects of light versus dark, their imagery mirrored their perception. This makes sense because these contrast sensitivity functions are known to reflect activity in early cortical areas.

Nevertheless, in closing this section we wish to note that the idea that tacit knowledge figures into imagery is not entirely off-base. Pylyshyn is correct in observing that imagery does not automatically obey the laws of nature. However, this does not imply—as he argues—that the mechanisms underlying imagery do not do *any* work in helping one solve problems via "mental simulations." Mental simulations are imagined scenarios that mimic what one would expect to happen in the corresponding actual situation, and depictive representations play a key role in such reasoning because they make *explicit and accessible* aspects of shape and spatial relations that otherwise need not be evident. For example, consider what occurs when you have a pile of luggage and must pack it efficiently into a car's trunk. You can visualize the bags in various positions and locations, mentally moving them around until you "see" a good configuration—all before you even begin to haul a single bag off the ground. The image makes explicit the shapes and spatial relations in a way that allows you to conduct a mental simulation.

Failure of Mechanistic Accounts

Why does imagery not always mimic perception? It is important to note that imagery and perception do not rely on identical neural mechanisms. Although most of the brain areas activated by either imagery or perception alone are activated in common (Ganis, Thompson, & Kosslyn, 2004; Kosslyn, Thompson, & Alpert, 1997), not all areas are activated in common. Critically, imagery does not rely on mechanisms used in purely bottom-up processing. And, in fact, every example in which imagery does not mimic perception relies on *sustained input* from bottom-up processing mechanisms, such as is required in order to track a moving object. For example, we know that some neurons in the retina specifically register different wavelengths of light; it is not surprising that feedback connections to the occipital lobe originating in the temporal lobe cannot trigger such input for sustained periods of time. If such mechanisms existed, we would be prone to vivid hallucinations during perception. Top-down processing is transient, possibly in part because the input from these systems is relatively weak (both because feedback connections tend to be relatively diffuse and because the timing of top-down signals is probably not as precise as that of signals driven by an external stimulus)—and hence top-down influences are easily interrupted by bottom-up input.

In contrast, not only do bottom-up signals tend to be stronger than top-down ones but they also can be driven for sustained periods of time by sensory input. Thus, even when mental imagery does affect mechanisms used in bottom-up processing, it does so less strongly than does sensory input: mental images are notoriously transient affairs (for reasons we discuss in chapter 5) and hence cannot drive mechanisms that require sustained input (which underlie Emmert's Law, the tendency for the size of an afterimage to appear larger with increasing perceived distance; see Grüsser & Landis, 1991). In addition, according to Schlack, Hoffmann, and Bremmer (2003), the ability to track a moving object smoothly (smooth pursuit) also depends on processes directly related to the retina. They state:

> The receptor stage, i.e. the retina, contains a specialised area with highest spatial resolution: the fovea. If we want to gain detailed information about a particular object, the gaze is adjusted such that the image of this object falls onto the fovea. If the object of interest moves, its image has to be stabilised on the fovea by matching eye velocity to target velocity and correcting for positional errors. The respective eye movements are called smooth pursuit eye movements (SPEMs). Such eye movements are mainly controlled on the basis of afferent information about visual motion on the retina ("retinal slip") in combination with extraretinal information about eye movements and eye position. (p. 551)

In short, considering the nature of neural mechanisms offers principled reasons for distinguishing between imagery tasks where performance mimics that of the corresponding perceptual tasks and imagery tasks where performance is different. The tacit knowledge account does not.[1]

The fact that imagery does not always mimic perception actually poses a bigger problem for tacit knowledge accounts than for mechanistic accounts. When imagery mimics perception, a tacit knowledge perspective leads one to take the finding as an obvious result of participants' tacit knowledge about vision. However, if the results of imagery experiments simply show that participants mimic perception when told to use imagery, why shouldn't they mimic perception in all tasks? This is a major problem for tacit knowledge accounts in tasks in which participants clearly know the correct answer from perceptual experience. For example, colors cannot be easily mixed in imagery (see Kosslyn, 1981) even if the participant has had experience mixing paints (see figure 3.4). If a tacit knowledge account is correct, people should have no problem mimicking perception in this task.

Cognitive Penetrability

In the present context, we must distinguish between two facets of the concept of cognitive penetrability. On the one hand, cognitive penetration occurs when a person's beliefs, attributions, or expectations alter a phenomenon. Such effects are expected simply from the idea that top-down processing mechanisms used in perception are also used in imagery (as is elaborated in chapter 5). On the other hand, and potentially more damaging to mechanistic theories, this idea implies that images have no properties other than those that the imager assumes they have. This view was championed by Sartre well before Pylyshyn adopted the idea. Sartre, in particular, seems to be making two different points, one of which is correct and one of which is not. First, he correctly asserted that because we create images, we are not surprised by what they represent; for example, we do not intend to visualize a horse and then suddenly discover that we are visualizing a French poodle. It is difficult to imagine how a useful representational system—of any sort—could function otherwise; these systems evolved to help us remember information, reason, solve problems, and so on—not as a form of entertainment.

Second, he also asserted, incorrectly, that images do not allow us to make novel discoveries. In fact, Finke and his colleagues (e.g., Finke, 1990) have shown that people can combine patterns and notice emergent forms that were entirely unexpected. For example, participants were shown three of the shapes illustrated in figure 3.5 and told to rotate, shift, or change them until they fit together to produce a possible object. After two minutes, the participants wrote down the name of the thing that they created and then drew it on a page. Figure 3.6 shows some examples of objects they produced.

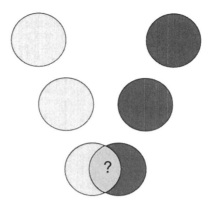

Figure 3.4. Pylyshyn (2002, 2003) argues that imagery is not like perception, based in part on the observation that people cannot visualize colors and combine them mentally to represent accurately the new color that would result from the combination. However, color mixing begins with events in the retina, whereas imagery relies on mechanisms used in the later phases of perceptual processing. Thus, it is not surprising that imagery cannot engage all mechanisms used in color perception—particularly those used in the very earliest phases when color mixing occurs. Note also that this finding does not inform us, one way or the other, about whether imagery representations depict shapes. See color insert. (From Pylyshyn, Z. W. [2003]. Return of the mental image: Are there really pictures in the head? *Trends in Cognitive Neuroscience*, 7[3], 113–118.)

The patterns were in fact recognizable objects on fully 40.5 percent of the trials, and the judges agreed that 15 percent of those patterns were creative.

Many additional studies followed up the original work by Finke and his colleagues. For example, other researchers have asked whether the procedure works with forms other than geometric shapes and simple drawings. The answer is "yes": Mental synthesis is just as easy and effective when people visualize common objects (Helstrup & Anderson, 1996). In addition, researchers have found that actually asking people to use visual imagery to construct new objects leads them to perform much better than if they were told to use a verbal strategy (Helstrup & Anderson, 1991). This finding is interesting from the point of view of the imagery debate: if images are in fact represented as propositional descriptions, why wouldn't a verbal strategy—which directly produces such representations—be more effective than a visual strategy, which requires several additional steps to produce these language-like representations? In fact, describing the forms actually seems to hurt performance: For example, the participants in another study were asked to say "la la la" as they interpreted mental images. The researchers hypothesized that saying "la la la" would interfere with the participants' ability to verbally describe the visualized

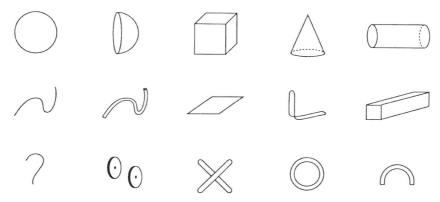

Figure 3.5. The patterns that were used by Finke to examine creative inventions in imagery. Participants were shown three of the patterns and were told to visualize and mentally arrange the patterns to create a novel object. (From Finke, R. A. [1990]. *Creative imagery: Discoveries and inventions in visualization.* Hillsdale, NJ: Erlbaum.)

forms (for example, by naming objects or parts), but would not interfere with the ability to interpret a depictive representation. As predicted, the participants performed better when they said "la la la" as they interpreted the images than when they were not told to say those syllables. Why? Because using language apparently gets in the way of interpreting patterns in mental images (Brandimonte, Hitch, & Bishop, 1992), and the participants' saying "la la la" prevented them from using a language-based strategy.[2]

Such findings are consistent with many reports about the role of imagery in creativity (e.g., Miller, 2000). Einstein (1945) famously emphasized these properties of imagery in his descriptions of how he used imagery in reasoning—for example, by imagining what he would see if he chased a beam of light and caught up with it (and in fact was surprised to note that what he would see in the image did not correspond to what he had ever in fact seen).

Moreover, the role of imagery in memory retrieval relies on just this property of not knowing (explicitly) the contents of one's images. Police interviewers now regularly induce eyewitnesses to visualize the scene of a crime simply because the image *can* surprise witnesses, reminding them of aspects of the situations that were not explicitly encoded in descriptions (Fisher, 1995; Fisher, Geiselman, & Amador, 1989). Indeed, the mundane use of imagery to answer questions about relatively subtle visual or spatial characteristics, such as "What shape are a cat's ears?" or "In what hand does the Statue of Liberty hold the torch?", depends on this characteristic of imagery. If one already believes that cats have pointed ears, why form an image?

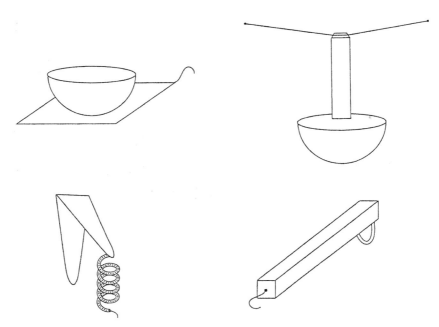

Figure 3.6. Some examples of novel objects produced by the participants who were shown the patterns illustrated in figure 3.5. From upper left, clockwise: the "child-proof bowl," the "hip exerciser," the "shoestring unlacer," and the "hanging extension cord." (From Finke, R. A. [1990]. *Creative imagery: Discoveries and inventions in visualization.* Hillsdale, NJ: Erlbaum.)

One might claim that the experience of imagery is a result of recalling visual content—but if that is true, then why do people stop reporting the use of imagery after they have answered the question three times in succession? In our view, after one answers this sort of question repeatedly, one simply adds a new representation of the content in a verbal format (e.g., "the ears are rounded") and thus no longer needs to use an image.

In our view, imagery is useful in large part *because* it can lead to the unexpected. Imagery allows one to anticipate the consequences of "trying something out" before actually doing it. In fact, imagery can allow one to anticipate the consequences of trying something—such as catching up with a beam of light—that one cannot actually do. We stress that in order to serve this function, one's beliefs must modulate imagery. As illustrated by the theory described in chapter 5, depictive representations are embedded in a processing system, and it is the system as a whole that accomplishes tasks.

The Null Hypothesis

By formulating his own position as the "null hypothesis" that must be dis-proved by others, Pylyshyn (2002) takes it for granted that propositional representations (or "symbol systems," as he sometimes calls them) are the default format. Why should the idea that propositional representations are used in all human information processing be the default? Barsalou (1999), for one, argues that modality-specific representations do virtually all of the work that has sometimes been ascribed to symbol systems—and points out that there is in fact very little evidence that true symbol systems of the sort Pylyshyn invokes are used in human cognition. Barsalou's arguments led us to take pause when considering Pylyshyn's choice of terminology. All stu-dents of statistics are taught that one cannot affirm the null hypothesis, and the same would appear to be true of this incarnation. Instead, to be taken seriously, tacit knowledge accounts must be supported by independent evidence.

Assessing Tacit Knowledge

How would one collect evidence for the tacit knowledge account? Pyly-shyn (2002) asserts that whether participants have tacit knowledge of a phenomenon cannot be assessed by asking them or by testing what they know about the phenomenon. However, if participants in an experiment can use tacit knowledge to produce responses like those they would have made in the corresponding perceptual situation, it is not clear why they shouldn't be able to imagine themselves in the experiment and describe what they would do. But when Denis and Carfantan (1985) gave people descriptions of imagery experiments and asked them to predict what would happen, only a small minority of the participants correctly predicted the results of mental image scanning or rotation experiments. Pylyshyn simply dismisses these findings as irrelevant because people may not have con-scious access to tacit knowledge, but the findings clearly reflect what people believe to be true. Pylyshyn cannot have it both ways: if people supposedly rely on their beliefs when actually performing the task, why can't the sim-ulation allow them to note what they believe would happen when they are asked to simulate performing the task?

Pylyshyn argues that responses can often change depending on how the question is asked, which is no doubt true. However, for this assertion to have theoretical force, we would need to know why asking questions in some specific ways taps particular aspects of one's beliefs, whereas asking questions in other ways taps other aspects of one's beliefs. Otherwise, whenever one assesses tacit knowledge and finds no evidence for it, proponents of such accounts could always claim that participants do have the requisite type of tacit knowledge but were not queried in the right way. This observation points to a larger problem with tacit knowledge accounts: they are in principle post hoc, given the lack of any clear method of assessing the sort of tacit knowledge that purportedly is used in imagery experiments.

Evaluating the Tacit Knowledge Accounts of Key Imagery Phenomena

Do tacit knowledge accounts and related nondepictive accounts illuminate the actual findings? Let's take a closer look.

Image Generation

Do participants simply mimic perception when they need to do so? Such an account would not explain why forming an image can facilitate subsequent perceptual processing of the same stimulus. For example, Nielsen and Smith (1973) found that visualizing schematic faces facilitated evaluating such faces, and Kosslyn, Cave, et al. (1988) found that visualizing a letter in a grid facilitated deciding whether an X mark would or would not fall on the letter, relative to a condition in which the image was not generated in advance.

Scanning

The tacit knowledge account for image scanning is strained, for several reasons: First, there is no evidence that people believe that attention is shifted incrementally during visual perception. The one study that asked people to predict their behavior in image scanning tasks failed to find evidence of such beliefs (Denis & Carfantan, 1985). This lack of evidence makes sense: in vision, we typically shift attention by making rapid saccades, which produce the phenomenology of one point of view being replaced by another. Moviemakers long have taken advantage of our comfort with such transitions, making sharp cuts from one scene to another. The only time we scan smoothly in perception is when we track objects, at which point we are attending to the object itself (by definition). Nevertheless, the time to scan an image increases with distance even when objects are not being tracked.

In addition, no depictive theorist (including our group) has claimed that scanning is *always* used as part of image inspection. If the task does not require shifting focus from one locus to another in order to "see" a part or property with high resolution, scanning would not be required. Kosslyn (1994, pp. 339–341) discusses ways in which "pop-out" can occur in imagery, where characteristics of the imaged object are immediately passed on for later processing (without needing to be focused on following scanning). For example, in the study in which lights go on and off at different locations, a point of light could be seen even with very low resolution (in the periphery) and would not require shifting focus. This type of task is most likely accomplished with spatial representations in the parietal lobe (see Sereno et al., 2001).[3]

Finke and Pinker (1982, 1983) and Pinker, Choate, and Finke (1984) reported a lengthy series of experiments investigating this issue many years ago. These scanning experiments are important because they were the first studies to lead the participants to scan spontaneously. As illustrated in figure 3.7, in this task participants view an array of dots, which is then removed, or they study the array in advance; after the dots have been memorized, an arrow is presented, and participants must say whether it would have pointed at one of the dots if the arrow were superimposed on the array. The result is that the time to decide increases linearly with the distance from the arrow to the target dot. However, Pylyshyn claims that this increased time to scan may be due to "attentional crowding," which leads to more difficult discriminations among dots that are farther away. Although the evidence we turn to shortly shows that attentional crowding is not the main factor causing these effects in visual imagery, we note that even if it were, this would be evidence for a depictive representation. The

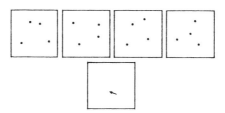

Figure 3.7. Stimuli used by Finke and Pinker (1982). The participants first studied an array of dots (e.g., one of the four at the top), which they memorized. Once the array had been removed, an arrow was presented and the participants decided whether it would have pointed at one of the dots if the array were still present. The participants were never explicitly instructed to scan or to form images. (From Kosslyn, S. M. [1983]. *Ghosts in the mind's machine.* New York: Norton.)

very notion of crowding implies being arrayed closely in space; it simply is not clear how crowding effects could occur without a depictive representation.

The potential problem of perceptual crowding was eliminated by Dror and Kosslyn (1993), who adapted the Finke and Pinker paradigm as follows. They replaced dots with a square doughnut-like display, shown in figure 3.8; each of the four sides of the display was composed of a set of contiguous small squares, most of which where white (17) and some black (3). After the display was removed, an arrow was presented in the empty center space of the display, pointing directly to the location previously occupied by a target square. The task was simply to classify as black or white the square that was pointed to by the arrow. For present purposes, it is important to note that crowding effects between the black squares would not occur: the distance between them (relative to their eccentricity) is well above that required to produce attentional crowding (e.g., Intriligator & Cavanagh, 2001), regardless of the position of the arrow. As in the previous scanning experiments, response times increased with increased distance from the arrow to the square, consistent with the inference that people scanned the image (as they did in fact report during debriefing). The more recent image scanning experiments do not ever mention the word *imagery* in the instructions, let alone *scanning*. Thus, there is no hint in the instructions that the participants should simulate what it would be like to

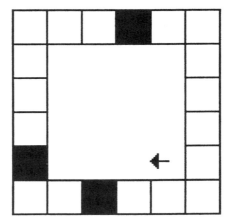

Figure 3.8. The stimulus used by Dror and Kosslyn, which rules out the "perceptual crowding" argument. Crowding between the black squares could not occur because the distance between them is too large. (From Dror, I., & Kosslyn, S. M. [1993]. Mental imagery and aging. *Psychology and Aging, 9,* 90–102.)

perceive the corresponding situation—but nevertheless, the results are as predicted, with increased time to scan increased distance.

Zooming

As many people have become aware after the advent of inexpensive high-resolution printers, smaller does not necessarily mean blurrier. Thus, it is not clear that part of the definition of smaller implies blurrier. Moreover, the effects of size are evident even when size is manipulated indirectly (Kosslyn, 1975), and later memory is poorer for objects that were visualized at a small size than at a larger size—even when participants were not aware that they would receive a later memory test (Kosslyn & Alpert, 1977). The tacit knowledge account is weak when there are no task demands that lead participants to mimic what they would expect to perform in the analogous perceptual situation.

In contrast, depictive theory can account for such findings by appeal to the facts that: (1) the neurons in the visual buffer have relatively short connections, (2) these connections are primarily inhibitory, and (3) top-down influences are not sustained or strong enough to overcome all of the inhibition. Thus, when objects are visualized subtending small visual angles, the local effects of inhibition will make them blurrier, with fewer details evident than when they are visualized subtending larger visual angles; with larger objects, the inhibition will not disrupt widely separated portions of the image as strongly as it affects nearby portions. Hence, details of the object will be obscured in small images but distinguished in larger ones. In contrast, in perception, the bottom-up input from the eyes is sustained and sufficiently strong to overcome much of the inhibition among neurons that register even nearby points in the visual field.

Rotating

The tacit knowledge account fails to explain why mental rotation results are obtained when no instructions to use imagery are provided and thus no task demands to mimic perception exist (Shepard & Cooper, 1982). Moreover, this account fails to explain many subtle aspects of these findings. For example, in some experiments participants are asked to begin to rotate an image, and at some variable time after they start, the stimulus to be evaluated is actually presented; for example, the participants might rotate an image of an uppercase letter, and then be asked to decide whether a presented letter faces normally or is mirror-reversed. The perceptual stimulus is either at the same orientation as the imaged stimulus (as estimated on the basis of the time it would take for participants to mentally rotate the image a specific amount) or at another orientation. Participants can evaluate perceptual patterns faster when they are presented at the same orientation as an image of that pattern than when they are presented at another orientation (Cooper & Shepard, 1973). This finding indicates that the image primes the presented percept most strongly if they are at the same orientation. If the image was represented propositionally, it is not clear why orientation would have such effects (in this case, differences in orientation would correspond to differences in the parameter values of described angles).

Another attempt to undermine depictive accounts would set aside the tacit knowledge account and instead claim that the rotation operation represents a series of intermediate positions. This account is irrelevant for the current issue—it says nothing about the format of the representations. In addition, such an account is entirely post hoc for a propositional theory because a description of spatial relations can be altered as easily to specify a large change as to specify a small change (e.g., from a 10-degree orientation of a line to a 90-degree orientation versus a 15-degree orientation). Moreover, when people are asked to "erase" an initial image and form a second one at a new orientation, they find this much more difficult than mentally rotating (Kosslyn, 1980), which does not make sense if rotation consists of simply changing parameter values for angles.

In a depictive representation, however, one only needs to assume that (a) separate parts of the patterns are shifted individually, which makes sense because images preserve a part structure and parts are regenerated individually, and (b) that the parts are not displaced by precisely the same amount, but that there is instead variability that is proportional to the absolute magnitude—much like what occurs in actual movements (cf. Decety & Jeannerod, 1995). If so, then if parts were to be shifted in large increments, the image would become scrambled. By moving the parts in small increments, the image is less distorted at each juncture and easier to realign (see Kosslyn, 1980). This account hinges on the notion of "distance" as an inherent characteristic of the representational buffer (the visual buffer in our theory), which has no place in propositional theories. Moreover, this account hinges on the idea that a representation is literally moved, which is consistent with both the original functional magnetic resonance imaging study by Cohen et al. (1996) and more recent evidence by Podzebenko, Egan, and Watson (2005) that show that mental rotation engages area MT, which responds selectively to motion during perception. Such findings not only counter a tacit knowledge account of mental rotation but also are evidence against the possibility that mental rotation is achieved by constructing a series of static images (if that were the case, one would not predict activation in motion-sensitive area MT).

Image Organization

According to tacit knowledge accounts, the finding that images have an internal organization simply indicates that people are aware (unconsciously) that the corresponding object was perceptually organized. In this case, their propositional description of the object would capture the organization of the object, making explicit and accessible some characteristics but not others. This view predicts that aspects of shapes that are included in a stored description can simply be looked up in memory, but computation would be required to infer aspects of shapes that are not explicitly described. However, this factor per se does not predict response times or error rates. In several studies, van der Kooij, Thompson, and Kosslyn (2005) asked participants to visualize uppercase letters and to evaluate whether they included specific properties. Some of these properties (such as straight lines) had been mentioned frequently by other participants who were asked to describe the letters, whereas other properties (such as the D-shaped enclosed space in the uppercase letter *P*) were never mentioned.

The hypothesis was that if propositional accounts are correct, participants should be able to judge more quickly whether a named property is present in a letter if that property is explicitly encoded. Nevertheless, participants could "see" the different sorts of properties (those that are frequently mentioned in descriptions and those that are only implicit in a depiction) equally easily in their images. Of course, one might claim that the descriptions did not correspond directly to what had been stored. But surely the basic elements of a shape, such as the strokes used to compose it, would be very likely to be included in a description, whereas emergent properties, such as the shape of enclosed areas, would be less likely to be so included. In contrast, a depictive representation should make explicit and accessible the various aspects of shape, and hence these findings were not surprising from the perspective of such theories.

These results are what one would predict if images were like actual pictures. But if so, then we would expect images to be as easily reorganized and reconstrued (i.e., reinterpreted) as pictures in general. However, the research on reconstruing images of shapes (such as the ambiguous duck/rabbit figure, or a rotated version of a map of Texas) shows that images are not like pictures in this regard. Nevertheless, to reconstrue the image at all requires properties and characteristics that are explicit and accessible in a depiction but are not necessarily explicit and accessible in another format. For example, Rouw, Kosslyn, and Hamel (1997, 1998) reasoned that if images rely on depictive information, then people should be able to extract "low-level" visual properties (such as whether edges meet to form a T junction or Y junction) as well as "high-level" visual properties (such as whether a part is symmetrical). If participants form a description of objects, it is unlikely that they would include low-level properties; such properties are only important insofar as they contribute to higher-level shapes, such as the shape of a specific part. Thus, participants either visualized previously studied line drawings (in an imagery condition) or actually viewed them (in a perception condition), and determined whether specific low-level or high-level properties were present. Not only could participants extract low-level properties during imagery, but the relative ease of extracting high-level versus low-level properties was the same in imagery and perception.

In addition, Peterson and her colleagues (Peterson, 1993; Peterson, Kihlstrom, Rose, & Glisky, 1992) found that part-based reconstruals (such as being able to reconstrue the wife/mother-in-law ambiguous drawing; see figure 3.9) were easier than reference-frame realignments (in which one or more global directions are reassigned in the image, as in the Necker cube or rabbit/duck ambiguous figures). However, they rarely found figure/ground reversals with imagery. Moreover, these researchers found that the process of reconstruing imaged patterns is highly sensitive to suggestions, hints, and strategies.

We have asked literally hundreds of people to participate in a simple demonstration: They are asked to visualize an uppercase version of the last letter in the alphabet, and then rotate it 90 degrees clockwise. They then are asked whether it is now another letter. And, if so, which one? The vast majority of people have no difficulty reconstruing the initial image after it is rotated. Why is this task (based on one reported by Shepard & Feng, 1972) so easy, but some other image reconstrual tasks (such as those requiring rotating a map of the state of Texas) so hard?

The first step toward answering this question is to realize that the reinterpretations and reconstruals are not computed by early visual cortices per se. Rather, depictive representations in these areas provide information to later visual processes, which actually interpret input (as we elaborate in chapter 5). Viewed from this perspective, Kosslyn (1994) stressed that imagery has limited capacity, both in how much information can be retained (as just discussed) and in how easily specific operations can be performed.

Rollins (2001) argues that this account fails to explain why participants can retain equally complex images in other tasks, such as when they are

Figure 3.9. The ambiguous "wife/mother-in-law" figure. (From Boring, E. G. [1930]. A new ambiguous figure. *American Journal of Psychology, 42*, 444.)

required to scan an image of a map. He notes that the map used by Kosslyn, Ball, and Reiser (1978) is complex, containing seven specific objects and a convoluted contour. Why can people maintain an image of the map in the scanning task but not operate on comparably complex images in other tasks? Rollins raises a good point, but on reflection we can offer the following replies.

To begin, we note that Rollins's notion assumes that a single sort of processing capacity limit applies to all tasks. Mast and Kosslyn (2002) demonstrated that this is not the case: depending on the precise nature of the task, different processes will be used—and each process has its own limitations. Specifically, Mast and Kosslyn (2002) asked forty-four people to study the ambiguous figure illustrated in figure 3.10. Depending on its

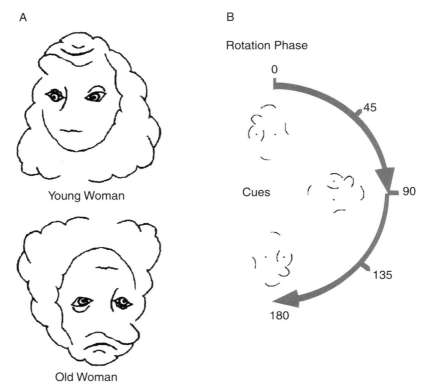

A

Young Woman

Old Woman

B

Rotation Phase

0

45

Cues

90

135

180

Figure 3.10. The ambiguous figure used by Mast and Kosslyn (2002). Participants studied one version of the figure and later were asked to rotate their image incrementally until it was completely upside down. Many of the participants were able to reinterpret the figure in its other form. (From Mast, F. W., & Kosslyn, S. M. [2002]. Visual mental images can be ambiguous: Insights from individual differences in spatial transformation abilities. *Cognition, 86,* 57–70.)

vertical orientation, this figure either resembles an old woman or a young woman. The participants studied one version of the figure (old or young woman), and knew nothing of the task while they studied it. They learned their version of the figure by completing a drawing based on fragmentary cues. When they initially completed a drawing (on translucent paper), their drawing was placed over the original, and the participants were asked to correct any discrepancies in their mental image. The procedure was repeated until they could accurately reproduce the image on paper. The participants then were given the fragmentary cues and were asked to visualize the figure as vividly as possible. Then the cues were rotated in steps, until they were upside down. The participants were asked to visualize the figure as completely as possible at each step of the way, until the figure was upside down. After visualizing the figure upside down, participants were asked what the picture looked like. In all, sixteen participants were able to reinterpret the image correctly without perceptual input (these were called recognizers), whereas eighteen were not able to do so (these were called nonrecognizers).

Here's the most interesting twist to the experiment: after they had learned the figure, the participants completed four mental imagery tasks that were designed to assess their ability to inspect images for specific parts, "see" aspects of imaged patterns with high resolution, compose images from separate parts, and rotate images. Participants who performed well on the mental rotation imagery task were more likely to be recognizers than to be nonrecognizers. And only differences on the rotation task predicted the ability to perform the ambiguous figure task. The authors drew two major conclusions: (1) alternative interpretations of an ambiguous figure can be discovered, even spontaneously, but especially when people are given ways to cope with the cognitive load; (2) individual differences in mental imagery ability, and particularly the specific ability of mental transformation predicted success in the task—which relied on just this ability for successful performance. The take-home message is that failure to reinterpret an image says nothing about the format of the representation but volumes about the nature of the task per se; tasks that tax one's information processing abilities are—not surprisingly—difficult to do!

In addition, even if the crucial limitation is the amount of time that an image can be retained, differences in tasks are still relevant: some tasks require more processing than others, and thus are more susceptible to a fading image (as discussed in chapter 2). Moreover, according to our theory, images are maintained by being regenerated repeatedly. If so, then tasks that can be accomplished without modifying the image, such as image scanning, should be easier than those that require reorganizing, restoring, and then regenerating an altered image, and should be easier than tasks that require maintaining an image for long periods of time.

An alternative type of account of reconstruals (Kosslyn, 1994) is based on the notion that people describe shapes as well as encode the actual visual information. The stored description then plays a role in how one organizes a shape in an image. How? The verbal coding can direct attention, and, depending on what one attends to, objects are organized in different ways. For example, returning to our earlier example of viewing a Star of David, one can attend to two large overlapping triangles or a hexagon surrounded by six small triangles. Depending on how one attends to the pattern, different parts are stored and later used to form the image. According to this view (which is a variant of one proposed by Rollins, 2001), a stored description later directs attention, when one inspects the imaged object. For example, if part of a shape was initially encoded as "the top," this specification later will need to be overridden if one wants to reinterpret or reconstrue the image such that another part is the top (cf. Reisberg, 1996).

In short, the fact that reinterpretation of mental images is highly sensitive to hints and strategies does not undermine the claim that images can depict information. A key question is whether the image representation in the visual buffer is retained long enough to be reinterpreted. An appropriate hint may lessen the load on short-term memory (Rouw et al., 1997). In addition, the fact that hints help one to reinterpret objects in images may arise not simply because they help to circumvent capacity limits but also because they help one to override ineffective attentional strategies. Furthermore, the processes that transform the image and interpret it may also be limited, as demonstrated by Mast and Kosslyn (2002)— and hints may help overcome such limitations by sparing one the effort of making false starts, using inappropriate but taxing transformations or strategies.

Finally, even when objects in mental images can be reinterpreted, this process appears different from what occurs in perception. For example, Peterson et al. (1992; see also Peterson, 1993) showed that reference-frame reversals (such as reassigning what is the vertical versus horizontal axis) are dominant in vision but are less common in mental imagery, whereas the opposite is true for part-based reconstruals. They conclude that

> it is now clear that mental images of pictures of ducks and rabbits, and snails and elephants (and not just familiar letters like J's and D's), can be reversed—just as the corresponding pictures can be . . . Whether images are as reversible as pictures is another matter, but the fact of reversibility indicates that perception and imagery share processes that penetrate to the level at which reference frames are established, and before recognition and interpretation occur. (Peterson et al., 1992, p. 121)

Imagery, as we have noted repeatedly, is not the same as perception; images suffer limitations not present in vision—which in turn affects the ease of processing images. In our view, the issue is not whether reinterpretations and reconstruals always occur, or even whether they are easy in mental imagery. The issue is whether they *ever* occur. If the raw material can be used even in some situations, this is evidence that images depict the information needed to reinterpret and reconstrue. And that is the issue: whether images depict.

Mutually Exclusive Accounts?

Knowledge and beliefs (of any sort, not just tacit) can affect imagery—and in fact knowledge and beliefs must be drawn upon when one uses imagery to mentally simulate what one believes would happen in a corresponding actual situation. But this is not to say that tacit knowledge is necessarily an alternative to the sorts of mechanisms we propose. Tacit knowledge accounts say nothing about the format of the representations used to store and use information. Tacit knowledge must be represented in the brain, and there is no reason why it cannot be represented—at least in part—by depictive representations.

Additional Tacit Knowledge Theories

We must consider two additional attempts to use tacit knowledge to explain imagery phenomena. These theories are more elaborated than the bare-bones ideas discussed above.

Perceptual Activity Theory

A relatively new theory of imagery is closely related to tacit knowledge accounts, but is even more extreme. *Perceptual activity theory*, as it is called, rejects the very idea that there are internal representations. For example, in the words of Thomas (2002, p. 211):

> Visual experience, O'Regan [1992] holds, arises not from the
> presence of representations in the brain but from the active
> exercise of our "mastery of the relevant sensorimotor con-
> tingencies" (O'Regan & Noë, 2001) as we explore our visual
> surroundings. *Perceptual activity theory* holds that imagery arises
> from vicarious exercise of such mastery; a sort of play-acting of
> perceptual exploration. (Thomas, 1999)

Presumably, tacit knowledge underlies the "mastery of the relevant sensorimotor contingencies." If this theory is correct, then we are indeed misguided in trying to draw inferences about the nature of internal representations from empirical findings.

We have four responses to this challenge. First, this view apparently asserts that all stored information is embedded in processes that link stimuli to responses; within the framework of Schacter (1987), this is equivalent to claiming that all information is stored as "implicit" memories. It is a sad commentary on the field that we need to revisit the question of whether "explicit" internal representations exist at this late juncture; such representations are not embedded in a particular process but can be retrieved in a wide range of circumstances and processed in new ways. As Tolman (1948) pointed out so long ago, even rats can store "explicit" memories: they can learn a spatial layout, not simply stimulus-response relations. Humans are even more gifted; we can in fact use working memory to operate on stored information in novel ways—which requires having internal representations of the sort that underlie explicit memory (Schacter, 1987).

Second, the empirical support for perceptual activity theory hinges on evidence that the motor system is used in imagery. For example, Laeng and Teodorescu (2002) found that people had similar patterns of eye movements when they generated an image as they did when they initially studied the stimulus perceptually (in preparation for the subsequent imagery task); moreover, image generation was relatively slow if participants were prevented from perceptually scanning the stimulus when they studied it or when they later visualized it. These and similar findings (see Laeng & Teodorescu, 2002) are indeed consistent with perceptual activity theory. However, such findings are also consistent with depictive theories—and were actually predicted by Kosslyn (1994), who noted that eye movements can serve as spatial retrieval cues, helping one to access the next to-be-visualized part in sequence. In fact, the theory of Kosslyn (1994) easily accounts for all of the data that are consistent with perceptual activity theory but *also* accounts for data that support depictive representations—about which perceptual activity theory is silent.

Third, Kosslyn, Thompson, Sukel, and Alpert (2005) provide neural evidence against this theory. In this study the participants first memorized the appearance of figures (sets of connected bars) either by (a) memorizing one segment at a time, with each one being presented in the appropriate relative location, or (b) memorizing verbal (written) descriptions, as shown in figure 3.11. The participants later visualized the figures and made judgments about whether a shown X would fall on or off the figures if they were in fact present. If perceptual activity theory is correct, when asked to visualize the figures, the participants should mimic the sensorimotor contingencies that were present when they learned the figures initially. In this case, this mimicry would produce very different patterns of brain activation in the two conditions. Namely, we would expect activation in language-related areas (e.g., Broca's and Wernicke's areas) when the participants generated an image based on verbal descriptions and activation in areas that govern eye movements (e.g., the frontal eye fields) when they recalled the locations of individual segments. No such activation was

PRE-SCAN AMALGAMATION LEARNING

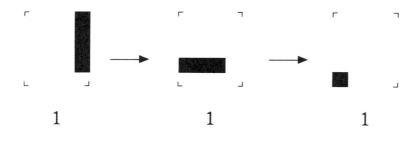

1   1   1

PRE-SCAN VERBAL LEARNING

Figure 1
- A vertical bar extends from the upper right corner downward to just before the end of the column
- attached to the left end of the first bar is a horizontal bar extending leftward to the end of the row.
- attached to the bottom end of the second bar is a vertical bar extending downward to the bottom left corner.

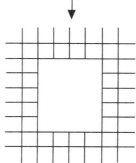

Figure 3.11. Kosslyn, Thompson, Sukel, and Alpert (2005) asked participants to encode figures either by seeing one segment at a time (*top*) or by reading a verbal description (*bottom*). In separate conditions, participants later visualized the figures that were amalgamated perceptually or encoded verbally, and then decided whether an X mark would fall on the figure if it were present in a set of brackets. The results from these two conditions were compared. (From Kosslyn, S. M., Thompson, W. L., Sukel, K. E., & Alpert, N. M. [2005]. Two types of image generation: Evidence from PET. *Cognitive, Affective and Behavioral Neuroscience, 5,* 41–53.)

detected. Instead, as shown in figure 3.12, strikingly similar patterns of activation were produced in the two conditions, which is consistent with the claim that they created comparable internal representations in the two cases. Moreover, the activation pattern was consistent with our general theory of depictive imagery (as summarized in chapter 5).

Fourth, perceptual activity theory is stated at an entirely verbal level. Our strong sense is that if this theory were actually fleshed out in enough detail to be simulated on a computer, it would incorporate key aspects of our theory. Both the mastery of sensorimotor contingencies of O'Regan and Noë and the "play acting of perceptual exploration" of Thomas (1999) rely on mechanisms in which one anticipates the perceptual consequences of operating on the world in specific ways. As we discuss in chapter 5, we theorize that depictive images are generated via the same priming process used to anticipate seeing objects during perception—but this priming is so strong that it actually evokes a pattern of activation in the visual buffer.

Finally, our bet is that if its advocates developed this alternative theory, perceptual activity theory, in detail, they could not escape having to delineate the nature of internal representations.

Attention Allocation Theory

An alternative attempt to undermine depictive theories would instead argue that there is no depictive image representation but rather that "imagery" is in fact simply attention allocation. In this case, tacit knowledge presumably guides where one attends. Specifically, when asked to form an image, the participant would rely on "visual indexes" (thinking that a "specific part of the image would be where a speck on the wall is," or "another part may be at the corner of the wall"; Pylyshyn, 2002, p. 168). Presumably, according to this account, each part is attended to separately, and thus it would require more time to generate images of more complex objects.

This account essentially hinges on the idea that shapes can be reduced to spatial representations that indicate the locations of parts and characteristics. One piece of evidence against such an account is evidence that people can visualize object properties, such as color, shading, texture, and other characteristics. Although such findings do not implicate any specific format, they do undermine the attention allocation theory. For example, studies have shown that when participants are asked to project images of color onto a gray display, regional cerebral blood flow is increased in the right-hemisphere "color area" of the human brain—and blood flow is reduced in this area when participants are asked to "drain" color from a

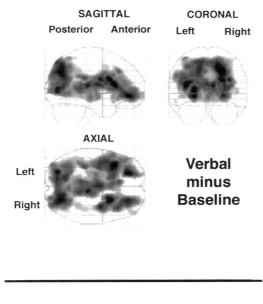

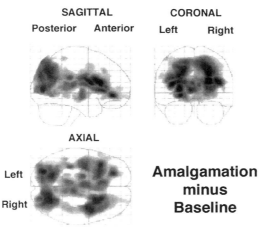

Figure 3.12. In spite of minor differences between the two forms of encoding illustrated in figure 3.11, when brain activation from both conditions was compared to a baseline, the pattern of activation was strikingly similar. These results suggest that regardless of the method of encoding, comparable image representations were created and processed. The activated network was consistent with the subsystems we propose in our theory. (From Kosslyn, S. M., Thompson, W. L., Sukel, K. E., & Alpert, N. M. [2005]. Two types of image generation: Evidence from PET. *Cognitive, Affective and Behavioral Neuroscience, 5,* 41–53.)

visible display (see Howard et al., 1998; Kosslyn, Thompson, Costantini-Ferrando, et al., 2000). Such specific responses in the brain to distinct aspects of imagery are difficult to understand in terms of spatial attention per se. Moreover, although attention to nonspatial features of the stimulus (e.g., color) can increase activation in visual areas that encode those features (e.g., Saenz, Buracas, & Boynton, 2002), the activation increases reported in Howard et al. (1998) and Kosslyn, Thompson, Costantini-Ferrando, et al. (2000) were found with stimuli that did not contain the crucial feature—there was no color in the display—and hence it is difficult to explain these findings in terms of feature attention.

Consider another approach to ruling out the view that imagery and attention are essentially the same process. This tack would rely on showing that factors that affect spatial attention do not affect imagery. One example of such research was reported by Podgorny and Shepard (1978). In one condition, participants viewed a grid in front of them and then visualized filling in specific cells in the grid to depict a block letter. The inclusion of grid lines makes it easy to attend to the corresponding locations, much as one can "see" a letter on a tessellated tile floor by attending to specific rows and columns of tiles. In addition, in another condition Podgorny and Shepard removed the grid lines and asked participants to form images within an empty region—which did not mark locations to be attended. The time to determine whether a dot would have fallen on or off the letter (were it present, as it appeared in the mental image), varied for dots that were in different locations of the grid. Crucially, these variations were the same in both conditions, which is surprising if imagery is simply attention allocation: if the visual indexing hypothesis of imagery is correct, it should have been much easier to index specific locations when the locations—cells in grids—were clearly demarcated.

Moreover, forming an image of a different object actually interferes with perceiving an object if the image is visualized in the same location as the object (e.g., Craver-Lemley & Reeves, 1992), whereas focusing attention enhances perception (e.g., Nakayama & Mackeben, 1989). In addition, as will be discussed later, allocating attention and visualizing activate the brain differently (Slotnick, Thompson, & Kosslyn, 2005). Clearly, imagery is not simply attention. Indeed, in general, imagery results (such as image scanning) are obtained when eyes are open or closed. In fact, most imagery studies do *not* require "superimposing or projecting an image onto the perceived world" (Pylyshyn, 2002, p. 168); in the majority of studies, participants have their eyes closed—so how could they project images onto a visible scene? Furthermore, neuroimaging studies of imagery in which the participants closed their eyes to visualize have shown early visual cortex activation in the absence of activation in regions typically associated with spatial attention, such as the posterior parietal lobe (see Kosslyn & Thompson, 2003).

The key idea of the spatial indexing hypothesis is that the world provides the spatial properties, but how is this possible if the world is not being perceived? Pylyshyn (2002) speculates that some "iconic memory" of the projected scene or the object to be projected may persist for several minutes, which may explain how imagery tasks may be performed with eyes closed. There is no evidence for such long-lived afterimages—and in fact, such iconic images would either lead to smearing of the visual field or would be overwritten every time one moves one's eyes, and thus would be of limited use. In addition, imagery experiments typically rely on sets of stimuli, and during learning each would disrupt any afterimage produced by the prior one. Furthermore, these experiments usually are conducted many minutes after the stimuli have been memorized, longer than any afterimage could persist. In fact, often the stimuli are not even shown before the imagery study, because they are well learned, as in the case of letters of the alphabet. And exactly how is such an iconic image represented? This idea has a strong whiff of implying a depictive format.

The idea that the depictive properties of the representation are based on indexing locations in the world itself merely pushes the problem back a step. It is one thing simply to assert that the representation indexes specific locations and thereby inherits spatial properties, but quite another to specify how it does this. And that is the nut of the question. As it happens, parts of the posterior parietal lobes specify locations in topographically organized areas (Sereno, Pitzalis, & Martinez, 2001); if these representations underlie spatial indexing, then such representations are depictive.

Experimenter Expectancy Effects?

Task demands must be distinguished from *experimenter expectancy effects* (Intons-Peterson, 1983). When experimental expectancy effects are at work, participants respond to cues from the investigator that indicate how they should behave. We have so far focused on tacit knowledge accounts of the data, but some scholars have tried to explain away results from imagery experiments by appeal to this second sort of demand characteristic.

Most prominently, Margaret Intons-Peterson (1983) championed the idea that the imagery data could be understood simply as reflecting experimenter expectancy effects. She performed an experiment in which she compared scanning images to scanning physically present displays. Half of the experimenters were told that the image scanning should be faster and half were told that the perceptual scanning should be faster. She found that the experimenters' expectations influenced the results: when experimenters expected faster perceptual scanning, the participants produced this result; when they expected faster image scanning, there was no difference in overall times. Thus, the experimenters were somehow leading the participants to alter their responses. But even so, participants took longer to scan across longer distances, the effect that reflects the depictive properties of the underlying representation.

Goldston, Hinrichs, and Richman (1985) actually went so far as to tell the participants the predictions before the study (which is never done in ordinary psychological experiments). However, even when participants were told that the experimenter expected longer times with shorter distances, they still generally required more time when longer distances were scanned. Telling participants different predictions did affect the degree of the increase in scanning time with distance, but this result is not surprising; given the purposes of imagery in reasoning, one had better be able to control imaged events! In this case, participants may have simply been influenced to scan faster or slower, but the basic result—more time is required to scan longer distances—was not affected. What is impressive is that even when participants were, if anything, trying for the opposite result, they still generally took longer to scan across longer distances (see figure 3.13).

Jolicoeur and Kosslyn (1985) investigated further the claim that the increase in times with increasing distance scanned occurs only because participants respond to experimenter expectancy effects. They performed a series of experiments using Intons-Peterson's methodology. For example, they told one experimenter that they expected a U-shaped function, with the most time being required to scan the shortest and longest distances. The reason for this prediction, they explained, was that the four closest objects should be grouped into a single chunk—because of the Gestalt laws of organization—and so they are clustered together, making it difficult to scan among them. And the longest distances require more time than the medium ones because more scanning is involved. Nevertheless, in spite of explaining these "predictions" to the experimenter in advance, the results from this experiment were identical to those found previously: response times increased linearly with increasing distance. In additional experiments Jolicoeur and Kosslyn varied experimenter expectancy in different ways, none of which affected scan times. Indeed, these experimenters failed to replicate Intons-Peterson's original finding.

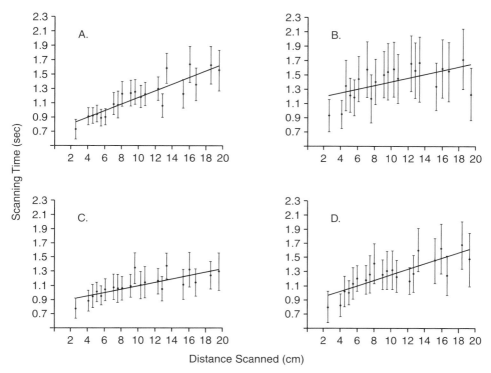

Figure 3.13. The time-distance function in the four conditions investigated by Goldston, Hinrichs, and Richman (1985). The participants were assigned to one of the following conditions: they were told that time to scan increases with distance (results in panel A); that time to scan decreases with distance (panel B); that there is no overall relationship between time to scan and distance (panel C); no expectations were given to the participants (panel D). Note that although the slopes of the functions were affected by the suggestions, time to scan generally increased with distance scanned. (From Goldston, D. B., Hinrichs, J. V., & Richman, C. L. [1985]. Subjects' expectations, individual variability, and the scanning of mental images. *Memory and Cognition, 13,* 365–370.)

What could be going on here? Many details of such experiments can differ from laboratory to laboratory (for instance, ensuring that participants always keep their fingers on the response buttons and having the experimenter read the instructions aloud versus having the participants read them silently), and these details could be critical for obtaining experimenter expectancy effects. The important point is that, whatever caused the experimenter expectancy effect in Intons-Peterson's study, these factors (if present) were not consequential in the original studies of image scanning.

Thus, these results cannot be explained away as simply reflecting how well participants can satisfy the expectations of the experimenter.

Similarly, such accounts cannot explain data from most imagery experiments. For example, Craver-Lemley and Reeves (1992) told half the participants that an image of vertical lines would help them detect a slight offset of perceived lines and told half the participants that the image would impair their performance—but the image interfered with perception for all participants (in spite of the fact that all apparently believed the "predictions").

Conclusions

The various attempts to explain away imagery results are strained. Although alternative explanations usually are possible for each of the individual results, different alternative explanations will be necessary to explain the different effects (such as the effects of size scale or of distance on scan times). In contrast, the depictive imagery theory addresses all of the results.

However, the strongest evidence against tacit knowledge accounts and for depictive representations comes from studies of the brain. Tacit knowledge accounts lose credibility when they require the participants to alter their brain activity in specific ways (even though they have no knowledge of what that activity is, tacit or otherwise!). In the following chapter we consider the nature of depictive representation in the brain in detail.

Notes

1. Pylyshyn makes much of a study on imagery-perception interactions in motion perception, in which imagery does affect perception, but in a counterintuitive way (Gilden, Blake, & Hurst, 1995). However, various methodological problems prevent drawing a strong conclusion from that finding, and recent studies have reported results entirely consistent with the idea that imagery and perception both rely on topographically organized areas even when processing motion (Winawer, Witthoft, Huk, & Boroditsky, 2005).

2. Anderson and Balsom (1997) summarize four lines of evidence that people actually use imagery to perform this task: (1) asking people to tap their finger in a spatial pattern disrupts their ability to perform the task much more than simple tapping (not in a pattern), which suggests that the spatial mechanisms are used in the task; (2) visual-spatial ability predicts performance, whereas verbal ability does not; (3) people tend to perform better when using imagery alone than when being

allowed to use pictures or make drawings; (4) people produce more discoveries when they are told to focus on the images instead of linguistic aspects of the task.

3. See especially Task 3 of Sereno, Pitzalis, & Martinez (2001), which shows— counter to Ingle's (2002) claim—that this representation is not used merely to guide saccades.

4

Depictive Representations in the Brain

The imagery debate hinges on the distinction between the format and the content of internal representations, the format being the type of code used to represent the shape of an object, and the content being the information conveyed. The issue is whether mental imagery makes use of representations that depict (perhaps in addition to those that also describe). Following many years of behavioral research, this debate reached an impasse: the results from these studies could be explained by theories that posited only propositional representations or by theories that also posited depictive representations (e.g., see Anderson, 1978). Modern neuroimaging techniques now provide an opportunity to press this issue forward, for two reasons.

First, researchers have documented that approximately thirty-two areas of the monkey cerebral cortex contain neurons that respond selectively to visual input; moreover, about half of these areas are topographically organized—they preserve (roughly) the geometric structure of the retina. Such areas use space on the cortex to represent space in the world (e.g., see Felleman & Van Essen, 1991; Fox et al., 1986; Heeger, 1999; Sengpiel & Huebener, 1999; Sereno et al., 2001; Tootell, Hadjikani, et al., 1998; Tootell, Silverman, et al., 1982; Van Essen, 1985). As discussed in chapter 1, these areas are not simply physically topographically organized—they function to depict information. The representations in topographically organized areas are depictions, not propositional descriptions.

Positron emission tomography (PET; e.g., Fox et al., 1986) and functional magnetic resonance imaging (fMRI; e.g., Sereno et al., 1995) have shown that such depictive areas are used during visual perception in the human brain. If these areas are activated when one visualizes, and disruption of these areas impairs the ability to visualize, this is strong evidence that the representations underlying visual mental images are not entirely propositional; rather, such evidence would show that at least some of these representations depict information and that such representations play a role in information processing.

The second reason neuroimaging results offer a way to break the impasse in the debate about imagery is that such findings cannot be explained by appeal to tacit knowledge. As we discussed in the previous chapter, some researchers have claimed that the results from studies of imagery arise because task demands are built into the experiments, which in turn activate tacit knowledge about perceived events (a phenomenon that is largely unconscious, such as our knowledge of how the surface of water will appear when a glass of water is tilted), which in turn leads participants to produce responses like those they believe (perhaps unconsciously) would occur in the corresponding perceptual situation. Findings from the brain would be truly definitive evidence against this position: no ordinary person has knowledge of how perception (and hence, according to the tacit knowledge account, also imagery) is processed in the brain—and thus people are not in a position to manipulate their brain activation (even if they had that ability) in accordance with tacit knowledge.

In the first part of this chapter, we summarize the arguments against the idea that topographically organized areas are used in visual mental imagery and the arguments that even if they are used, they play no essential role. In the second part, we address each argument in turn, considering counterarguments and evidence to the contrary. In the third part, we discuss a meta-analysis of studies of visual mental imagery (summaries of the studies are provided in the appendix). This meta-analysis untangles what might at first blush appear to be inconsistencies in the literature and provides strong support for the claim that topographically organized areas support depictive representations during visual mental imagery.

Do Topographically Organized Areas Depict Information?

Some researchers have tried to dismiss the evidence that depictive representations are functional in the brain. Such arguments can be divided into three classes, summarized below. We first summarize the arguments, and then consider them in detail.

Arguments against Neural Depiction

Some critics of the recent neuroimaging research have claimed that topographically organized areas in the human brain are not truly depictive. For example, area 17 (also known as area V1, the striate cortex, and the primary visual cortex) is organized so that objects that subtend small visual angles activate posterior portions of the area, and objects that subtend larger visual angles activate more anterior portions of the area (e.g., Fox et al., 1986). Larger objects do not necessarily occupy a larger amount of the area, so how can we infer that the area is truly depicting information?

In addition, the idea that topographically organized regions in the brain support depictive representations purportedly is flawed because vision does not accumulate information in an internal display to produce a panoramic view of the world; this is a subjective illusion. Every time the eyes move, the information in early visual structures is replaced by the new input. So, how can theorists claim that neural structures used in vision also support depictive representations in mental imagery? In criticizing our claim that topographically organized visual areas depict information, Dennett (2002, p. 190) asserts: "It has yet to be established when and how *vision* utilizes image processing!" He continues:

> Vision isn't television. The product of vision is not a picture on the screen in the Cartesian Theater (Dennett 1991). The fleeting retinal images punctuated by saccades are the first images, and they are not the last, as Julesz (1971) demonstrated by showing perception of depth in random dot stereograms that requires image-processing after the optic chiasma. But which subsequent cortical processes also exploit any of the informational properties of images? The *eventual* "products" of vision are such things as guided hand and finger motions, involuntary ducking, exclamations of surprise, triggering of ancient memories, sexual arousal . . . and none of these is imagistic in any sense, so assuming that the events in their proximal causal ancestry are imagistic is rather like assuming that power from a hydroelectric plant is apt to be wetter and less radioactive than power from a nuclear plant. The raw retinal data are cooked in many ways betwixt eyeball and verbal report (for instance). How cooked are the processes involved

in (deliberate or voluntary) mental imagery? (Dennett, 2002, p. 190)

Moreover, continuing this line of argument, critics have claimed that the very idea that the brain would create a copy of the visual world is flawed. This idea is nicely captured in the following quotation: "There is no evidence of the mental construction of images to be looked at or maps to be followed. The body responds to the world, at the point of contact; making copies would be a waste of time." These words were written by B. F. Skinner (1977, p. 6) but could have been written by many other critics of depictive theories of imagery. Pylyshyn (2002, p. 182, n. 14) asserts that vision "is not for turning one topographically organized pattern into another." Echoing this point, Dennett (2002) emphasizes that vision is used to identify objects and their properties and to guide and track movements—and none of these eventual goals directly relies on topographic maps. Dennett (2002) notes that electricity generated from hydroelectric plants is not wetter than electricity generated by other means—and thus, by analogy, topographically mapped areas may have no bearing on the representations actually used in vision.

Clarifying the Nature of Depictive Representation

Here we discuss why the arguments raised against depictive representations in the brain miss their intended target.

Representation within Topographically Organized Areas

Many neuroimaging findings have documented topographic organization in several areas of human visual cortex during perception (e.g., DeYoe, Bandettini, Neitz, Miller, & Winans, 1994; Engel et al., 1994; Hasnain, Fox, & Woldorff, 1998; Sereno et al., 1995; Van Essen et al., 2001). The high-resolution central (foveal) portions of these areas represent the central portions of the visual field, whereas low-resolution, peripheral portions of these areas represent more peripheral portions of the visual field. Space on the cortex is literally used to represent space in the world (more precisely, space on the cortex is used to represent a planar projection of space in the world, because the cortical areas are two-dimensional; information about depth is represented in a different manner, e.g., Tsao et al., 2003). Propositional representations have the property of being arbitrarily related to the objects they represent, whereas the relationship between an external visual stimulus and the activation it engenders in topographically organized areas is not arbitrary: points that are relatively close in space in the external world are represented by activation in nearby portions of these areas, and points that are relatively far in space are represented by activation in relatively separated portions within each of these areas.[1]

What about the question of why larger objects do not produce larger swaths of activation within these brain areas? This concern is based on a misunderstanding of how information is represented in topographically organized areas. First, neurons in the anterior portions of area 17 have larger receptive fields, which receive inputs from a larger region of space than do neurons in more posterior portions. Thus, activation in more anterior portions of this structure indicates that parts of the image are spaced farther apart and are less resolved than is the case when activation is in more posterior portions. This point is worth repeating, since it is often not appreciated: activation toward more anterior portions of this structure not only depicts larger extents but does so with poorer resolution. However, keep in mind that what is important is not how the area looks to an external observer but how it is interpreted by processes that operate on it in the brain. From this perspective, when neurons in the anterior portions of area 17 are activated, this is interpreted as specifying a larger portion of an object's surface.

The spatial organization of topographically organized areas in the human brain is complex, in part because numerous topographically organized areas must be connected to preserve the overall topography. Adjacent topographically organized areas meet at the horizontal meridian (i.e., the horizontal line through the fixation point in the frontal plane of one's visual field) or at the vertical meridian (i.e., the vertical line through the fixation point in the frontal plane). The most common way to establish that areas are topographically organized takes advantage of these facts. In this method, participants observe a narrow flashing wedge as it rotates slowly around a pivot, starting from the vertical. fMRI is used to track changes in activation over time as the stimulus moves. If the stimulus is vertical at the outset, activation will initially be detected along the vertical meridian, and as the stimulus rotates, this activation literally shifts over the cortex, toward the horizontal meridian. Because adjacent visual cortical areas abut at the horizontal (or vertical) meridian, this means that the wave of activation in one area will literally shift until it meets an incoming wave of activation from an abutting area—and researchers use the places where waves meet to establish the boundaries between topographically organized areas. We wish to emphasize that these waves reflect the precise position of the stimulus in space: as the stimulus moves, the activation is mapped, point-for-point, into the topographically organized areas. Each neuron in these areas registers a part of space, and the distance between neurons reflects the distance between the corresponding parts of space. However, the physical distance on cortex also reflects the resolution—with the same extent on an object's being represented by greater distances in the foveal region of cortex than in peripheral regions.[2]

And this brings us to the crucial point: connections to other areas compensate for the distortions in the actual (physical) representation—and thus the result is that the topographic areas function to depict shape accurately. This is a variant of the "Modigliani effect," named after the Italian artist Amedeo Clemente Modigliani (1884–1920), who famously painted and sculpted elongated figures. The question was once raised whether the painter actually saw the world the way he portrayed it. However, if Modigliani had in fact had distorted vision, which led him to see objects as elongated, the same distortions would operate when he painted, thereby compensating and leading him to produce a veridical depiction. But in the case of the brain, later brain areas compensate for the distortions introduced into earlier visual areas. Topographically organized areas depict, but do so within the context of the system as a whole.

The Role of Topographically Organized Areas in Perception

We must distinguish two separate issues. First, are depictive representations actually used in vision at all, no matter whether it is for a single fixation or only a portion of the visual field? Second, if so, how are such representations combined successively to produce the impression of seeing the entire visual field?

Regarding the first question, Dennett's (2002, p. 190) bald claim that we do not know whether vision uses depictive representations is a vast overstatement. The neuroanatomy reveals that these areas play a role in the earlier phases of visual processing, and neurological data indicate that these areas play a special role in the parsing of shapes into their component parts. For example, apperceptive agnosia results when there is diffuse neural death in these areas (usually due to carbon monoxide poisoning), which in turn characteristically disrupts the ability to organize input into objects and their parts (Vecera & Gilds, 1998).

The mere fact that, as noted in previous chapters, local damage to topographic areas produces localized scotoma demonstrates that the topographic properties of these areas play a role in vision. Moreover, studies in the macaque monkey, such as those by Roelfsema and Spekreijse (2001), clearly demonstrate that the visual topography of area V1 has a functional role in visual cognition. In this and related studies, monkeys had to trace a curve mentally (out of a set of two), without moving their eyes. During a random subset of trials, the monkey made a mistake and traced the wrong curve. These mistakes could be predicted by looking at the pattern of neural activation corresponding to the topographic representation of the two curves!

Certainly, we do not yet know everything there is to know about the functioning of topographically organized visual brain areas—but this is not necessary for present purposes. The depictive properties of such areas clearly play a role in visual perception.

Regarding the second question, what about the issue of how information from successive fixations is accumulated? Ingle (2002) notes that every time the eyes move, the material in the visual buffer (i.e., the set of topographically organized areas in the occipital lobe) is written over. Therefore, the buffer itself cannot integrate information from successive fixations. This fact is, however, completely irrelevant to the issue of whether visual processing exploits depictive representations. That said, we note that every time one's eyes move, the location of the stimulus that gives rise to the perceptual image is registered in the posterior parietal lobes, which keep track of where in space one is looking when a particular part of the field is encoded. Thus, one can store successive images (presumably in the temporal lobes) plus the loci of corresponding objects (in the parietal lobes), and the two sorts of information can be integrated downstream (as we discuss in chapter 5). Moreover, the parietal representation accounts for how we see three-dimensional images when two-dimensional depictive representations are used in vision; based on a variety of cues (such as retinal disparity, texture gradients, and occlusion) processed in earlier areas, the parietal lobes index each location in space with a distance. This representation allows one later to locate and fixate again on a particular object, if needed.

The Necessity of Interpretation

Is nothing in fact accomplished by "turning one topographically organized pattern into another"? To the contrary, there are good reasons for such mappings. For example, although the retina and area 17 have a similar spatial organization, the pattern of connections among neurons is radically different, because different information is processed in each structure. Indeed, area 17 not only has numerous short inhibitory connections, but also has neurons that compare input from two eyes (which obviously cannot be accomplished in a single retina); such information is important for segregating figure from ground and organizing perceptual units—which are not the tasks of the retina. A series of topographically mapped areas is computationally useful because their spatial organization makes explicit and accessible information needed to accomplish the initial phases of visual processing, and each phase takes advantage of transformations accomplished in earlier phases.

The fact that visual processing is not accomplished in one fell swoop was stressed by Marr (1982); vision is accomplished in a succession of small steps. We now know that visual input is processed in a set of successive brain areas, each of which abstracts specific types of information from processes that operate earlier in the sequence (e.g., Miyashita & Hayashi, 2000). The initial visual areas in cortex are topographically organized, but progressively later ones are increasingly less well organized topographically, until the latest ones in the temporal lobe no longer preserve the organization of the retina, or do so very loosely (Malach, Levy, & Hasson, 2002). Although not all visual processing relies on depictive representations, the evidence strongly indicates that depictive representations are in fact used during the early phases of visual processing.

Dennett's (2002) quip that electricity generated from hydroelectric plants is not wetter than electricity generated by other means is cute, but misses the mark. The topographical organization of early visual areas is not irrelevant in the end, after input has been fully processed. Dennett's notion is a little like saying that gasoline would only be important for automobiles if they moved ahead on a path of flaming fluids! Gasoline plays a key role in the sequence of events that allows an automobile to move, even if in the end it does not directly turn the wheels. Moreover, many features of an automobile, such as room for a gas tank and placement of an exhaust pipe so as not to allow fumes into the passenger compartment, emerge from use of an internal combustion engine. Similarly, the depictive properties of topographically organized areas play crucial roles in the early phases of visual perception, allowing the process to begin by making the spatial structure of an object explicit and accessible (with respect to processes that will operate on this representation). Furthermore, there is much evidence that the visual system is wired to allow information that is only implicit in the higher areas to be made explicit and accessible by reconstructing the shape in earlier areas. If so, then the stored representations are formed in part to have the ability to recreate such earlier, depictive representations—and this capacity is one factor that determines how the stored representations are organized.

Depictive Representation in Imagery

Even if topographically organized areas depict information during perception, they may not support depictive representations that are used during imagery. In this section, we consider this possibility and then consider evidence that supports the claim that depictive representations in the brain are used during visual mental imagery.

Do Topographically Organized Areas Depict during Imagery?

The following arguments have been made to undermine the view that topographically organized areas support depictive representations that are used during imagery.

First, even if topographically organized areas depict information during perception, they may function differently during imagery. For example, such areas register color (as a blob, with no specific shape), and this may be their sole function during imagery. In this case, the activation would not preserve properties of the shape per se. If so, then even if these brain areas are activated during imagery, this would not indicate that depictive representations are used; rather, the depictive properties of the representation, if any, would not play a functional role in imagery.

In addition, even if representations formed in topographically organized areas depict information, they may play no functional role in imagery. It is possible, for example, that the real work is done by higher-level areas, which are not topographically organized and presumably rely on propositional representations. In this case, because the areas are anatomically connected to earlier areas, they may incidentally activate the earlier areas—but such activation is entirely epiphenomenal (like the smoke from a cooking fire, which plays no functional role in the cooking process).

Furthermore, several researchers have reported that massive damage to area 17 does not disrupt visual mental imagery—which is evidence that this area does not play a functional role in imagery. For example, Chatterjee and Southwood (1995) studied a twenty-nine-year-old woman who had such massive damage to area 17 that she had been completely blind since the age of 15. Even though she could not tell whether a light was being shined into her face during perception, she nevertheless could answer visual imagery questions, such as whether upper-case letters have curved lines. Moreover, she reported that she was able to finish high school because she could visualize her studies. Other cases of cortically blind patients with preserved imagery have been reported (see Ganis, Thompson, Mast, & Kosslyn, 2003, for a review), although in most cases the tests of visual imagery have not been careful or systematic. Nevertheless, according to the propositional argument, even one case in which damage to area 17 does not affect imagery is sufficient to show that area 17 does not play a necessary role in imagery.

Dennett expresses his skepticism well in the following passage:

> Nobody denies that when we engage in mental imagery we *seem* to be making pictures in our heads—in some sense. The question is: Are we really? That is, do the processes occurring in our brains have any of the properties of pictures? More pointedly, do those processes *exploit* any of the properties of pictures? When you make a long-distance telephone call, there is a zigzag pattern of activity running through various media from you to your listener across the country, but if the curves and loops and angles happened to spell out "Happy Birthday" (as seen from space), this would be an image on the surface of the planet that was not exploited in any way by your information-transmission, even if it was a birthday greeting. . . . As Pylyshyn stresses, the evidence from neuroimaging studies is, so far, almost irrelevant to the points of contention. The presence of readable images of activity in the brain is *suggestive* of image-exploiting processes, probably a practical necessity for such processes to occur, but not conclusive. As Kosslyn (1994, p. 80) notes, in the long passage quoted by Pylyshyn, the issue is about a *functional* space, not necessarily a physical space. It's like computer graphics. As long as the data structures consist of properly addressed registers over which the operations are defined, the activity can be arbitrarily scattered around in space in the computer's memory without hindering the image-exploitation that is going on. (Dennett, 2002, p. 189)

Evidence that Topographically Organized Areas Depict during Imagery

Many studies have now been conducted to address the concerns about the role of topographically organized areas in imagery, as summarized below.

Depiction during Imagery

Do topographically organized areas depict shape during imagery? As a first step to demonstrating this, one must show that the appropriate brain areas are not simply activated during imagery (which could reflect their role in specifying nondepictive properties, such as color), but also that the shape of the imaged object modulates the specific pattern of activation. And in fact,

Kosslyn, Alpert, Thompson, Maljkovic, et al. (1993), Kosslyn, Thompson, Kim, and Alpert (1995), and Tootell, Hadjikani, et al. (1998) showed that images of objects that subtended smaller visual angles activated more posterior regions of area 17, as one would expect given the way area 17 functions in perception, and many other studies (see the appendix) have documented that visual imagery activates topographically organized cortex. However, one might argue that the variations in location merely reflect the difficulty of the task. With such concerns in mind, the facts about how topographically organized areas depict have been used in recent studies to provide exceptionally strong evidence that imagery relies on depictive representations.

First, Klein et al. (2004) asked participants to visualize checkered bow tie–like patterns; these patterns were either oriented vertically or horizontally. While participants performed this task, Klein et al. recorded activation in area 17 (using event-related fMRI). For the majority of participants, when they visualized the shape vertically, activation was focused along the vertical meridian of area 17; in contrast, when they visualized the shape horizontally, activation was focused along the horizontal meridian. This finding is particularly interesting because activation was also recorded while the participants actually viewed the shape in the two orientations—and the resulting patterns of activation in area 17 were extraordinarily similar to those recorded during imagery.

Second, Slotnick, Thompson, and Kosslyn (2005) mapped the visual areas activated by imagery using an analog of the standard visual mapping technique, illustrated in figure 4.1. In all, they had participants take part in four separate conditions. One was a standard perception condition, where two flickering checkerboard wedges (lined up at their points, so that the stimulus resembled a bow tie) rotated around a central fixation point. The remaining three conditions relied on another stimulus, which consisted of only the outer arcs of the two opposing wedges used in the perception condition. These arcs rotated around the center fixation point just as the entire pattern rotated during the perception condition. During one of the conditions (imagery), the participants visualized the checkerboard stimulus wedges used in the perception condition, filling in the space between the arcs. In both the perception and imagery conditions, a red dot occasionally appeared, and participants indicated whether it fell on or off the stimulus (visible or visualized). The results from the imagery condition were similar to those observed in actual perception: in both cases, there was clear evidence of activation in topographically organized areas, particularly areas 17 and 18.

However, one might object that the imagery effect merely reflects the fact that the participants had to pay attention to the region within the

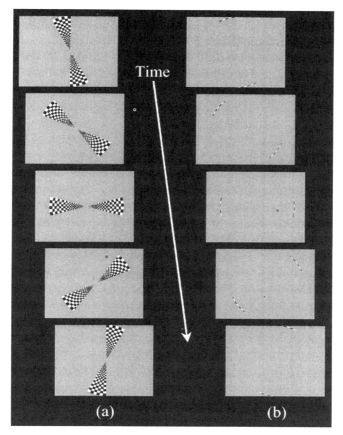

Figure 4.1. The stimulus displays used by Slotnick, Thompson, and Kosslyn (2005). See color insert. (From Slotnick, S. D., Thompson, W. L., & Kosslyn, S. M. [2005]. Visual mental imagery induces retinotopically organized activation of early visual areas. *Cerebral Cortex, 15,* 1570–1583.)

wedges. To counter this view, two attentional conditions were included. In one, the participants distributed attention over the field while observing the rotating arcs; in the other, they focused attention to the region between the two rotating arcs. Not only were the retinotopic maps obtained in imagery similar to those obtained in perception, but these maps were more pronounced than those obtained in either attention condition (although some retinotopic activation was observed even in the attention conditions, the pattern of activation in these conditions suggested that this was most likely due to the presence of the rotating arcs, which could be observed in peripheral portions of the visual field) (see figure 4.2). Thus, the imagery-induced activation could not be attributed to attention per se. Rather,

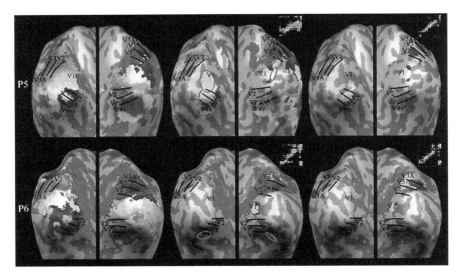

Figure 4.2. Retinotopic maps elicited from two participants during perception (*left*), imagery (*center*), and attention (*right*) in the Slotnick, Thompson, and Kosslyn (2005) experiment. Reversals of color in the map mark borders between visual areas (not intensity of activation). The blue ovals indicate areas where retinotopic activity induced by imagery was significantly greater than retinotopic activity induced by attention. See color insert. (Adapted from Slotnick, S. D., Thompson, W. L., & Kosslyn, S. M. [2005]. Visual mental imagery induces retinotopically organized activation of early visual areas. *Cerebral Cortex, 15,* 1570–1583.)

depictive imagery makes explicit and accessible properties of shapes—using representations of the same sort used during the early phases of visual perception.[3]

Depictive Representations Are Functional during Imagery

At least three results have demonstrated that activation in topographically organized visual cortex does play a functional role and is not simply epiphenomenal.

First, Kosslyn (1978) developed a technique for measuring the "visual angle of the mind's eye." As noted earlier, Farah, Soso, and Dasheiff (1992) used this technique to study a patient before and after the occipital lobe in one cerebral hemisphere was removed for medical purposes. The angle subtended by imaged objects was reduced by approximately half its initial size following the surgery—but only in horizontal, not vertical, extent. This result makes sense because the occipital lobe in each hemisphere represents

the contralateral portion of space, but vertical extent is represented re-
dundantly in both hemispheres. In short, the size of the patient's images
was directly related to available functional tissue in topographically organized portions of the occipital lobe, which demonstrates that such cortex
plays a functional role in the representation of mental images.

Second, Kosslyn, Pascual-Leone, et al. (1999) used repetitive transcranial magnetic stimulation (rTMS) to disrupt the function of area 17. In
this technique, a coil is placed against the skull, and a large magnetic field is
generated for a very brief period of time. This field activates the neurons
directly under the coil (within a region of about a cubic centimeter). When
magnetic pulses are delivered repeatedly, evoking repeated neural responses,
the neurons eventually become desynchronized and do not function
well together. Thus, rTMS can temporarily impair the functioning of a
brain region for a few minutes after its administration. Before applying
such stimulation, Kosslyn, Pascual-Leone, et al. (1999) asked participants to
memorize a stimulus that contained four sets of black-and-white stripes; a
previous study had shown that area 17 was activated when the participants
later visualized this stimulus and mentally compared the stripes (e.g., in
terms of their relative width). In the rTMS study, after the participants had
memorized the stripes, rTMS was either applied directly to calcarine cortex
(the anatomical landmark of area 17) or (in a control condition) was aimed
to miss this area. Within minutes after the TMS was applied, the participants
were asked to visualize sets of stripes and compare them, indicating their
responses by pressing one of two buttons (one button to indicate that the
first named set of stripes had more of the named dimension, and another
button to indicate that the second named set of stripes had more of the
named dimension). Response times and error rates were recorded.

The results of this study were as predicted: every participant required
more time to perform the task if the rTMS administered just prior to the task
had been aimed at calcarine cortex than if it had missed this area. Moreover,
performance was degraded to the same degree following rTMS when the
participants performed either the imagery or perception version of the
task—as expected if topographically organized visual cortex plays a role in
both perception and imagery. If activation in topographically organized
visual cortex during imagery is simply epiphenomenal, playing no functional
role in processing, then disrupting such activation should not have disrupted performance in an imagery task. The fact that disrupting this brain
area disrupted performance in an imagery task is evidence that this area
plays a functional role in performing that task.

Third, TMS is a good source of converging evidence, but it is known
that TMS can disrupt brain areas remote from the site of stimulation (via

anatomical connections; e.g., Beckers & Zeki, 1995; Munchau, Bloem, Irlbacher, Trimble, & Rothwell, 2002). Thus, these results would be most compelling if the contributions of other areas could be ruled out. Kosslyn, Thompson, Kim, Rauch, and Alpert (1996) did just this, using a statistical technique that allowed them to isolate the contribution of area 17 to specific behavior. They asked people to visualize uppercase letters, and then to decide whether each had a specific property (such as curved lines or an enclosed space). They used PET to assess regional cerebral blood flow (rCBF), which reflects how activated a part of the brain is; measures of rCBF in PET can easily be compared across participants. The results revealed that the less blood flow to area 17, the slower the people responded. But more than this, this correlation between the amount of activation in area 17 and response times remained significant even after correlations between rCBF in other areas were forced into a stepwise multiple regression before the values in area 17 were entered into the equation, and thus the contribution of other areas to the variations in response times was statistically removed. In short, variations in blood flow in area 17 per se were related to variations in behavior; this relation was not an artifact of correlations in blood flow between area 17 and other brain areas.

However, one could question whether the activation in topographically organized visual cortex during imagery reflects the representation of shape or instead reflects the effects of modulation due to attention. If the effect were simply due to attention, these findings would not speak to the issue of whether a depictive format is used during mental imagery. Consider: "I have argued that a visual expectation, even one that involves detailed shapes and locations, does not need to be more than a spatial distributions [sic] of attention over a real scene, which is very different from a picture or a pattern of activity on a Tootell Display" (Pylyshyn, 2002, p. 226).

We have the following responses to this concern. (1) As we noted in the previous chapter, forming an image in a particular patch of space *interferes* with perceiving different stimuli in that location—which is exactly the reverse of what one finds when people focus attention at a particular patch of space (e.g., compare Craver-Lemley & Reeves, 1992, for imagery, with Nakayama & Mackeben, 1989, for attention). Clearly, imagery and attention are not identical. (2) Further evidence for the differences between imagery and attention was provided by Kosslyn, Alpert, Thompson, Maljkovic, et al. (1993), who used PET to compare performance under two conditions—visualizing letters in a grid and deciding whether an X mark would fall on the letter (the imagery condition), and watching the grid and responding as quickly as possible when an X mark disappeared (the attention control

condition). Topographically organized visual cortex was activated significantly more strongly in the imagery condition than the attention condition.
Moreover, as just discussed, Slotnick, Thompson, and Kosslyn (2005) found
a similar result, using a very different task. (3) Ishai et al. (2002) found no
additional activation of area 17 when they compared a condition in which
participants visualized objects with a condition where they visualized objects
and had to attend to specific characteristics of the image (and, because there
was more activation for images based on recently seen stimuli than images
based on information stored in long-term memory (LTM), a ceiling effect is
unlikely in the latter condition). If imagery and attention were essentially the
same process, requiring attention in addition to imagery should have increased activation. (4) In many imagery experiments the participants keep
their eyes closed. It is not clear what is being attended to in this situation,
given that there is no external stimulus. If the object in the image is being
attended to, then attention would modulate the representation of the
object—and thus activation of topographically organized visual cortex
would still provide evidence that this cortex plays a role in representing the
image.

The notion that attentional effects might explain the activation of area
17 during imagery is not the only possible alternative explanation. One
could also argue, following Ishai et al. (2002), that area 17 is activated
primarily when images are formed on the basis of recently encoded stimuli.
If this were true, then it is possible that there is some residual activation in
this area due to perception, which is boosted by the effort of forming a
mental image. In this case, the activation in area 17 would not indicate that
a depictive representation is used in imagery. However, even in that study,
topographically organized visual cortex was found to be activated (albeit
less so) when images were formed on the basis of information stored in
LTM.[4] Thus, although it is possible that participants can form more vivid
or accurate images on the basis of more recently encoded stimuli, this
factor does not explain the activation of topographically organized visual
cortex.

Last, we note that a die-hard tacit knowledge theorist could argue that
the results do not necessarily rule out a tacit knowledge theory, that is, the
idea that participants are using their knowledge of perception to mimic
(perhaps unconsciously) their behavior in the corresponding perceptual
situation. Specifically, perhaps they use tacit knowledge to move their eyes
during imagery, mimicking what they believed would occur in perception.
One might then argue that it was the eye movements that produced the
observed effects in early visual cortex. Could such "perceptual behavior"
explain the imagery results? We think not: Kosslyn and Thompson (2003)

found that scanning a visual image—which was probably often accompanied by eye movements—did not independently predict when areas 17 or 18 (both of which are topographically organized) are activated. In fact, scanning per se was correlated with decreased activation in topographically organized visual cortex during imagery (as can be seen in the meta-analysis presented later in this chapter). This finding is consistent with that reported by Paus, Marrett, Worsley, and Evans (1995), who showed that eye movements actually decreased activation in topographically organized visual cortex. Thus, if participants used tacit knowledge in this way, we would expect results opposite from those actually obtained.

Counterevidence from the Effects of Brain Damage

In addition, what about the finding that some patients who have brain damage in area 17 can nevertheless perform imagery tasks? One possible account for this result rests on the idea that the tasks may not have required object-based visual imagery. For example, one of us once saw a patient who had major damage to her occipital lobes. When asked whether the uppercase letter *A* had any curved lines, she literally drew it in the air, and then responded, "No." She clearly was using kinesthetic feedback to answer. Her ability to draw need not have been guided by visual imagery; rather, purely spatial or motoric information would have been sufficient to allow her to make the response.

Another account focuses on the fact that topographically organized areas are present not only in the occipital and parietal lobes, but at many levels of hierarchy in the pathways within these systems (e.g., Felleman & Van Essen, 1991). However, as one progresses more deeply into the brain, the receptive fields of these areas become larger—and hence the resolution presumably declines. Thus, it is possible that only high-resolution imagery requires the lowest-level areas, such as area 17. If so, then such patients should have great difficulty when the task requires using high-resolution visual images, such as required to compare which of two similar sets of stripes has wider stripes. To our knowledge, such a study has never been conducted.

Finally, it is worth noting that the phenomenology of imagery may not even arise from parts of the visual system per se, even parts that have relatively low resolution. Rather, the experience of seeing may arise from much later brain areas; Crick and Koch (1995), for example, speculate that parts of the frontal lobes must receive input in order for one to have a conscious experience. It is also possible that such experiences are somehow produced when stored perceptual memories are activated, in the temporal lobes.

Counterevidence from Neuroimaging?
Understanding the Literature

Our approach to resolving the imagery debate has focused on the role of topographically organized visual areas in cortex. Patterns of activation in these areas clearly use space on the cortex to represent the corresponding space in the real world, and thus depict information (within the context of the system as a whole). However, the neuroimaging data that implicate these areas in visual mental imagery are mixed. Scores of neuroimaging studies of visual mental imagery have now been reported, with approximately half reporting activation of either primary visual cortex (which, as noted previously, is also known as area 17, area V1, the striate cortex, and the calcarine cortex), which is the first cortical area to receive input from the eyes, or the second visual area (also known as area 18 and area V2). Crucially, both of these areas are known to be topographically organized in humans (e.g., Sereno et al., 1995). Enough studies have not found such activation to make us take pause. If imagery is not systematically related to activation of these areas, our case is seriously undermined. In fact, Pylyshyn (2002) dismisses such neuroimaging findings out of hand.

In this section, we show that the neuroimaging data do in fact provide strong support for the use of depictive representations during imagery. To do so, we consider a variety of accounts for the mixed results by employing two complementary approaches to analyze the factors that govern when areas 17 and 18 (hereafter referred to as the topographically organized visual cortex) are activated during visual mental imagery. We conducted two types of analyses. First, we adopted a theory-driven approach and considered predictions of specific theories. We used three classes of theories to produce hypotheses concerning the factors that determine when imagery activates topographically organized visual cortex. Following this, we drew on a recent review of the neuroimaging studies of imagery (Kosslyn & Thompson, 2003) to report a novel type of meta-analysis. Specifically, each study was coded 1 or 0 according to whether or not topographically organized visual cortex was activated. In addition, each theory was associated with independent variables that should predict activation of topographically organized visual cortex, if that theory is correct. Each study then was coded for the presence or absence of each of these variables (each variable was considered independently of the others when codes were assigned for each study). Stepwise logistic regression analyses were conducted to identify which of the correlated variables specifically predict the presence of activation in topographically organized early visual cortex.

(Logistic regression is like ordinary multiple regression, except that the dependent measure is 1/0 data, and what is being computed is not percent of variance accounted for but rather the accuracy of predicting the 1/0 probability. The results of such analyses yield a chi-square score, which indicates the degree to which the values of the independent variables predict the probability.) These analyses allowed us to identify which variables predict activation, and the variables are identified with predictions of specific theories.

Second, we adopted a variable-driven approach, without any initial reference to different theories. To begin, variables were identified that distinguished the various studies. The 0/1 codings of whether topographically organized cortex was activated were then regressed (again using logistic regression analysis) on the independent variables. We observed which differences among studies predicted the presence or absence of activation in the topographically organized visual cortex. We then related these results back to the theories of interest.

Three Classes of Theories

For purposes of the analyses of the literature, we considered two very general classes of theories. In addition, we considered the notion that purely methodological factors affect whether and when activation in the topographically organized visual cortex is detected. In what follows we summarize the models (based on the key properties that define each class of theory) that were used in subsequent analyses, and we note how the studies were coded in order to evaluate the models. The appendix presents a summary of the neuroimaging studies that were analyzed.

Perceptual Anticipation Theories

Perceptual anticipation theories center on the idea that mental images arise when one anticipates perceiving an object or scene so strongly that a depictive representation of the stimulus is created in the topographically organized visual cortex (cf. Kosslyn, 1994; McCrone, 2001; Miyashita, 1995; Neisser, 1976). In this view, visual long-term memories of shapes are stored in an abstract code in the visual memory areas of the inferior temporal lobes. At least in the monkey brain, such memories are stored using a population code, where entries in different combinations of columns in the cortex specify a shape (Miyashita & Chang, 1988; Tanaka, Saito, Fukada, & Moriya, 1991). According to perceptual anticipation theories, the local geometry of the surfaces of shapes is only implicit in the visual long-term memory representation of shape, and is made explicit and accessible by generating patterns of activation in topographically organized visual cortex (which implement the visual buffer of our theory). Indeed, direct connections from the inferior temporal lobe to area 17 exist in the monkey brain (Barone, Batardiere, Knoblauch, & Kennedy, 2000; Clavegnier, Falchier, & Kennedy, 2004; Douglas & Rockland, 1992; Rockland & Drash, 1996; Rockland, Saleem, & Tanaka, 1992; Suzuki, Saleem, & Tanaka, 2000; Vezzoli et al., 2004); however, these efferent connections are diffuse—image generation is not simply "playing backward" stored information, but rather is necessarily a constructive activity (see Kosslyn, 1994; we discuss this in more detail in chapter 5).

In contrast, spatial representations—such as those used to guide navigation—are stored in topographically organized areas of posterior parietal cortex (Sereno et al., 2001); thus, accessing this information should not require generating patterns of activation in areas 17 and 18. And in fact, Thompson and Kosslyn (2000) conducted a meta-analysis of fMRI, PET, and single photon emission computed tomography (SPECT) neuroimaging studies to examine the relationship between activation in the posterior parietal cortex and eleven independent variables. They found, as expected if spatial representations are stored in this region, that greater activation in the posterior parietal cortex was predicted by the necessity to perform a spatial transformation, such as mental rotation, of the image. As noted in chapter 1, we distinguish between object-based images (which specify shapes and properties of shapes, such as color) and spatial images (which need not specify shape at all, but instead indicate spatial relations). We here focus on identifying the conditions under which object-based images—which are the focus of the debate—occur.[5]

This class of theories posits that the act of "looking for" a characteristic in an imaged object or scene leads one to generate an image of that characteristic. However, such theories do not require that one need to be anticipating that one will *actually* be seeing (or hearing, or feeling, depending on the modality) a specific stimulus in the environment when generating an image. An image can be generated for any reason, or even without a specific goal (e.g., during daydreams), and images can be combined or created in novel ways such that one has not necessarily seen what one is imaging. Nevertheless, in all cases the mechanisms used to generate images rely on processes used to anticipate perceiving stimuli.

According to perceptual anticipation theories, long-term visual memory may include characteristics that were not also encoded propositionally or verbally (such as the shape of an animal's ears), and thus reconstructing the shape in the topographically organized early cortex affords an opportunity to reinterpret the pattern. Generating the image makes the object's geometric properties explicit and accessible to other processes (such as those that classify shapes, which may involve processes that rely on propositional representations). In this case, the pattern of activation in topographically organized visual cortex, once present, is subsequently processed like corresponding patterns of activation that arise during perception (for a detailed theory, see Kosslyn, 1994). In addition, perceptual anticipation theories posit that representations can be reparsed and reorganized only when a pattern is reconstructed in topographically organized visual areas. Such processing often requires one to note high-resolution details of an imaged object or scene.

Perceptual anticipation theories lead us to expect activation in topographically organized visual cortex when the following three conditions were met.

1. Participants had to "see" a detail with high resolution on an imaged object or scene to perform a task. For purposes of the analysis, if the task (which could simply be visualizing an object or scene in vivid detail) required noting a part or characteristic that subtended 1 degree of visual angle or less, as seen from the participant's perspective, it was coded as requiring "high resolution," and assigned the value 1; otherwise, it was coded as 0. This criterion was chosen to be conservative: foveal vision subsumes about 2 degrees of visual angle, and that number was halved.
2. Participants had to visualize a specific example of an object that was likely to have such high-resolution details. A study was coded as 1 if the participants were to visualize specific patterns or objects (i.e., exemplars, which typically were memorized in advance of, and in preparation for, the study) and 0 if they visualized prototypes or categories of objects.
3. The task required participants to inspect properties of shapes (not spatial relations). A study was coded as 1 if it required inspecting parts, color, or characteristics of shape and 0 if it required judging spatial relations. As noted in chapter 1, distinct neural systems are used to encode and process properties of shapes versus spatial relations.

Propositional Theories

Propositional theories are based on the ideas presented by Pylyshyn (1973, 1981, 2002, 2003), and center on the claim that mental images are not represented as images at all but rather are descriptions. These descriptions

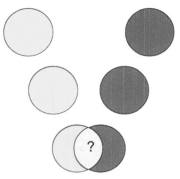

Figure 3.4. Pylyshyn (2002, 2003) argues that imagery is not like perception, based in part on the observation that people cannot visualize colors and combine them mentally to represent accurately the new color that would result from the combination. However, color mixing begins with events in the retina, whereas imagery relies on mechanisms used in the later phases of perceptual processing. Thus, it is not surprising that imagery cannot engage all mechanisms used in color perception—particularly those used in the very earliest phases when color mixing occurs. Note also that this finding does not inform us, one way or the other, about whether imagery representations depict shapes. (From Pylyshyn, Z. W. [2003]. Return of the mental image: Are there really pictures in the head? *Trends in Cognitive Neuroscience, 7*[3], 113–118.)

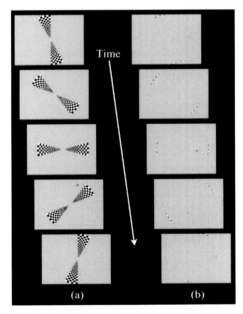

Figure 4.1. The stimulus displays used by Slotnick, Thompson, and Kosslyn (2005). (From Slotnick, S. D., Thompson, W. L., & Kosslyn, S. M. [2005]. Visual mental imagery induces retinotopically organized activation of early visual areas. *Cerebral Cortex, 15,* 1570–1583.)

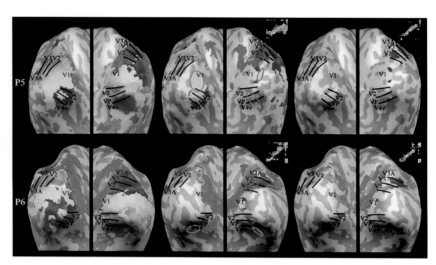

Figure 4.2. Retinotopic maps elicited from two participants during perception (*left*), imagery (*center*), and attention (*right*) in the Slotnick, Thompson, and Kosslyn (2005) experiment. Reversals of color in the map mark borders between visual areas (not intensity of activation). The blue ovals indicate areas where retinotopic activity induced by imagery was significantly greater than retinotopic activity induced by attention. (Adapted from Slotnick, S. D., Thompson, W. L., & Kosslyn, S. M. [2005]. Visual mental imagery induces retinotopically organized activation of early visual areas. *Cerebral Cortex, 15,* 1570–1583.)

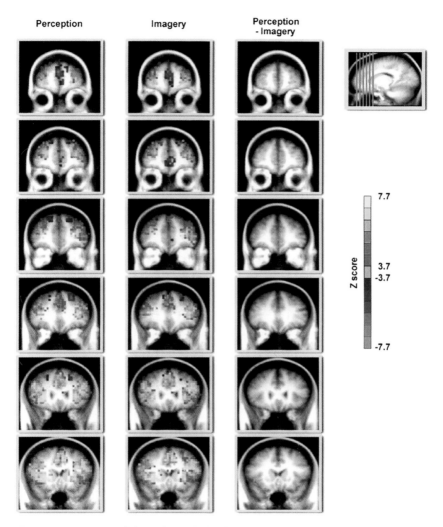

Figure 5.7. Six coronal slices through the frontal lobe. See figure 5.8 for details.

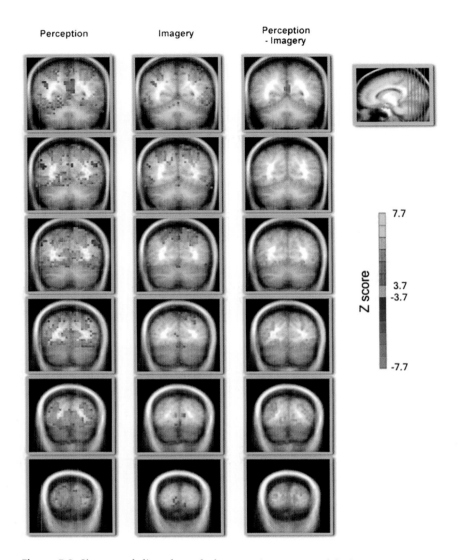

Figure 5.8. Six coronal slices through the posterior portion of the brain. The image is a composite of data from fifteen participants. The sagittal view at the top right shows the position of the sections. Activation maps are shown for the perception condition (*left*), the imagery condition (*middle*), and the contrast (perception > imagery). The overlap in activation between imagery and perception was far less than in the frontal lobe. (From Ganis, G., Thompson, W. L., & Kosslyn, S. M. [2004]. Brain areas underlying visual mental imagery and visual perception: An fMRI study. *Cognitive Brain Research, 20,* 226–241.)

rely on the same abstract symbolic codes used in language. For example, a visual form can be described in terms of the presence of certain elementary forms (such as cylinders and cones) and the spatial relations among them (cf. Biederman, 1987; Marr, 1982).

We were tempted to try to derive predictions about which specific areas should be activated during imagery if a propositional theory is correct. This proved impossible, in large part because no detailed versions of propositional theories of imagery have been developed. One's first impulse is to assume that language-related areas should be activated if such theories are correct, but this does not follow: propositional theorists argue that all cognition relies on such representations, including those used in perception; moreover, lower animals might use propositional representations to describe visual forms in the absence of language. Thus, without a detailed theory of how such a representational system would function, we cannot even begin to hypothesize which parts of the brain would be recruited during such processing.

Because this class of theories is relatively vague, it is difficult to generate positive predictions that distinguish it from other theories; this class of theories is distinguished in large part by what it rejects rather than what it posits. However, it does make one strong claim that can allow us to rule it out. Specifically, propositional theories do not assign a special role to the topographically organized visual cortex in imagery; such cortex is hardwired to represent depictions of surfaces, not sets of abstract codes combined into language-like descriptions. Thus, these theories would not predict activation of such cortex, and—critically—such observed activation would be ascribed to noise, having no orderly relation to the neural activity that actually underlies imagery processing. If so, then the appearance of such activation should be most evident when the following three conditions were met.

1. Relatively small numbers of participants were tested, and thus spurious variations could have a large impact on the results. The range of participants used in the published studies varied from four to eighteen; based on a median split, all studies with eight or fewer participants were coded as 0, and studies with nine or more participants were coded as 1.
2. Less sensitive techniques were used, which would allow noise more easily to affect the results. This was the only variable that was not binary: for testing the propositional theories, if a 3T or 4T fMRI (the *T* stands for *Tesla*, a measure of the strength of the magnetic field produced) was used, the task was scored 1; if 1.5T fMRI was used, it was scored 2; if PET, 3; and if SPECT, 4.

3. A resting baseline was used, and thus participants could engage in activities, such as talking to themselves, perhaps in anticipation of the next set of test trials. These activities might produce hypometabolism in the topographically organized visual cortex—and thus when this level of activation is compared with that in the imagery condition, the appearance of activation by the test condition would result.[6] A median split of the interstimulus intervals used in the studies employing a no-stimulation phase (most common in fMRI between periods of stimulation) as a baseline revealed that the median duration was sixty seconds. These studies were simply divided into two sets, those with no-stimulation intervals over sixty seconds and those with no-stimulation intervals at sixty seconds or less. Thus, to be considered as "rest," a no-stimulation condition had to consist of more than sixty seconds. If a study used a resting baseline, it was coded as 1; otherwise it was coded as 0.

Methodological Factors Accounts

Finally, we can take the exact opposite stance of propositional theories, and assume that topographically organized visual cortex should *always* be activated during visual imagery. According to methodological factors accounts, the perceptual anticipation process is taken to an extreme: the mere act of visualizing is enough to induce a pattern of activation in topographically organized visual cortex. If so, then the issue becomes methodological—identifying the factors that limit researchers' ability to detect such activation. Note that methodological factors accounts and perceptual anticipation theories are not mutually exclusive: it is possible that methodological factors mask the activation that should be evident only during visualization of high-resolution characteristics. We consider here the purest form of methodological factors accounts to derive simple predictions; specifically, activation of topographically organized visual cortex is more likely to be detected when the following three conditions were met.

1. Larger numbers of participants were tested, and hence the results should have been more stable.
2. More sensitive neuroimaging techniques were used, and thus activation could more easily be distinguished from noise.
3. A resting baseline was not used. Previous studies have shown high levels of activation in topographically organized visual cortex during rest (e.g., Kosslyn, Thompson, Kim, et al., 1995). Thus, when this level of activation is compared with that in the imagery condition, activation due to imagery is removed.

Evaluating the Three Classes of Theories

The studies reviewed in the appendix were coded independently by two authors (W.L.T. and S.M.K.), using the criteria associated with each model.[7] After coding each of the studies, logistic regression models were constructed to discover how well each class of theories predicted when the topographically organized visual cortex was activated. Each set of three variables was entered into a separate simultaneous logistic regression equation, which indicated how well the combination of those variables predicted the probability that topographically organized visual cortex was activated during imagery. The results for each of the models were as follows.

Perceptual Anticipation Theories

When the three variables associated with perceptual anticipation theories were considered, the likelihood ratio test for the entire model was highly statistically significant, and the residual did not even approach significance (for details of the statistical tests, see Kosslyn & Thompson, 2003). Two variables contributed to the predictive power of the model: namely, whether participants had to note high-resolution details of shapes (as defined earlier) and whether they had to visualize shapes (not spatial relations). The use of an exemplar image was not a significant predictor.

Propositional Theories and Methodological Factors Accounts

The likelihood ratio test for the entire model was again highly significant, and the residual again was not significant. Two variables contributed to the predictive power of this model—specifically, the type of baseline and the sensitivity of the technique. The variable *number of participants* was not significant. The direction of the predicted values was exactly the opposite of what was expected on the basis of propositional theories, and in line with methodological factors accounts. Studies that did not use a resting baseline were more likely to evince activation in topographically organized visual cortex, and the more sensitive the neuroimaging technique, the more likely that activation was detected. This last finding is evident in the simple proportion of fMRI studies in which such activation was detected versus those that did not find such activation, fully 19:8 if individual studies and conditions are considered (many articles reported multiple studies or conditions, such as the two events per trial in Klein, Paradis, Poline, Kosslyn, & Le Bihan, 2000; see the appendix). In contrast, the corresponding proportion for the much less sensitive SPECT technique is 2:7. As is clear, both perceptual anticipation theories and the methodological factors accounts predicted patterns of activation in topographically organized visual cortex during visual mental imagery. We reiterate that these theories are not mutually exclusive.

Variable-Driven Analyses

Although we are interested in testing the theories per se, we can only do this via specific models that represent each one. One could object to the way the models were operationalized, claiming that more appropriate variables could have been identified and coded. Rather than attempt to elaborate the models and test them again post hoc, it seemed prudent to adopt the opposite tack. Independent of any theory, differences among the studies were coded and analyses conducted to discover whether any of these differences predicted the probability of activation of the topographically organized visual cortex. After discovering which variables best predict activation in the topographically organized visual cortex, it would make sense to discuss which theories were most closely related to those variables. After reading the literature and attempting to identify ways in which the studies differed, an additional fifteen variables were formulated. The two coders independently classified each study according to the presence or absence of each variable.

First, the variables were simply correlated with each other, as well as with the presence or absence of activation in topographically organized visual cortex. As is evident in table 4.1, numerous variables were positively correlated with activation, but many others were not. However, many of these variables were intercorrelated, and thus these correlations are difficult to interpret. The next step was to ask which variables were independently the most important predictors of activation. A logistic multiple regression analysis (as is appropriate when the dependent measure is 1/0) was conducted to answer this question, which relied on a stepwise forward regression procedure in which the contribution of the most important independent variable was removed before the second-most important independent variable was determined and entered, and so forth, until no additional independent variables predicted the probability of activation in topographically organized visual cortex (see Cohen, Cohen, West, & Aiken, 2003; Menard, 2002; and Tabachnick & Fidell, 1996, for more information on logistic regression). Only the nine variables that were significantly correlated with activation in the topographically organized visual cortex were considered; this was reasonable, given that there were a total of fifty-nine observations (and if we had too many variables, it would be trivially easy to fit the observations).

Table 4.1
Correlations of Each of the Independent Variables with the Topographically Organized Visual Cortex Activation

Variable	Description	r	p	Number of tasks
Ambient light	At least some light was present in the room at testing	.26	.05	23
Categorical relations	Qualitative spatial relations such as left-right and above-below	−.14	.30	18
Color or texture	Coded positively if the task required visualizing color or object texture	.17	.20	.40
Coordinate relations	Specification of metric distances	−.16	.23	23
Explicit encoding as image	Participants learned visual patterns prior to the experiment	.02	.87	36
Eyes closed	The participant's eyes were closed during imagery	−.16	.23	41
Familiar stimuli visualized	Objects in the image were common, everyday objects, as opposed to objects of an unusual shape that participants had never seen before	−.01	.91	35
High-resolution details	"Seeing" a detail with high resolution on an imaged object to perform a task	.59	<.0001	27
Image inspection	The imaged pattern had to be interpreted for the participant to perform the task correctly	−.09	.52	29
Shorter image retention time	Image retention time was high if it exceeded six seconds (the image would begin to fade)	−.01	.94	43
Exemplar image	Specific patterns or objects, typically memorized in advance of the study	−.08	.52	39
No participant selection	Participants were not selected for their spatial imagery abilities	.47	.0002	48
No scanning	Participants were not required to shift their attention from one part of the image to another	.34	.008	44
Nonresting baseline	The baseline condition was not a resting state	.50	<.0001	47
Nonspatial processing	Properties of shapes, not spatial relations	.52	<.0001	38
High number of participants	Nine or more	−.09	.52	29

(continued)

Table 4.1
(Continued)

Variable	Description	r	p	Number of tasks
Prototype image	Standard, canonical versions of objects from long-term memory	.05	.71	21
Resolution	Considered high if the image contained a part that subtended 1° of visual angle or less (although participants need not have evaluated such parts)	**.53**	.0001	33
(Shorter) task duration	Imagery task lasted five minutes or less	**.30**	.02	36
Task performed	Participants performed a task to verify that they had used imagery as requested	−.12	.37	32
Technique sensitivity	3T or 4T fMRI was the most sensitive technique used, then 1.5T fMRI, PET, and SPECT	**.48**	.0001	59[a]

Note. Significant correlations appear in boldface type. The number of imagery activation tasks (studies or conditions within studies, out of a total of fifty-nine) reporting the presence of the characteristic is indicated in the far right column; the remaining tasks reported the opposite value of the variable. r = correlation coefficient; p = probability of the r value's being due to chance; T = Tesla; fMRI = functional magnetic resonance imaging; PET = positron emission tomography; SPECT = single photon emission computed tomography. [a]3T or 4T fMRI: 11; 1.5T fMRI: 16; PET: 23; SPECT: 9.

As indicated in table 4.2, the overall model was significant, and the residual was not significant. The first variable entered into the equation was the requirement to note high-resolution details; the second variable was the requirement to visualize shapes (not spatial relations); and the third variable was the sensitivity of the technique. All of these variables were highly statistically significant.

Implications of the Results

The meta-analyses allow us to conclude that the literature is not littered with random results or unreplicable quirks. Specifically, theory-driven analyses allow us to rule out propositional theories and collect evidence consistent with perceptual anticipation theories and methodological factors theories. In addition, a variable-driven analysis identified three variables that predicted all of the systematic differences in the probability of activation across studies. Two of

Table 4.2
Summary of Logistic Forward Selection Multiple Regression

Variable entered	df	Chi-square	p
Step 1: High-resolution details	1	20.82	<.0001
Step 2: Nonspatial images	1	15.62	<.0001
Step 3: Technique	1	13.17	<.0001
Residual chi-square			.81

Note. Independent variables significantly correlated with the dependent variable were used in this forward stepwise regression; *df* = degrees of freedom; *p* = probability of the Chi-square value's being due to chance.

these variables (the requirement to note high-resolution details and the requirement to visualize shapes rather than spatial patterns) were associated with perceptual anticipation theories, and the other one (the sensitivity of the technique) was associated with methodological factors accounts. We now consider each of the variables that were identified, in turn.

First, one theoretically interesting result was that the requirement to inspect details of shapes with high resolution—but not the requirement to use high resolution in general (which included having to make fine spatial distinctions)—predicted activation in topographically organized visual cortex. This result is of interest in part because Mellet, Tzourio-Mazoyer, et al. (2000) explicitly set out to discover whether the requirement to use high resolution in an imagery task would lead to activation of the topographically organized visual cortex. They failed to find such activation. However, their task required judging the relative heights (a spatial relation) of portions of two geometric forms, not inspecting details of their shapes. To inspect a detail of a shape, one must focus on only a portion of an overall pattern and match the shape of this portion to another (stored either in visual memory or in another part of the image). According to perceptual anticipation theories, the act of searching for a detail in a mental image results in actually placing that detail in the image, which apparently leads to activation in topographically organized visual cortex. Alternatively, the image may need to be reorganized to "see" a specific part or detail; this process would also require operating on a high-resolution depictive representation, which activates the topographically organized visual cortex. The failure to find that visualizing a specific example predicts activation in topographically organized visual cortex may simply mean that one or both of these processes is equally effective with images of prototypes.

Thompson, Kosslyn, Sukel, and Alpert (2001) explicitly studied the requirement to visualize patterns with high resolution and found that

visualizing sets of black-and-white stripes activated topographically organized visual cortex. However, differences in the resolution of the stripes
used as stimuli did not affect the degree of activation. Rather than resolution of the stimuli per se, the relevant variable appeared to be the difficulty of making the discrimination required for the task, which did not
differ for the stimuli used in that study. That is, the critical variable was the
level of resolution required to make the judgment, rather than the resolution of the stimuli themselves. This finding directly confirms the results
of the regression analysis. However, this finding in turn raises a crucial
issue: could activation in topographically organized visual cortex simply
reflect difficulty per se? One might argue that more difficult tasks generally
activate the topographically organized visual cortex. However, difficult
spatial tasks have been administered in many neuroimaging experiments in
which topographically organized visual cortex was not activated. For example, verbal working memory tasks and spatial working memory tasks do
not activate topographically organized visual cortex (Smith & Jonides,
1997, 1999). Thus, difficulty per se cannot explain the present findings.

Second, also of interest was the finding that the topographically organized visual cortex was not activated when the task required spatial—and
not shape-based—processing. In an earlier meta-analysis with the then-
extant literature, Thompson and Kosslyn (2000) found that spatial processing predicted activation of the posterior parietal cortex—and not
occipital cortex—during imagery tasks. This finding is consistent with the
claim that the parietal lobes process spatial images (see chapters 1 and 5).
Because these spatial representations are stored topographically (cf. Sereno
et al., 2001), there is no reason why they would need to be reconstructed in
the topographically organized regions of visual cortex. In contrast, at least
in the monkey, shape representations are not stored topographically, and
thus accessing this information may require generating patterns of activation in topographically organized visual cortex. In addition, this result is
consistent with Mazard, Tzourio-Mazoyer, Crivello, Mazoyer, & Mellet's
(2004) meta-analysis of PET studies. The authors of that meta-analysis
considered the results from nine mental imagery studies conducted in their
laboratory, seven of which required spatial imagery and two of which required depictive imagery. They found that topographically organized visual
cortex was activated when participants performed depictive imagery tasks
but was actually deactivated when they performed spatial imagery tasks.[8]

Third, it is not surprising—if one accepts the idea that depictive imagery relies on topographically organized areas of cortex—that activation in
such areas was more likely to be reported when more sensitive techniques
were used. The fMRI studies may have proven more sensitive for several

reasons: First, part of the increased power of fMRI arises from the ability to analyze data from individual participants. Thus, the activation maps from multiple individuals do not need to be averaged and a spatial transformation is not necessary, as is required in traditional PET analyses (see, e.g., Fox, Mintun, Reiman, & Raichle, 1988; Fox & Pardo, 1991). Cohen and Bookheimer (1994) argue that this is an enormous advantage because the spatial transformation necessarily results in lower signal-to-noise ratios; Watson et al. (1993) demonstrated this clearly in a combined study using fMRI and PET. In addition, fMRI allows researchers to include a larger number of replicates (and thus obtain greater statistical power) than is possible with PET or SPECT. Finally, given the properties of magnetic resonance, we would also expect greater signal-to-noise ratio with higher field strengths, and, indeed, some reports have found greater magnitude differences with increased field strength (Frahm, Merboldt, & Hnicke, 1993; Kwong et al., 1992; Ogawa et al., 1992; Thulborn, Waterton, Matthews, & Radda, 1982). However, the increment in sensitivity with higher fields remains controversial because the variation in magnetic resonance noise also increases with higher magnetic fields. Nevertheless, there is enough evidence for increasing sensitivity along the spectrum from SPECT to 4T fMRI for us to consider this as a possible source of variation in the observed results.

Considering data from individual participants may be a critical aspect of most fMRI designs, as is evident when one considers the nature of individual differences in blood flow in the topographically organized visual cortex during imagery. As discussed earlier, Kosslyn, Thompson, Kim, Rauch, and Alpert (1996) found that blood flow in area 17 correlated negatively with response times during a visual imagery task. A similar analysis was performed by Klein et al. (2000), who also found a negative correlation between activation in area 17 and response times. The results from the analysis of individual differences also bear on the sensitivity of the technique in the following way: examination of Kosslyn, Thompson, Kim, Rauch, and Alpert's (1996) data reveals that approximately 25 percent of the participants did not have more blood flow in area 17 than the adjusted grand mean for the whole brain. This estimate is consistent with the results from the fMRI neuroimaging studies of visual imagery reviewed in the appendix, in which an average of about 24 percent of the participants were nonresponders (based on the studies in which analyses of data from individual participants are clearly reported and in which there were at least some positive findings). Given that some studies reported only a group analysis yielding negative results, this is probably an underestimate of the actual percentage of nonresponders (see, e.g., Handy et al., 2004).[9]

Conclusions

The virtues of turning to the brain should now be clear, and we press this approach forward in the following chapter. We showed in this chapter that the claim that visual mental images depict is consistent with key facts about the brain and the relevant behavioral findings. Moreover, neither the anatomical properties of topographically organized areas nor their role in imagery can be explained by appeal to tacit knowledge theories.

However, although many neuroimaging studies have documented that the topographically organized cortex is activated when people visualize, many other studies have failed to find such activation. The meta-analyses summarized here made sense of what at first glance might appear to be a chaotic set of empirical findings (reviewed in the appendix). When people visualize shapes with high resolution, depictive representations are in fact created. The theory summarized in the following chapter allows us to understand these findings, and also to understand why spatial imagery tasks do not activate topographically organized areas.

One strong prediction that emerges from our interpretation of the results is that if the topographically organized visual cortex represents the geometric properties of surfaces of shapes during imagery, then the precise pattern of activation should reflect the shape of the object in the same way it does during perception. Moreover, if a small part of topographically organized visual cortex is impaired, either from a very localized lesion (as might occur after a small tumor is removed) or from very focused TMS, only a small portion of an imaged object should be obscured—and the precise portion should depend on the size, orientation, and position of the imaged object. As the methodologies used in cognitive neuroscience continue to improve, it should be possible to test these strong predictions.

Notes

1. We must note that in the topographically organized areas there are some cases in which points close by in external space are not close by on the cortical surface. For example, if one takes two dots, one just above the horizontal meridian, one just below, their representation in area V2 will be far away because of how the upper and lower visual fields are represented in V2. Topographic areas typically represent only the upper or lower half of a single hemifield. As we would expect, perceptual effects arising from this neuroanatomical configuration can be measured psychophysically (Rubin, Nakayama, & Shapley, 1996). Nonetheless, the system interprets this pattern correctly. We again emphasize that the depictive properties of these areas

emerge from the way they are connected to areas downstream. The fact that these areas function to depict information within the context of the system is clear: the location of damage in topographically organized brain areas is directly related to the loci of blind spots in the visual field, and magnetic stimulation of different parts of such cortex produces phosphenes in the corresponding locations in space (see also chapter 1).

2. One might argue that the crucial variable is not the actual physical distance on cortex, but rather a kind of "functional distance" defined by connectivity among neurons in a brain area. Start by taking the extreme case, where physically distant neurons are connected directly to each other and thus function as if they were adjacent, whereas physically nearby neurons are connected indirectly to each other via intermediate neurons and thus function as if they were very far apart. If the neurons in an area were so arranged, would the area in fact depict? Now take a less extreme case, where physically distant neurons tend to have more intermediate neurons between them—and thus, the crucial variable is not actual distance on the cortex but rather the number of connections that intervene among neurons. Would such an area still depict?

We have two responses to this concern (which was expressed to us in conversation by the distinguished philosopher Ned Block): (1) In point of fact, most connections between neurons in topographically organized areas are short and inhibitory (at least in the monkey brain, about which we know considerably more than we do about the human brain). This is a good example of how neuroanatomy constrains theory. We cannot simply posit an arrangement of connections by fiat; there is a physical device, and there are known facts about how it is constructed (and how it operates). (2) The fact that topographically organized areas are physically depictive is irrelevant for present purposes. The neurons in these areas could be interconnected arbitrarily, but as long as *fixed* connections to areas farther downstream "unscramble" the activity in earlier areas appropriately, the earlier areas will functionally depict. We know that such an orderly mapping to later areas occurs because of the systematic relations between loci that are damaged in an area and loci in the visual field where blind spots appear.

3. Slotnick et al. also found that such imagery induced activation in the motion area MT. This finding is of interest because motion-related activity in this area has been directly linked to conscious awareness of a moving stimulus (Britten, Newsome, Shadlen, Celebrini, & Movshon, 1996; Britten, Shadlen, Newsome, & Movshon, 1992; Shadlen & Newsome, 1996; Zeki & ffytche, 1998).

4. Moreover, many other researchers have found activation in the topographically organized visual cortex when images are formed on the basis of information stored in LTM—specifically, Chen et al. (1998), Goldenberg and colleagues (Goldenberg, Podreka, Steiner, et al., 1989; Goldenberg, Steiner, Podreka, & Deecke, 1992; with high-imagery sentences); Handy et al. (2004); Klein, Paradis, et al. (2000); Kosslyn, Alpert, Thompson, Maljkovic, et al. (1993, Experiment 3); and Lambert, Sampaio, Scheiber, and Mauss (2002). On the other hand, some studies that required participants to form images based on recently encoded stimuli failed to find activation in topographically organized visual cortex (Ghaëm et al., 1997;

Knauff, Kassubek, Mulack, & Greenlee, 2000; Mellet, Tzourio, Denis, & Mazoyer, 1995; Roland & Gulyás, 1995; and Wheeler, Petersen, & Buckner, 2000). In short, this variable—whether information resides in STM or LTM at the time the image is formed—does not explain why area 17 is activated during some types of imagery.

5. Some theorists (e.g., Milner & Goodale, 1995) have argued that the posterior parietal lobes do not represent spatial information per se, but rather represent information to be used in guiding action ("how," not "where"). However, spatial relations are used in many contexts, not just in guiding movement. For example, a landmark is an object that has a specific spatial relation to something else (e.g., a turn in a path). In fact, there is a growing body of literature that implicates the posterior parietal lobes in coding "categorical spatial relations," such as those captured by spatial terms (e.g., "above," "inside," "connected to"; for a review, see Laeng, Chabris, & Kosslyn, 2002). These spatial relations specify categories, which are too broad to be useful in guiding motion. For example, knowing that a desk is "in front of" you is not sufficient to allow you to navigate around it. Such categories would be useful in describing the structure of a multipart shape, such as a bicycle, because the same description could apply even if the object were contorted in various ways. There is also evidence that the posterior parietal lobes are involved in processing "coordinate" spatial relations, which specify precise metric distances, which would help you navigate around a desk that was in front of you. Thus, we adhere to the notion, originally proposed by Ungerleider and Mishkin (1982), that the posterior parietal lobes encode spatial information—not simply information to be used in guiding movements.

6. However, this class of theories does not predict that some activities, such as daydreaming, would (or even could) lead to hypermetabolism in the topographically organized visual cortex; such a prediction rests on the idea that visual mental imagery does in fact rely on topographically organized areas to depict shape.

7. In this and all other codings used in this analysis, the two judges were at least 85 percent reliable in all cases (and on average about 93 percent reliable); when the judges disagreed, a brief discussion invariably resulted in consensus.

8. Mazard et al. (2004) also found that performance on the mental rotations test (i.e., the MRT; Vandenberg & Kuse, 1978), which assesses how well one can rotate images of multi-armed shapes, correlated positively with blood flow in area 17 in the depictive imagery tasks; this is the opposite result from that reported by Kosslyn, Thompson, et al. (1996) and Klein et al. (2000). In Mazard et al.'s analysis, the correlation was computed on a restricted range of scores—the participants were selected on the basis of having high scores on the MRT—and thus must be interpreted with caution. The authors suggested that this effect may reflect general imagery ability, which is possible. However, Kozhevnikov and Kosslyn (2000) found that the ability to use object-based imagery was actually negatively correlated with the ability to use spatial imagery (see also Kozhevnikov, Kosslyn, & Shephard, 2005). In addition, Kozhevnikov, Hegarty, and Mayer (2002) presented evidence that people high in spatial ability tend to generate and use "schematic" (i.e., spatial) images, as opposed to depictive images. Viewed in this light, it is possible that

object-based imagery was actually more difficult for the participants who scored highest on the MRT, and hence these participants had to expend more effort—which produced more blood flow in area 17—to perform the task.

9. It is not clear why some participants are nonresponders; the reasons may include physiological differences in function as well as anatomical differences that make the BOLD response particularly difficult to detect in some brain regions. In any case, nonresponder participants have been observed across different cognitive domains, not only in imagery (Davis, Kwan, Crawley, & Mikulis, 1998; Hedera et al., 1998; Lee, Jack, & Riederer, 1998). For additional details on the analysis of non-responders, see Kosslyn & Thompson (2003).

5

Visual Mental Images in the Brain

Overview of a Theory

One of the lessons we have learned from studying mental imagery is that neurophysiology and neuroanatomy can play a key role in theorizing about cognitive events. In our view, the "mind" is "what the brain does." (Or, more precisely, "mental processes" are one of the primary functions of the brain.) Thus, knowing about what specific areas of the brain do and about the connections among brain areas can place major constraints on theories of mental processing. And, as we discussed earlier, such constraints can—as Anderson (1978) suggested—prevent theorists from inventing theories of representations and processes willy-nilly. The value of such neurological constraints is nowhere more apparent than in mechanistically oriented theories of visual mental imagery—nor is it more important, given the types of criticisms that have been levied against such theories.

In this chapter we outline a neurologically plausible theory of visual mental imagery that posits depictive representations. Our goal is not to review the theory in detail (see Kosslyn, 1994), but rather to provide enough information to show that depictive representations can in fact function effectively within a plausible information-processing system. We also demonstrate that neuroscientific data are in fact relevant to settling the question as to whether depictive representations are used in imagery.

Visual Processing Mechanisms

Visual processing can be divided into two general types, "sensory" and "perceptual." Sensory visual processing is driven primarily (if not purely) by sensory input, whereas perceptual processing makes use of stored information. A fundamental assumption of the present approach is that visual imagery evokes many of the same processing mechanisms used in visual perception. This assumption is important because the neuroanatomy and neurophysiology of vision are relatively well understood, and hence we gain considerable leverage for understanding imagery if visual imagery relies largely on visual perceptual mechanisms.

Subsystems of Visual Perception

Our theory of imagery is built on a theory of visual object identification. Object identification, like all other mental functions, is not accomplished by a single process. Rather, just as there are many processes involved in storing and recalling memories (Schacter, 1996; Squire, 1987), there are many processes involved when we come to know what an object is and facts about it (for instance, that it's a purse). Our theory is an attempt to decompose such visual processing into a set of subsystems, each of which accomplishes a specific part of the overall task. Figure 5.1 illustrates the subsystems that we hypothesize to be used in both visual mental imagery and visual perception. We begin by considering the hypothesized role of each processing subsystem in perception, and then consider how the system functions in visual mental imagery.

Visual Buffer

As we noted earlier, at least thirty-two distinct areas of cortex are involved in visual perception in the monkey brain (Felleman & Van Essen, 1991), and probably more in the human brain. Some of these areas (about half in the monkey brain) are topographically organized; such areas use space on cortex to represent space in the world (e.g., see Felleman & Van Essen, 1991; Fox et al., 1986; Heeger, 1999; Sengpiel & Huebener, 1999; Sereno et al., 1995; Tootell, Hadjikani, et al., 1998; Tootell, Silverman, et al., 1982; Van Essen, 1985). These areas are not simply physically topographically organized, they function to depict information. As we've discussed in previous chapters, not only does activation in these areas reflect the geometric structure of the planar projection of a stimulus, but also damage to

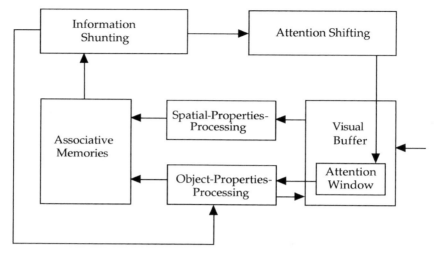

Figure 5.1. The subsystems hypothesized to implement visual perception and imagery processing.

discrete portions of these areas produces scotomas—blind spots—that are localized in space according to where the damage occurs. As noted in chapter 1, we group the topographically organized areas in the occipital lobe into a single functional structure, which we call the *visual buffer.*

That said, the visual buffer is in fact what we called a hybrid representation in chapter 1. Each point in the topographically organized areas represents more than the presence or absence of a point in space. Rather, properties such as color, intensity, depth and motion are also specified at each location, using a symbolic (propositional) code. Furthermore, the representation is not necessarily complete; parts of the object may be omitted and other parts may be represented incompletely (largely because one did not pay attention to them). The representation is not a picture.

Attention Window

There is more information in the visual buffer than can be processed in detail; thus, an attention window selects some regions of the visual buffer for further processing (Brefczynski & DeYoe, 1999; Cave & Kosslyn, 1989; Posner & Petersen, 1990; Treisman & Gelade, 1980). The attention window can be covertly shifted either to new locations in space (e.g., Posner et al., 1980; Sperling, 1960) or to different objects (e.g., Egly, Driver, & Rafal, 1994).

Object-Properties-Processing

The visual buffer can be said to convey information only insofar as its contents are processed further; if the brain regions that make up the visual buffer were entirely isolated, they might as well not exist. And in fact, there are massive connections from the topographically organized areas of the occipital lobe to other areas of the brain. One set of connections runs from the occipital lobe to the inferior (i.e., lower) temporal lobe (e.g., Desimone & Ungerleider, 1989; Haxby et al., 1991; Kosslyn, 1994; Mishkin, Ungerleider, & Macko, 1983; Ungerleider & Mishkin, 1982). There is good evidence that visual memories are stored in portions of the inferior temporal lobe (e.g., Fujita, Tanaka, Ito, & Cheng, 1992; Tanaka, Saito, Fukada, & Moriya, 1991). At least in the monkey, such memories are not stored topographically, but rather are stored using a *population code*: each cortical location contains neurons that respond selectively to combinations of values along a large number of different visual dimensions, and it is the sum total of the set of activated neurons that specifies object properties (e.g., Fujita et al., 1992; Miyashita & Chang, 1988; Tanaka et al., 1991). Because these representations do not use space to represent space and generally do not meet our definition of "depiction" (see chapter 1), they cannot be considered to depict. These areas not only store information about shape and shape-related properties, such as color, but also match input to such stored information. According to our theory, these areas implement the *object-properties-processing subsystem*, which analyzes properties such as shape and color. During perception, input from the attention window is compared to stored visual representations in this subsystem, and an object is *recognized* if the input matches a stored representation.

Spatial-Properties-Processing

We not only can recognize objects but also can localize an object's position (or the positions of the object's parts) in space. How is this accomplished? The brain evolved a strategy of "divide and conquer." The object-properties-processing system essentially throws away information about location—which allows it to recognize objects in different locations (Gross & Mishkin, 1977). But at the same time it is operating, a second system registers location. Such processing is accomplished along a pathway that runs from the occipital lobe to the posterior parietal lobe (e.g., Haxby et al., 1991; Kosslyn, Thompson, Gitelman, & Alpert, 1998; Ungerleider & Mishkin, 1982). The posterior parietal lobe processes properties such as location, size, and orientation (Andersen, Essick, & Siegel, 1985). According to our theory, these areas implement the *spatial-properties-processing* subsystem.

At first glance, it may not appear that there is a principled distinction between the object-properties-processing and spatial-properties-processing systems. As anyone who has looked very closely at a computer screen or a comic strip knows, shapes can be represented by configurations of points—and shapes rely entirely on how those points are placed relative to each other in space. Nevertheless, we can distinguish the way points function in shape versus spatial representations, as follows: In shape representations, the individual points are only important insofar as they give rise to configural properties, such as edges that are straight or curved or regions that are open or enclosed. These configural properties emerge from the juxtaposition of the entire set of points. In contrast, in spatial representations a single point holds a privileged role as the origin: the locations of other points are specified relative to the origin. The origin can be one's body (or a part thereof) or a specific object or spot in space; there is no comparable point in a representation of shape. Thus, the spatial-properties-processing system attempts to locate objects, parts or characteristics relative to an origin, not to organize shapes into figure and ground and match these units to units stored in memory (which is the province of the object-properties-processing system).

The parietal cortex that implements at least part of the spatial-properties-processing subsystem is topographically organized, and thus at least some of the representations used in this system are depictive (Sereno et al., 2001). As one of its functions, the spatial-properties-processing subsystem represents a map of the locations of objects or parts of objects in space (Mesulam, 1990); this *object map* indicates the locations of objects in a scene or parts of an object. The object map is important in part because every time the eyes move, a different representation is produced in the visual buffer. The object map indexes the locations of successive representations of shape; the shapes at those locations may be stored in the object-properties-processing subsystem. In addition, object maps allow the world to serve as a kind of external store (O'Regan & Nöe, 2001): we know where something is located, allowing us to go back for a second look. The object map itself may be stored (cf. Squire, 1987). Finally, we hypothesize that the object map represents units across the entire visual field, not just what one is paying attention to; thus, one knows that there is an object (or part or characteristic) at a location before one shifts attention to see what it is. In contrast, the object-properties-processing system processes almost exclusively output from the attention window.[1]

Associative Memories

During perception, the flow of information does not stop in the object-properties-processing and spatial-properties-processing subsystems. Outputs from both of these subsystems feed into associative memories. These outputs allow associative memory to specify links among representations, creating a propositional description of the structure of an object or scene. A short-term associative memory structure is implemented in the dorsolateral prefrontal areas, retaining information on-line about which objects are in which locations (Rao, Rainer, & Miller, 1997; Wilson, O'Scalaidhe, & Goldman-Rakic, 1993). A long-term associative memory structure appears to be implemented in various structures, including Wernicke's area, the angular gyrus, the anterior temporal lobe, and classic "association cortex" (e.g., area 19; for evidence, see Kosslyn, Thompson, & Alpert, 1995). The outputs from the object-properties-processing and spatial-properties-processing subsystems are compared to representations stored in associative memory. If the input matches a stored representation, one has access to the information associated with that stored representation—and hence has *identified* an object. When one has identified an object, one knows its name, what categories it belongs to, and so forth. (Recognition, which occurs in the object-properties-processing subsystem, merely indicates that a stimulus is familiar.) If the object cannot be immediately identified, the best-matching representation in long-term associative memory is treated as an hypothesis about the viewed object.

Information Shunting

According to the theory, when input to long-term associative memory does not clearly implicate a specific object, representations of distinctive parts and characteristics of the best-matching object that are activated by the input are registered by an information shunting subsystem (cf. Gregory, 1970; Neisser, 1967, 1976). This subsystem guides a top-down search by passing information to other subsystems. That is, we humans are not passive perceivers but instead actively seek information to help confirm or disconfirm hypotheses about what we are seeing. The information shunting subsystem serves two functions: First, it provides information that allows other subsystems to shift the focus of attention to the presumed location of a distinctive part or characteristic. Second, at the same time, the information shunting subsystem sends information about the distinctive part or characteristic to *prime* the corresponding representation in the object-properties-processing subsystem (cf. McAuliffe & Knowlton, 2000; for evidence of such priming in perception and imagery, see Kosslyn, 1994, pp. 287–289; McDermott & Roediger, 1994). Priming facilitates the ability to encode an expected part or characteristic. Portions of dorsolateral prefrontal cortex (DLPFC) implement this subsystem (e.g., Damasio, 1985; Koechlin, Basso, Pietrini, Panzer, & Grafman, 1999; Luria, 1980; Posner & Petersen, 1990; note that DLPFC is a huge region, and we are not claiming that its only function is to implement the information shunting subsystem).

Attention Shifting

The process of actually shifting the focus of attention to a new location or object involves a complex subsystem, implemented in the superior parietal lobes, frontal eye fields, superior colliculus, thalamus and anterior cingulate (Posner & Petersen, 1990). Other brain regions may also be involved in this complex process (see Corbetta, Miezen, Schulman, & Petersen, 1993; LaBerge & Buchsbaum, 1990; Mesulam, 1981; Posner & Petersen, 1990). This system not only can shift the location of the attention window (such as occurs when one scans over an afterimage) but also can shift the eyes, head, and even body so that new information is registered. Although relative locations are stored in the spatial-properties-processing subsystem and indexed in long-term associative memory, they need not be linked to eye movements.

In perception, if the object is familiar and seen from a familiar point of view, it may be recognized (i.e., matched to a visual representation in the object-properties-encoding system) and identified (i.e., matched to a representation in long-term associative memory) via purely bottom-up processing. If the object cannot be recognized and identified relatively quickly via bottom-up processing (driven solely by the material encoded at first glance), then top-down processing is allowed to run to completion. Such processing is driven by stored information, and not only directs attention to the location where one should find a diagnostic part or characteristic but also primes the representation of that part or characteristic in the object-properties-processing system.[2] In this case, after attention is appropriately shifted, a new part or characteristic is encoded into the visual buffer, and a second cycle of processing commences. If the new part or characteristic matches the primed representation in the object-properties-processing subsystem, the part or characteristic is recognized, and this information may be enough to implicate a single representation in long-term associative memory. If so, then the object has been identified. If not, either additional parts or characteristics of that object are sought or a new hypothesis is used to guide search.[3]

Visual Processing during Mental Imagery

One important feature of the present theory of imagery is that it was grounded in facts about the mechanisms that operate during perception; it was not simply created ad hoc to explain data (for details, see Kosslyn, 1994). Two crucial aspects of this theory are that (1) the flow of information among the subsystems is highly constrained by the nature of neuroanatomical connections among brain areas in human and nonhuman primates and (2) the postulated properties of the various subsystems are constrained by what is known about the underlying neuroanatomical organization of the brain areas that implement these subsystems. For example, unlike the earlier theory of Kosslyn (1980), we do not simply stipulate that the visual buffer has spatial properties like those of an array in a computer; we appeal instead to neuroanatomical facts to justify this assumption, which cannot be adjusted to suit the theorist's whims. Moreover, the nature of the connections is a major determinant of the functional properties of representations *within the system.* In particular, the fact that the topography of early visual areas is mapped in an orderly way to increasingly later visual areas indicates that topographical characteristics of the representations in these areas are used in the system. This a crucial point, which obviates Dennett's (2002) concern that the processes used in imagery have not been characterized in enough detail to know how properties of the representations would affect performance. We are not considering representations and processes in isolation, but rather in the context of the processing system as a whole.

The first important distinction that arises from the theory is between two general classes of visual mental images: spatial and depictive. Spatial images correspond to an object map (which, as discussed earlier, specifies the locations of objects or their parts) created on the basis of information stored in long-term memory, whereas depictive images correspond to a pattern of activation in the visual buffer created on the basis of information stored in long-term memory. According to the present theory, both sorts of imagery rely on four types of functions: image generation, inspection, maintenance, and transformation. These functions were identified in the course of trying to build computer simulations that mimic imagery (Kosslyn, 1980, 1994), and subsequently justified by studies of the effects of brain damage on imagery (e.g., Farah, 1984) and neuroimaging studies (e.g., Kosslyn, 1994; Kosslyn, Ganis, & Thompson, 2001; Thompson & Kosslyn, 2000). The operation of the system in both cases is summarized below.

Image Generation

As discussed in chapter 1, different formats make different information explicit and accessible, which is why different representations are used in different phases of processing in the visual system. The initial phases of visual representation in the cortex rely on topographic representations, in which space on cortex is used to represent space in the world. As perceptual processing progresses in the brain, these maps become less precise, and the representations become more abstract. The final phases of representation (in what we refer to as the object-properties-processing subsystem implemented in the ventrolateral temporal cortex) apparently rely on representations in which population codes are used to specify the shapes of objects (Tanaka, 1996; Tanaka et al., 1991). These representations make explicit and accessible characteristics of shape that tend not to vary when objects are seen from different perspectives, which is useful for comparing input to memories of previously seen shapes. However, because visual memories are stored in this more abstract format during perception, in order to recall the local geometry of shape it is necessary to *generate* mental images in topographically organized areas. Generating images causes the local geometry to become explicit and accessible, in much the same way that playing a DVD makes the local geometry of the stored images explicit and accessible (to us humans) on a TV screen.

A key part of our theory is that visual information is stored in a way that allows the system to reconstruct the shape, if need be. Why? Because it is not always clear from the outset what information may be relevant to solving a given task, the representations preserve as much of the input as possible—thus respecting Marr's (1982) famous "Principle of Least Commitment" (which advocated retaining as much information as possible for as long as possible in the processing sequence). Think of this by analogy to giving someone directions on how to get a specific restaurant from a particular metro stop. You might look up the location of the stop and restaurant on a map, and then describe the optimal route verbally. But you would not then discard the map and save only the verbal description! Who knows what other routes you will need to look up in the future? Similarly, although the visual system appears to encode automatically whatever one pays attention to, this does not require that all of the encoded information will be retained. But retaining it makes good sense: one cannot know in advance which aspects of the input will be required to perform specific tasks, and thus throws away as little as possible. Instead of discarding information, we propose that—if possible—the information is transformed into more concise forms and stored.

The theory posits that image generation begins by a process of first looking up a description of a spatial layout in long-term associative memory. If a spatial image is all that is required by the task, stored information is unpacked to create an object map in the spatial-properties-processing subsystem (in the posterior parietal lobes). The object map specifies the relative locations of objects, or parts of a single object, but does not indicate depictive properties of shape. Although all processing occurs in parallel, and thus one typically generates an image of shape at the same time one generates a spatial image, not all forms of processing may be useful for performing a specific task. For some tasks, for example, to make judgments on the spatial relations between objects, it is not necessary to visualize the shape of an object or its surface characteristics; rather, generating an object map is sufficient. Because the spatial-properties-processing subsystem makes explicit and accessible spatial information, spatial imagery does not rely on reconstructing a representation in the visual buffer. Consistent with this claim, Levine, Warach, and Farah (1985) found that damage to the inferior temporal lobes (which implement the object-properties-processing system in our theory) could disrupt the ability to visualize objects but not sets of directions, and damage to the posterior parietal lobes (which implement the spatial-properties-processing system) had the reverse effect.

If a depictive image of a single shape is required for a task, the information shunting subsystem accesses long-term associative memory and shunts a representation of the shape to be visualized to the object-properties-processing subsystem. This abstract representation indexes the corresponding stored representation of the shape and activates it just as occurs when one's expectations prime one during perception. According to the theory, this stored shape representation is primed so strongly that activation is propagated backwards, inducing a representation of a part or characteristic in the visual buffer (which corresponds to the depictive image itself). Indeed, as discussed earlier, researchers have documented direct connections from inferior temporal lobe to area 17 in the monkey brain (Barone et al., 2000; Clavegnier et al., 2004; Douglas & Rockland, 1992; Rockland & Drash, 1996; Rockland et al., 1992; Suzuki et al., 2000; Vezzoli et al., 2004); area 17 is the first and largest cortical area to receive input from the eyes (and, as noted earlier, is topographically organized). In order to reconstruct the shape appropriately, parameter values must be set for the mapping function from the object-properties-processing subsystem to the visual buffer; these values specify the size and location of the imaged pattern in the buffer. The theory posits that processes operating on the object map in the spatial-properties-processing subsystem can set these values, based on spatial properties (size and location) of the object.[4]

If a depictive image of a multipart shape is required for a task (for example, a bicycle, with all of its individual parts), an object map is created at the outset, which specifies either the layout of an object (what Kosslyn, 1980, previously called the "skeletal image") or the layout of a scene. In this case, the information shunting subsystem accesses long-term associative memory and shunts a representation of the location of the most distinctive part or characteristic to the attention-shifting subsystem. Guided by the object map, the attention-shifting subsystem positions the attention window at the appropriate location in the visual buffer at the same time that the index of the part is shunted to the object-properties-processing subsystem, and the relevant stored representation is primed so strongly that activation is propagated backwards, inducing a representation of a part or characteristic in the visual buffer. Again, in order to reconstruct the shape appropriately, parameter values must be set for the mapping function from the object-properties-processing subsystem to the visual buffer, as noted above. This entire set of processes is repeated for each additional property or part (or object, in a scene) to be depicted.[5]

Image Inspection

If one has visualized object properties, and hence an image representation is formed in the visual buffer, one *inspects* the imaged pattern by shifting the attention window over it to encode properties (e.g., as would occur if one were asked what shape are a cat's ears and so visualized a cat's head and examined the shape of its ears). Imaged patterns are recognized by matching the input to stored visual memories in the object-properties-processing subsystem, just as is done during perception. One can shift the focus of attention incrementally (as we will describe shortly), scanning the imaged object; in contrast, parts or characteristics may "pop out," that is, they may be inspected without scanning. Kosslyn (1994, pp. 339–341) discusses ways in which pop-out can occur in imagery, where characteristics of the imaged object are immediately passed on for later processing (without needing to be scanned to and then focused on following scanning).

Similarly, image inspection involves encoding spatial relations using the spatial-properties-processing subsystem, just as in perception. If a spatial image (i.e., only an object map) has been generated, novel spatial relations can be extracted using the spatial-properties-processing subsystem— just as would occur if the stimulus were being viewed (see Kosslyn, 1994). Image inspection is in fact a key part of image generation and vice versa. It is often the act of trying to inspect an imaged object that leads one to generate images of specific parts and properties (see Kosslyn, 1994); the two abilities—image generation and image inspection—work in tandem. Consistent with this claim, Kosslyn, Thompson, Shephard, et al. (2004) examined correlations between brain activity and performance on tasks that selectively tapped different imagery processes. Image generation and image inspection clearly drew on some of the same frontal and thalamic areas— which may underlie the common use of image inspection (the thalamus is clearly involved in fixating attention; e.g., Posner & Petersen, 1990) and image generation (the frontal lobes are involved in sequencing, and image generation in particular; e.g., Kosslyn, Thompson, & Alpert, 1997).

Nevertheless, although they often work in tandem, the two processes are distinct: image inspection is the process of interpreting an image including an object, part, or characteristic (for object-based-imagery) or a specific location, size, or orientation (for spatial imagery). Such processing is logically distinguished from the process whereby an image is created on the basis of stored information. In addition, one can inspect an image that is retained from perceptual input (i.e., formed by closing one's eyes and maintaining the image), without generating it on the basis of information stored in long-term memory. And, on the other side of the coin, one can generate an image but only inspect closely a selected part of it—but the other parts are still in the image. Moreover, in spite of some overlap, the brain areas that predict performance in image generation and image inspection tasks are largely distinct (Kosslyn, Thompson, Shephard, et al., 2004).

Image Maintenance

An object-based image begins to fade as soon as it is formed. The fact that such images fade quickly makes sense if they share the same topographically organized occipital cortex used in visual perception. As noted in chapter 1, in perception, one does not want smearing every time the eyes move and a new image is projected into cortex. So the neurons in the topographically organized areas that implement the visual buffer do not retain representations for long. This same property implies that object-based mental images also will be difficult to retain. One can maintain such an image by re-activating the visual memory representations in the object-properties-processing subsystem.

Image Transformation

Finally, one also can *transform* an imaged pattern. At least two mechanisms can be used to transform objects in images. On the one hand, objects in images can be transformed if one anticipates what one would see if one were physically to manipulate the object. Such anticipation leads to priming (in the same way that generating a depictive image relies on mechanisms used in priming), but now an existing image is transformed in accordance with one's expectations (e.g., Kosslyn, Thompson, et al., 2001; Shepard & Cooper, 1982). On the other hand, one can anticipate what one would see if an external force were to manipulate an object (e.g., by rotating it). Kosslyn, Thompson, Wraga, and Alpert (2001) and Wraga, Thompson, Alpert, and Kosslyn (2003) found that the primary motor cortex is activated when participants anticipate what they would see if they personally manipulated an object, but not if they anticipated what they would see if an external force manipulated it. In both cases, we theorize that image transformations are accomplished by altering the object map and thereby modulating the mapping function from the object-properties-processing subsystem to the visual buffer. (In chapter 3 we provided one possible reason why the transformation itself is incremental.) We elaborate on this mechanism in the following section.

Explaining Basic Phenomena

Any theory of imagery must address core empirical findings. Although there are literally hundreds of distinct phenomena that have been documented in scientific literature on visual mental imagery, we will treat the ones summarized in the following section as the most central; each of these findings has been replicated many times (e.g., see Finke, 1989; Kosslyn, 1980, 1994; Shepard & Cooper, 1982). We have mentioned many of these findings in previous pages, but now will pull them together and address them within the context of the theory; our goal is not to explain the findings in detail, but rather to provide enough of an explanation to make it clear that there is no in-principle problem in developing an adequate account.

Image Generation Findings

The most fundamental fact about imagery is that we can produce mental images at all. As just summarized, the theory posits an image generation process in which depictive images are formed by repeating a series of operations for each additional part or characteristic (or object, in a scene). This iterative process explains why there is a linear increase in time to generate images of objects for each additional part or characteristic they include (e.g., Kosslyn, 1980; Kosslyn, Cave, et al., 1988). In order to place each part in the appropriate location, one must have a representation of shape that makes explicit and accessible the shapes of other parts in the image, which is necessary to "see" how to position properly an additional part or characteristic. Depictive representations have this virtue.

Image Scanning Findings

As noted in chapter 2, a large body of literature now indicates that the time to scan across an imaged object typically increases linearly with the distance scanned (for a review, see Denis & Kosslyn, 1999). As summarized in the preceding chapter, in the original experiments (Kosslyn, 1973; Kosslyn, Ball, & Reiser, 1978) participants were asked to close their eyes, visualize an object, and mentally focus on a specific location. They then heard the name of a property that might or might not have been present on the object (e.g., an anchor for a boat). Their task was to look for the named property, and to press one button if they found it and another if they looked but could not find it. The earliest experiment (Kosslyn, 1973) made no mention of scanning in the instructions, but some later experiments (e.g., Kosslyn, Ball, & Reiser, 1978) explicitly asked participants to scan. More recent experiments (e.g., Dror & Kosslyn, 1993; Finke & Pinker, 1983) eliminated not only instructions to scan but also to use imagery; these studies relied on tasks that require imagery to perform, and thus instructions to use imagery were not necessary.

When the relevant portions of the image are clearly "visible," the theory explains these results by positing that the attention window is shifted over the image (Pinker, 1980). However, this account fails to explain an interesting twist in the findings (Kosslyn, Ball, & Reiser, 1978): if participants are asked to zoom in on a part of the image, so that much of the imaged object has overflowed, they nevertheless can scan either to another part that is still visible in the image or to a part that has overflowed the image (i.e., they scan "off-screen"). In fact, an equal increment of time is required to scan between two parts that both are initially visible on the image as to scan the same distance from a part that is initially visible to one that was initially overflowed and is not visible.

The theory accounts for such findings by appeal to an image transformation process. By analogy, when a TV camera pans across a scene, the image on a monitor shifts across the screen. Similarly, the imaged object (such as an island with different landmarks positioned at different locations) is translated incrementally across the visual buffer, with more time being required for larger shifts. This translation operation is accomplished by changing the mapping function from the object-properties-processing subsystem to the visual buffer; such modulation relies on updating the spatial coordinates of the part of the object being focused on, which is accomplished by altering the object map in the spatial-properties-processing system.

This theory thus explains how the time to scan can increase linearly with distance scanned, in spite of the fact that the visual buffer is anisotropic (as described earlier, the foveal region is over-represented in topographically organized areas). It also explains the ability to scan "off-screen."

Image Zooming Findings

We also discussed earlier the fact that if one begins with an image of an object that seems to subtend a small visual angle (hereafter referred to as a "small image"), more time is generally required to detect parts or otherwise inspect the shape than if one begins with an image that fills the visual field (Bundesen & Larsen, 1975; Kosslyn, 1975, 1976; Sekuler & Nash, 1972). As discussed, the inhibitory connections in topographically organized areas typically are short, and thus when a lot of spatial variation is packed into a small region strong input is required to overcome the inhibition. In visual perception, the bottom-up input is sufficiently strong that fine variations in shape are preserved in the representation; in imagery, the top-down input is relatively weak, so weak that the local inhibition blurs nearby characteristics of the image, obscuring details. When the image is formed at a larger size (i.e., so it seems to subtend a larger visual angle), this local inhibition does not obscure the details.

Thus, in order to overcome the blurring effects that are apparent when the image is formed at a small size, the mapping function from the object-properties-processing subsystem to the visual buffer is altered; such modulation is accomplished by updating the spatial coordinates of the part of the object being focused on, which is accomplished in the spatial-properties-processing subsystem. In this case, the coordinates are changed so that the object in turn seems closer, which reveals the locations where distinct parts (e.g., the whiskers on the head of a cat) belong. As these "foundation parts" (as Kosslyn, 1980, called them) become distinct in the depictive image, additional details of the parts that belong there can be generated—thereby fleshing out the image as one zooms in on the object. Again, as is the case with image generation in general, depictive representations facilitate this operation by making explicit and accessible information about the shapes of parts and characteristics, which helps one position subsequent parts and characteristics as they can be fit into the image (i.e., the object becomes large enough that grain constraints do not prevent their being generated).

Image Rotation Findings

The farther one must rotate an image, the more time is required (Shepard & Cooper, 1982). Again, this image transformation relies on incrementally modulating the mapping function from the object-properties-processing subsystem to the visual buffer. This process would alter the orientation of the pattern in the visual buffer itself—a prediction that is supported by neuroimaging findings (Klein, Dubois, et al., 2004).

However, rotating an object in an image requires solving a problem that is not present during image scanning or zooming: Because detailed parts and characteristics of an image are stored and generated individually, the part structure is preserved in the image (as summarized in the following section). Thus, simply altering the mapping function from the object-properties-processing subsystem to the visual buffer so that each part is rotated would result in each part's being rotated independently, which would disrupt the overall shape of the pattern.[6] It is necessary to rotate around a common origin for the object as a whole, keeping the individual parts aligned. According to the theory, this is accomplished by shifting the parts along arcs around the central axis while rotating them so that they continue to be aligned the same way, relative to the central axis.

In fact, Just and Carpenter (1976) monitored eye movements while people mentally rotated Shepard-Metzler figures, and were able to isolate three distinct phases of processing. First, individual parts that superficially correspond to each other in the two figures to be compared are identified. The aim is to isolate portions of the figures that may potentially be rotated into congruence with each other. Second, these parts are then rotated individually, and compared to each other along the way, keeping the entire figure aligned. This is a stepwise process where transformations are performed incrementally until the two segments are close enough in orientation to be compared. And finally, the two figures are compared in the final confirmation stage, after the same rotation process is applied to other portions of the figures, to verify that the figures can be brought into congruence. Similar processes were suggested by Metzler and Shepard (1974). Thus, the rotation process is remarkably complex, and requires an intimate interplay between the transformation operation and image inspection (to track the relations among parts).

Image Organization Findings

Visual mental images are organized into parts. For example, we noted earlier that Reed (1974) and Reed and Johnsen (1975) found that participants require more time and make more errors when asked to see whether there is a hexagon in an image of a Star of David than they do when asked to see whether there is a triangle. Why? The image of the Star was originally encoded as two overlapping triangles, and its image was subsequently generated as such. Once each part is generated, it begins to fade. Thus, the parts cohere as separate units in the visual buffer, according to the Gestalt Law of Common Fate (or "Common Fade," in this case). Kosslyn, Reiser, et al. (1983) asked participants to memorize the geometric figures illustrated in figure 5.2 either as sets of relatively many, small contiguous forms (such as a hexagon surrounded by six small abutting triangles for the Star of David) or as sets of relatively few, large overlapping forms (such as two overlapping triangles). When later cued to generate an image of the figure, the participants required more time when the figure had been learned as having more units. This finding indicates that the participants did in fact store the figure as it was originally organized. Moreover, participants required less time to "see" that a pattern (e.g., a hexagon) was present in the image when that pattern was congruent with the organization originally learned—which is also good evidence that the image had an internal organization. Nevertheless, depictive representations do provide an opportunity to override an initial

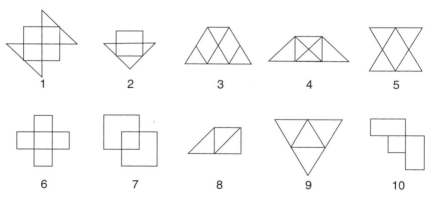

Figure 5.2. The geometric figures that Kosslyn, Reiser, Farah, and Fliegel (1983) asked participants to memorize as relatively few large overlapping forms or relatively many small contiguous forms. (From Kosslyn, S. M., Reiser, B. J., Farah, M. J., & Fliegel, S. J. [1983]. Generating visual images: Units and relations. *Journal of Experimental Psychology: General, 112,* 278–303.)

organization—for example, although they required relatively more time, participants could see a large overlapping triangle even when they learned the star pattern as a hexagon surrounded by six abutting small triangles. Thus, as we discussed in chapter 4, depictive images may in fact be reinterpreted.

Comparing Processing during Imagery and Perception

A central assumption of our approach, which we have emphasized repeatedly, is that imagery and perception share underlying neural processes, and there is ample evidence for this view (e.g., for reviews, see Farah, 1988; Finke & Shepard, 1986; Kosslyn, 1994; Kosslyn, Thompson, & Alpert, 1997; Kosslyn & Thompson, 2003; Thompson & Kosslyn, 2000; Tippet, 1992). One line of investigation has demonstrated that imagery interacts with like-modality perception and vice versa. Visual imagery, for example, can reduce visual perceptual acuity; moreover, the effect is modulated by the location of the imaged stimulus, with greater interference if the image is formed directly over the perceptual stimulus. Other studies have shown that, under some circumstances, research participants confuse having visualized a stimulus with actually having perceived it (Finke, Johnson, & Shyi, 1988; Intraub & Hoffman, 1992; Johnson & Raye, 1981).

A second line of research has documented overlapping brain activity in visual perception and visual mental imagery. We review these findings in the appendix. A third line of evidence for shared processing between visual imagery and like-modality perception has focused on the effects of brain lesions. Many researchers have reported parallel deficits in imagery and perception in patients with brain damage (see Ganis, Thompson, Mast, & Kosslyn, 2003, for a review). In a classic study, Bisiach and Luzzatti (1978) demonstrated that patients afflicted with *unilateral visual neglect*, who ignore half of space during perception, may also neglect the same half of space during imagery. There is also evidence that patients with brain lesions who cannot recognize faces perceptually also cannot visualize faces (e.g., Shuttleworth, Syring, & Allen, 1982).

These findings might convey the impression that imagery is simply perception in the absence of the immediate stimuli. However, the sum total of the extant empirical literature paints a more complex picture. For example, some patients with brain lesions may be impaired in perception but have preserved imagery abilities. Bartolomeo, Bachoud-Levi, De Gelder, et al. (1997) and Bartolomeo, Bachoud-Levi, and Denes (1998), for example, report cases of patients with severe impairments in perception who can visualize shape as well as color. These results demonstrate that the two systems are only partially overlapping, which should not be a surprise: imagery is based on stored information that has already been organized, whereas perception requires segregating figure from ground, along with recognizing and identifying a perceived object.

Although we have focused primarily on the role of the topographically organized cortex in imagery, because such cortex supports depictive representations, equally important is the question of how such representations are processed within a broader system. As we've emphasized repeatedly, the properties of a representation only arise in the context of how they are processed. Thus, our laboratory has devoted much effort to investigating the view that visual mental imagery does in fact draw on mechanisms used during visual perception. We now summarize some of the more important findings in some detail, in part because they provide direct support for the specific theory we have developed.[7]

Test 1: Activation of the System during Perception

We began by focusing purely on perception, examining whether the system of processes we hypothesize in figure 5.1 is plausible. Specifically, Kosslyn, Alpert, Thompson, Chabris, et al. (1994) showed participants a line drawing of a common object on the computer screen at the same time that a word was heard. The participants were asked to judge whether the word was an appropriate name for the drawing. In the experimental condition, participants viewed the drawing from a noncanonical (i.e., unusual) perspective, as shown in figure 5.3 (bottom). This condition was contrasted to a baseline, in which participants viewed the drawings from a typical point of view (also shown in figure 5.3 [top]). The theory leads us to expect that in the baseline condition, the objects would be identified quickly and easily, largely via a single bottom-up cycle through the visual system. In contrast, when the objects were seen from an atypical perspective, we would expect additional processes to be engaged in order to identify the object. In particular, the prediction was that the visual input would serve to create an hypothesis about the identity of the object. Based on that hypothesis (e.g., "this object kind of looks like a cat"), one would look up stored information about the hypothesized object (e.g., "should have a tail and pointed ears"), would shift attention to the appropriate place where a distinctive property would be expected (e.g., to the cat's head, to look for ears) and would seek out additional information by encoding more characteristics. If one or more properties that are consistent with the hypothesized object are present, then one might identify the object (i.e., the hypothesis that it is a cat, for example, would be confirmed).

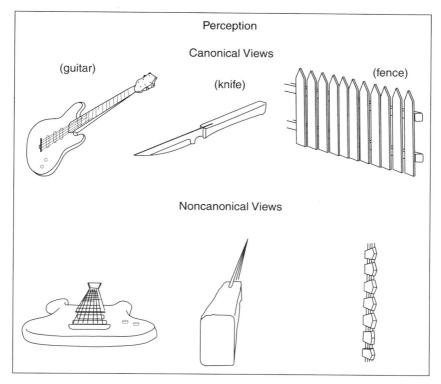

Figure 5.3. Examples of objects seen from canonical (typical) and noncanonical (unusual) perspectives, as used by Kosslyn, Alpert, Thompson, Chabris, et al. (1994). (From Kosslyn, S. M., Thompson, W. L., & Alpert, N. M. [1997]. Neural systems shared by visual imagery and visual perception: A positron emission tomography study. *NeuroImage, 6,* 320–334.)

And, in fact, Kosslyn, Alpert, Thompson, Chabris, et al. (1994) found evidence that a system of processes was engaged when participants had to identify objects seen from unusual points of view, relative to when they identified objects seen from common points of view. As predicted by our theory, additional activation occurred in brain areas that we hypothesized to implement specific processing subsystems illustrated in figure 5.1: (1) the visual buffer, implemented in Brodmann's areas 17 and 18 (the two first cortical areas to receive input from the eyes during visual perception); (2) the object-properties-processing subsystem, implemented in parts of the inferior temporal gyri; (3) the spatial-properties-processing subsystem, implemented in the posterior parietal lobes; (4) the long-term associative memory system, implemented in the angular gyrus and nearby area

19; (5) short-term associative memory, implemented in the dorsolateral prefrontal cortex; (6) the information shunting system, implemented in dorsolateral prefrontal cortex; and (7) the attention-shifting subsystem, implemented in the superior parietal lobes, frontal eye fields, superior colliculus, thalamus, and anterior cingulate. The only unexpected activation appeared in the precentral gyrus.

In short, the results during perception were remarkably consistent with our predictions, which is important because the theory was formulated primarily on the basis of data from nonhuman primates. Thus, these findings show that we were safe in our assumption that we could generalize from the monkey to human brain when theorizing about visual processing.

Test 2: Shared Processing in Imagery and Perception

So many brain areas were activated when participants evaluated objects shown in noncanonical perspectives, compared to objects shown in canonical perspectives, that the results might seem rather unspecific. That is, one might wonder what would have occurred by chance during any difficult task. The theory predicts that a system of areas should be activated, and thus there's no avoiding complex results if the goal is to track the footprints of the entire system working.

One way to address the problem is to show that a very similar set of areas is activated in two tasks that appear very different, but that the theory predicts should engage the same underlying processes. Kosslyn, Thompson, and Alpert (1997) used PET to study which brain areas are drawn upon by visual mental imagery and visual perception, and which areas are drawn upon by one function but not the other. In order to underline the strength of the predictions with respect to the overlap between imagery and perception, participants were given tasks that appear very different. In spite of the surface differences between the tasks, the theory leads us to expect the underlying neural processes to be largely overlapping when the two functions are compared.

Specifically, the theory predicts that the same system of brain regions described above should be activated during visual mental imagery as when objects seen from noncanonical views are identified; in both cases, the entire system outlined in figure 5.1 should be engaged. In this study, Kosslyn, Thompson, and Alpert (1997) asked participants to perform the same perceptual task just described. In addition, the participants performed an imagery task used by Kosslyn, Alpert, Thompson, Maljkovic, et al. (1993, experiment 2, which was based on a task invented by Podgorny & Shepard, 1978). Superficially, the perceptual and imagery tasks appear very different. No object identification is required in the imagery task, nor are any words or names associated with objects. Instead, in a baseline condition, participants first see a lowercase letter followed by a 4×5 grid. One of the grid's cells is marked with an X, and the participants merely make a response (by pressing a pedal) when they perceive the grid. In the imagery task, the same sequence of events occurs, but now the lowercase letter at the beginning of the trial sequence serves to cue the participants to visualize the corresponding uppercase block letter within the grid. After visualizing the appropriate letter within the grid, the participants were to decide whether, if the letter were present, the X mark would fall on or off the letter. This task requires generating an image of the letter in the grid (see Kosslyn, Cave, et al., 1988; Kosslyn, Alpert, Thompson, Maljkovic, et al., 1993).

According to our theory, the same processes used to identify an object seen from a noncanonical point of view should also be used in this imagery task. In the imagery task, a description of the shape of the block letter (indicating the shapes of segments and how they are connected) would be stored in long-term associative memory. The search for this information would be driven by the information shunting subsystem, and the attention-shifting subsystem would be used to focus attention at the locations where letter segments should be placed. However, instead of testing an hypothesis about the identity of the object or letter, as one would do in perception, in imagery one would generate an image (of a letter segment, for example) at the appropriate location. According to our theory, the same mechanism that is involved in priming the stored representation of a distinctive part that one expects to see during perception is also used to prime the representation during imagery. In imagery, however, the priming is strong enough that the representation is evoked in early visual cortex, reconstructing the shape of the object in the visual buffer (see Kosslyn, 1994, for a discussion of the neural computational mechanisms that may be at work in this process, as well as the underlying anatomy and physiology). Once the representation has been reconstructed in the visual buffer, object and spatial properties then can be processed anew, as they would in perception proper.

Figure 5.4 illustrates the brain areas activated in common in the imagery and perception comparisons (specifically, imagery minus the detection of the grid versus noncanonical minus canonical picture identification), and figure 5.5 illustrates the brain areas activated in imagery but not top-down perception and vice versa. As is evident, about two-thirds of the areas were activated in common. Moreover, those areas activated in common are neatly organized by our theory: the activation of left area 18, a topographically organized early visual area, implicates the visual buffer. A region in the left

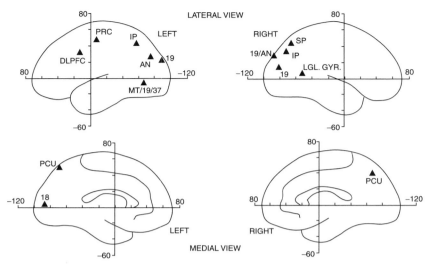

Figure 5.4. Brain areas found to be activated in common in imagery and top-down perception by Kosslyn, Thompson, and Alpert (1997). (From Kosslyn, S. M., Thompson, W. L., & Alpert, N. M. [1997]. Neural systems shared by visual imagery and visual perception: A positron emission tomography study. *NeuroImage, 6,* 320–334.)

occipitotemporal junction (in the vicinity of the left middle temporal gyrus and the right lingual gyrus) also was activated, which provides evidence that the object-properties-processing subsystem was used in both tasks. There was also evidence that the spatial-properties encoding subsystem played a joint role in these two tasks, as evidenced by the activation in inferior parietal lobule.

Similarly, bilateral activation in the vicinity of area 19 and the angular gyrus fits well with our theory. Long-term associative memory is thought to rely on these brain regions, and these sites of activation are very near to those identified by Kosslyn, Thompson, and Alpert (1995) when they studied the neural implementation of long-term associative memory processing. In addition, the specific locus of left dorsolateral prefrontal cortex activation, which replicated earlier findings, can be taken to implicate the information shunting subsystem in both tasks. The left-hemisphere lateralization of this area makes sense if the participants were looking up categorical spatial relations (Kosslyn, Thompson, Gitelman, & Alpert, 1998; see Chabris & Kosslyn, 1998; Laeng, Chabris, & Kosslyn, 2002). Finally, evidence for shared attention-shifting mechanisms was also detected, with

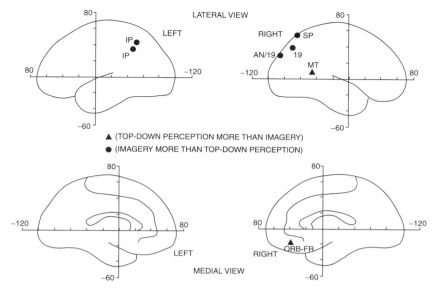

Figure 5.5. The brain areas where activation was greater during top-down visual perception than during visual mental imagery (triangles) and vice versa (circles) in Kosslyn, Thompson, and Alpert's 1997 study. (From Kosslyn, S. M., Thompson, W. L., & Alpert, N. M. [1997]. Neural systems shared by visual imagery and visual perception: A positron emission tomography study. *NeuroImage, 6,* 320–334.)

the bilateral activation of the precuneus and the superior parietal lobule on the right side (cf. Corbetta et al., 1993).

After examining the overlap between the two conditions, Kosslyn, Thompson, and Alpert (1997) also asked the opposite question: which areas play a greater role in imagery than in top-down perception, and vice versa? Figure 5.5 illustrates the brain regions where activation was greater in perception than in imagery. Only two foci of activation were detected. The opposite comparison documented areas where there was greater activation in imagery than in top-down perception; this comparison identified activation in five regions. These findings are also illustrated in figure 5.5.

In sum, fourteen of the twenty-one areas that were detected in these analyses were activated jointly by the two tasks, whereas two were activated solely in top-down perception and five were activated only in imagery, including two nearby sites in the inferior parietal lobule. The findings for imagery are not likely to have arisen from the grid stimuli because the effects of seeing these stimuli were removed by subtracting the baseline task (which presented identical stimuli).

Test 3: Activation during Maximally Similar Tasks

The PET studies conducted to compare imagery and top-down perception had two major limitations. The first is that the amount of overlap was calculated on the proportion of regions that were activated in common over a threshold, ignoring the extent of the activation. This can be misleading; for example, a common region in the dorsolateral prefrontal cortex might have been much smaller than a region in the parietal lobe that was activated only during one condition. A second limitation is that the imagery and perception tasks differed in many ways, which is likely to lead us to underestimate the amount of overlap that would be found in imagery and perception tasks that are more similar.

More recent studies have used stimuli and tasks that were more similar to each other (i.e., perceiving vs. imaging faces), but these studies have focused on occipito-temporal regions per se and have quantified the degree of overlap only in these regions. Moreover, these studies also had important limitations. For example, consider the study reported by Ishai, Ungerleider, and Haxby (2000); during the perception condition the participants passively viewed stimuli presented at a rate of one every second, whereas during the imagery condition they were asked to visualize stimuli from the same stimulus category at the same rate. Because there were no behavioral measures, it is difficult to know what the participants were actually doing in the two conditions. Furthermore, because it is unlikely that people can accurately visualize stimuli (particularly with high resolution) at the rate of one every second (Kosslyn, Reiser, et al., 1983), it is not clear whether the observed differences reflect intrinsic distinctions between visual mental imagery and perception or instead reflect other differences between the two conditions. Additional studies have examined the brain areas activated during mental navigation, but these studies did not focus on a direct comparison between actual navigation and mental navigation (Ghaëm et al., 1997; Mellet, Bricogne, et al., 2000).

We designed the next study to compare the upper bound of the similarity between visual imagery and visual perception. To do so, we devised a task that could be used in both imagery and perception conditions, so that differences in the pattern of brain activation observed in these two conditions could not be attributed to task differences. The visual mental imagery task consisted of closing one's eyes and forming a mental image of a previously studied line drawing, and then evaluating a probed relation (e.g., judging whether the object was taller than it was wide). The visual perception task was identical to the visual imagery task, with the only difference being that a faint picture was presented on a computer monitor

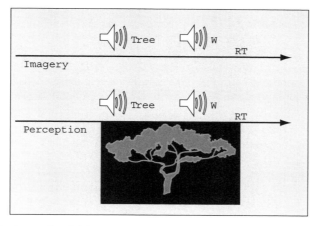

Figure 5.6. A sample trial from Ganis, Thompson, and Kosslyn's 2004 study. In the imagery condition (*top panel*), the participants first heard the name of an object, which cued them to visualize that object. They then made a judgment about the object (such as whether it was wider than high). In the perception condition (*bottom panel*), the drawing of the object appeared when the name was presented, and participants made their judgments while actually viewing the object. (From Ganis, G., Thompson, W. L., & Kosslyn, S. M. [2004]. Brain areas underlying visual mental imagery and visual perception: An fMRI study. *Cognitive Brain Research, 20,* 226–241.)

throughout each trial and participants evaluated the visible picture (see figure 5.6).

In this study we used functional magnetic resonance imaging (fMRI), which allowed us to quantify the amount of overlap by comparing the number of voxels activated in common during imagery and perception. This study thus allowed us to assess precisely the pattern of similarities and differences between the two activities.[8]

Because both visual mental imagery and visual perception are the products of the interplay of multiple cortical and subcortical regions, we expected both conditions to engage large sets of brain areas. However, because we used two versions of the same task in the perception and imagery conditions (thereby equating the key task requirements in these two conditions), we expected the overlap to be especially high in brain regions that are not involved in bottom-up processing.

The most striking result was the remarkably high overall proportion of voxels (volume pixel—the smallest defined [cube-shaped] part of a three-dimensional image) that were activated by both imagery and perception, about 92 percent. Because the analysis was by voxel, and not specific brain

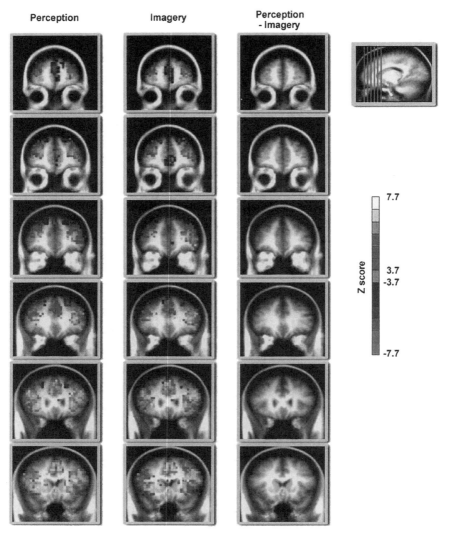

Figure 5.7. Six coronal slices through the frontal lobe. See figure 5.8 for details. See also color insert.

area, it is more difficult to fit the data directly to the predictions of the theory. Nevertheless, there was clear activation in areas that support each of the functions outlined in figure 5.1. Second, as shown in figure 5.7, we found complete overlap in the frontal parts of the brain: in all regions examined, the spatial pattern of activation was identical. Our theory posits that frontal cortex implements an *information shunting system* (among many other functions), which purportedly is involved in multiple aspects of visual mental imagery and visual perception (Kosslyn, 1994). In addition, numerous frontally based processes would be drawn upon in common in the perception and imagery versions of the task we used, including those involved in the retrieval of episodic information associated with the auditory probe, the maintenance of information about the judgment to be carried out during visual inspection, performing the visual evaluation, and the generation of the motor response.[9] In contrast, the posterior part of the brain was driven more strongly by perception than imagery. This makes sense, given that external stimuli are driving neural responses via bottom-up processing. Nevertheless, every voxel activated during imagery was also activated during perception (see figure 5.8).

Converging Evidence

One could argue that because neuroimaging results are merely correlational, many of the activated areas are essentially epiphenomena (like the LEDs on a control panel, they may simply be correlated with processing but not implement the processes themselves). One way to address this concern would be to disrupt the brain regions that are activated during a task and observe whether this impairs performance of visual imagery or visual perception tasks. For obvious ethical reasons, the human brain would never be intentionally lesioned simply in order to conduct a scientific study. However, accident and medical intervention sometimes do lesion the brain, and there is now a substantial body of evidence—accumulated over decades—documenting the effects of naturally occurring brain damage on performance.

As we would predict, many of the visual deficits following brain damage are also present in imagery, which suggests that distinct parts of the brain are used to process these different types of stimuli. For example, some patients who cannot report the shapes of a bear's ears from memory (using imagery) also cannot characterize the shape when shown a drawing of the animal. Such a deficit could arise following disruption of visual memories of different-shaped ears, which are matched to input during object recognition.[10] Caramazza and Hillis (1990) describe a particularly interesting instance of a common deficit in imagery and perception following brain damage. They studied a case of unilateral neglect, where damage to the parietal lobe led a patient to ignore the right-most portions of words while reading. Caramazza and Hillis found that when their patient was asked to spell words from memory, she made reading and spelling errors only on the right half of words. Moreover, the longer the word, the more letters she omitted. Such imagery-based neglect has been well-documented

Perception   Imagery   Perception
- Imagery

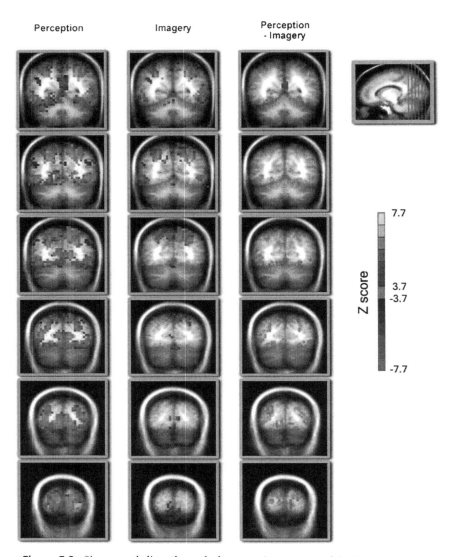

Figure 5.8. Six coronal slices through the posterior portion of the brain. The image is a composite of data from fifteen participants. The sagittal view at the top right shows the position of the sections. Activation maps are shown for the perception condition (*left*), the imagery condition (*middle*) and the contrast (perception > imagery). The overlap in activation between imagery and perception was far less than in the frontal lobe. See color insert. (From Ganis, G., Thompson, W. L., & Kosslyn, S. M. [2004]. Brain areas underlying visual mental imagery and visual perception: An fMRI study. *Cognitive Brain Research, 20,* 226–241.)

(e.g., Bisiach & Luzzatti, 1978), and extends to objects and scenes. Furthermore, these effects occur when the patient's eyes are closed and when he or she fixates straight ahead (e.g., Bisiach, Luzzatti, & Perani, 1979), and so cannot be an artifact of where one is actually attending in visible space. If a patient exhibits neglect during imagery, this condition is accompanied by neglect during perception, but not necessarily vice versa (see Bartolomeo, 2002); this dissociation might occur because neglect in visual perception may sometimes arise via the distracting effects of perceived visual stimuli (such as our reflexive tendency to look at parts of the field where there are sharp changes in intensity)—which don't affect imagery.

In addition to evidence from patients with naturally occurring brain lesions, further convergent evidence for the overlap in brain mechanisms between imagery and perception comes from the use of TMS to produce virtual, reversible lesions in circumscribed brain regions. We have already discussed the study reported by Kosslyn, Pascual-Leone, et al. (1999; see chapter 4), and now merely note that the findings support the view that common cortex is used in imagery and perception.

Possible Counterevidence

The theory covers a broad spectrum of phenomena and makes strong predictions, which leaves it vulnerable to counterevidence. This is a major virtue. But it also leads us to consider the possibility that our theory is not simply *potentially* falsifiable—but rather that it has already fallen prey to counterevidence. In this section, we review key empirical findings that have been raised to challenge the theory.

Overlap between Imagery and Perception?

We have claimed that imagery relies for the most part on the same cortical systems as visual perception. This idea is critical because it allows us to dismiss the problem of the homunculus and to explain many characteristics of imagery. But is it correct? Two major classes of findings have been raised as direct challenges to the idea that imagery and perception rely on common brain processes, and thus also challenge the theory we propose.

Effects of Brain Damage

If imagery and perception draw largely on the same neural mechanisms, why can brain damage affect one faculty but leave the other intact (see

Bartolomeo et al., 1998; Behrmann, Winocur, & Moscovitch, 1992; Ganis, Thompson, Mast, & Kosslyn, 2003; Goldenberg, Müllbacher, & Nowak, 1995; Jankowiak, Kinsbourne, Shalev, & Bachman, 1992)? Goldenberg (1993) reviews evidence that brain damage can selectively affect many different aspects of imagery, including shape, color, faces, spatial relations, and shapes of letters. He points out that such dissociations are inconsistent with damage to a general "image generation process."

Goldenberg (2002) claims that imagery and perception are sometimes dissociated because visual knowledge used in object recognition is embedded in processes used solely for recognition, and such knowledge cannot be used for imagery. Imagery, on the other hand, results from "explicit recall of semantic knowledge of the appearance of things" (p. 191). He states:

> I proposed that there are two kinds of knowledge of the visual appearance of things (Goldenberg 1992; 1998; Goldenberg & Artner 1991). Knowledge used in recognition is restricted to those features which permit a reliable identification of an object under varying circumstances. It neglects details like the shape of the bear's ears. There is a second store of visual knowledge within semantic memory. This knowledge includes information on features not necessary for recognition in addition to those used for recognition. The source of semantic visual knowledge may be an active interest in the visual appearance of objects, possibly enhanced by the high value given to visual arts in our culture and education (Armstrong 1996; Farah [1995]). The crucial point of this hypothesis is that knowledge used for visual recognition is completely embedded in visual recognition and cannot be used for any other purpose. Visual imagery is based exclusively on visual knowledge within semantic memory. If only this knowledge is lost, patients are unable to imagine the visual appearance of objects although the knowledge embedded in recognition enables them to recognize the same objects. (Goldenberg, 2002, p. 191)

In addition, based on the finding that neglect in imagery can be reduced if the patient moves his or her head as if looking at the neglected part of the scene (Meador, Loring, Bowers, & Heilman, 1987), some researchers have argued that the finding of neglect in imagery does not implicate a depictive representation. For example, Bartolomeo and Chokron (2002) suggest that "the 'perceptual' aspects of visual mental images might thus result not from the construction of 'quasi-pictorial' representations, but from the engagement of attentional and intentional aspects of perception in imaginal activity" (p. 185).

Contradictory Evidence from the Blind?

The blind show many of the skills and phenomena normally associated with visual mental imagery (e.g., Aleman, van Lee, Mantione, Verkoijen, & de Haan, 2001; Kerr, 1983; Marmor & Zaback, 1976). For example, in some studies the blind are asked to use their hands to explore a configuration of locations and then are asked to imagine the display and scan between specific pairs of locations. In such studies, the blind require more time to scan increased distances in images, even though they claim not to have any experience of imagery (Blanco & Travieso, 2003; Roeder & Roesler, 1998); however, their performance in imagery tasks is often not identical to that of the sighted participants (e.g., the blind may scan more slowly than do the sighted; Blanco & Travieso, 2003).

Contradictions: More Apparent than Real

At first blush, these findings might appear to be major challenges for our theory. But in fact the theory explains them without having to make any additional assumptions or posit convoluted processing.

Effects of Brain Damage

If imagery and perception draw largely on the same neural mechanisms, why can brain damage affect one faculty but leave the other intact? We would be surprised if imagery and perception could *not* be dissociated. As we have seen previously, they are not identical; rather, the two functions draw on most—but not all—of the same brain regions (Ganis, Thompson, & Kosslyn, 2004; Kosslyn, Thompson, & Alpert, 1997). The dissociations reflect damage to neural structures that are used by one function but not the other. On the one hand, if the cortex used only, or mostly, in perception (such as that used in the initial phases of edge detection) is damaged, cortical blindness or visual agnosias can occur in the presence of relatively intact imagery. On the other hand, if the experience of having a visual mental image arises when stored memory representations are activated (such as occurs when outputs from the visual buffer reach the object-properties-processing subsystem), such an experience should also arise when these memories are activated top-down. However, if topographically organized areas of the visual cortex are damaged, such imagery should be relatively low resolution (because it cannot take advantage of lower-level, high-resolution topographically organized areas), and patients should have difficulty reparsing or reorganizing visual forms. Moreover, given that the majority of brain processes are shared by the two functions, we would predict that simultaneous impairment of both systems should occur more often than dissociations. To our knowledge, these predictions have not been tested explicitly, in large part because vision is routinely assessed in patients with brain damage, but visual imagery functions are not often tested rigorously.

What about the evidence that brain damage can selectively affect many different aspects of imagery, including shape, color, faces, spatial relations, and shapes of letters? In our theory, image generation occurs when individual modality-specific representations are very strongly primed (so strongly that a depictive representation is engendered in the visual buffer, via efferent connections). If the stored representations are damaged, it will not be possible to activate them via such priming, and thus not possible to form the corresponding image. Such representations should be stored in the object-properties-processing subsystem, which is implemented in the temporal lobe; and in fact, studies of imagery deficits following brain damage indicate that the temporal lobe plays a key role in imagery for shape and color (Bartolomeo, 2002).

Now consider Goldenberg's (2002) idea that imagery and perception are dissociated because visual knowledge used in object recognition is embedded in processes used solely for recognition, and not for imagery. We have two responses. First, if visual information used in recognition were encapsulated so that it could be used for no other purpose, researchers should not have found that visual perception primes imagery, and vice versa (McDermott & Roediger, 1994; Kosslyn, 1994). Similarly, why would like-modality imagery interfere with perception, and vice versa, and why would imagery activate visual areas of the brain that clearly are used in object recognition? Second, if imagery were based purely on semantic knowledge, it is difficult to understand why it is so useful as a mnemonic device when one recalls episodic information, such as the particular items present on one's breakfast table (e.g., Galton, 1883).

In addition, we take issue with Bartolomeo and Chokron's (2002) idea that unilateral neglect in imagery reflects not depictive images but rather "the engagement of attentional and intentional aspects of perception in imaginal activity" (p. 185). This account omits a crucial point: what is it that is being attended to in imagery? We explain these results not in terms of the depictive representation in the visual buffer but instead by appeal to the "object map" in the spatial-properties-processing subsystem. (As we discussed earlier, according to our theory, this map depicts the locations of objects in a scene, parts of an object, or letters in a word.) By definition, neglect is based on attentional mechanisms that fail to process representations in a particular region of space. According to our theory, because the same spatial representation is used, the phenomenon can be observed in both imagery and perception; this representation relies on topographically organized parietal cortex.

Contradictory Evidence from the Blind?

Our theory allows us to understand why the blind can perform comparably to the sighted in some imagery tasks. These blind participants typically have suffered damage to neural structures (cortical or subcortical), not their retinas; this damage affects getting information into the object-properties-processing system. However, they still have intact spatial-properties processing, which can guide movements. Thus, such people can convert many shape-based imagery tasks into spatial tasks. For example, as we noted earlier, at least some such patients can decide which uppercase letters of the alphabet have any curved lines. They do so not by visualizing shape, but rather by moving as if printing the letters—and noting in which cases they produce a curved line.

The challenge is to isolate an aspect of visual imagery that cannot be captured easily by purely spatial representations. Arditi, Holtzman, and Kosslyn (1988) took up this challenge and focused on a fundamental visual characteristic: specifically, foreshortening. They found that the blind can accurately point to the left and right sides of objects when close to them, but—unlike blindfolded sighted individuals—the blind fail to appreciate that objects will subtend smaller visual angles as they move farther away. The blind cannot form object-based visual images. They can perform scanning using parietal-based spatial processing mechanisms—but do not represent truly visual properties, and thus cannot internally simulate what they would see if an object were viewed from farther distances.

Finally, Millar (2002) issues a cautionary note, pointing out that the vast majority of blind people have in fact had at least some visual experience and that there are clear relations between such experience and the subsequent ability to answer imagery questions (e.g., Schlaegel, 1953). Moreover, blind people appear to substitute images in numerous other modalities (not simply spatial representations) to accomplish tasks that may rely on visual imagery in sighted people. For example, Millar (2002) reports that when a blind colleague was asked to imagine his room at home, he reported "feeling cold air on his face, and hearing some form of echoing sound on entering his room late at night, touching his desk after walking a certain distance to the right, and hearing a difference in the sound of his footfall and in sensations underfoot on reaching the rug before the fireplace"

(p. 202). We have emphasized the role of spatial imagery as a substitute for object-based imagery, but Millar is quite right in noting that there are additional alternatives.

Critiques of the Theory

Our theory has not gone unnoticed by advocates of propositional and tacit knowledge approaches. In fact, in one article Pylyshyn went so far as to characterize elements of our theory as "grotesque" (Pylyshyn, 2003, p. 114). In this last section, we consider the major critiques.

Comparison to Propositional Theories

A theory may be best evaluated by comparing it to other theories. However, to our knowledge, there is no other detailed theory that addresses the same range of phenomena as ours. When he does consider mechanisms, Pylyshyn alludes to propositional theories. As Pylyshyn acknowledges, such a theory would be ad hoc—but, he claims, no more so than applying a set of external constraints to a matrix formalism (such as was used in the original theory of the visual buffer; see Kosslyn & Shwartz, 1977).

We have two responses to this concern. First, although it is clear that ad hoc assumptions are necessary for propositional theories, without attempting to work out the details of the accounts it is not clear whether such theories would be more or less ad hoc than depictive theories (although we again note that contemporary depictive theories are not ad hoc insofar as they are constrained by facts about the anatomy and physiology of the brain). Depictive theories have been developed in enough detail to be programmed as computer simulations since 1977 and have been developed to provide accounts for a wide range of imagery phenomena (e.g., Kosslyn, 1980, 1994). The only propositional theories of imagery that have been developed in such detail accounted for performance on a very limited range of tasks (typically only a single task; for examples, see Pinker & Kosslyn, 1983).

Second, the specific criticism about "applying a set of external constraints to a matrix formalism" applies only to the earliest depictive models of imagery, in which the visual buffer was modeled by an array in a computer (Kosslyn & Shwartz, 1977; see Kosslyn, 1980). As we have seen here and in previous chapters, one advantage of turning to neuroscientific evidence is that it provides additional motivation for this structure, and thereby eliminates any hint of ad hoc theorizing. The same would not be true of propositional theories.

Critique of Neural Constraints

Pylyshyn is not sanguine about our use of facts about the brain to guide theorizing. He claims that "the search for neural correlates or for neural mechanisms takes it for granted that we know what they are correlates of" (Pylyshyn, 2002, p. 217). He also claims that this depends on our having some idea of how these phenomena work and on (often questionable) assumptions about how function maps to neural structure. We fail to see the force of this point: one does not need a full-blown theory to obtain neural correlates of information processing in specific tasks. And once such "local correlates" are obtained, they are more grist for the theory mill.

In addition, Pylyshyn claims that we have backed off each time a counter-example is raised, "as they do when they admit that images are not exactly like any possible picture (e.g., they contain 'predigested information'—again Kosslyn's term), that they are laid out in a 'functional space,' that the process of inspecting images is not really like the process of visual perception or that even though the depictive display explains imagery phenomena its contents are not what we experience when we image" (Pylyshyn, 2002, p. 218.) Contrary to what is claimed, most of the specific instances Pylyshyn notes were in fact included in the theory implemented as a running computer simulation by Kosslyn and Shwartz in 1977. These characteristics of the theory followed from reasoning about the mechanisms, and not as responses to critics. For example, the fact that several eye movements are necessary to encode most objects into memory implies that different portions are encoded over time (as Pylyshyn himself has noted, when attacking the idea of a "panoramic display"). Thus, detailed depictive images will later be built up a part at a time. And if such images are generated a part at a time, then parts will begin to fade at different times. This "common fate" will preserve the internal organization of an imaged pattern. This line of reason led Kosslyn and Shwartz (1977) to preserve the part structure of imaged objects, based on the fact that they were built up from "predigested information." Given that images are based on information that was stored following perceptual processing, how could it be otherwise?

Pylyshyn also complains that every time another aspect of the theory is used to explain data, it reduces the explanatory power of the depictive representation; it is, in his words, "as if the behavior of an animated computer display is determined by an extrinsic encoding of the principles that govern the animation rather than by intrinsic properties of the display itself" (Pylyshyn, 2002, p. 178). In response, we must first note that, even in this computer display analogy, there is no way to avoid an object's going "off-screen" if the camera zooms in too closely; this is a result of an intrinsic property of the display (its size), as is the size at which details become obscured by grain effects. Properties of the display clearly play a role in governing some characteristics of the representations, even in this analogy. Moreover, those properties of the display—unlike the principles that are introduced to govern the animation—are not arbitrarily determined. One main reason we turned to a cognitive neuroscience approach is that it constrains the theory, both of the mechanisms and of the depictive representation itself. Unlike tacit knowledge accounts, depictive theories are constrained by factors in addition to the need to account for the imagery phenomena themselves.

In addition, we note that no task, from performing an imagery experiment to peeling a banana, can be accomplished by a single representation or process; a processing system must be engaged. We stress that the theory as a whole is used to explain data; no single aspect of a processing system operates in isolation. The situation is analogous to what one sees in physics: the explanatory power of the construct of gravity is weakened when one introduces the construct of wind—which is necessary to explain why leaves fall off trees the way they do. Like it or not, in the real world events typically are governed by multiple factors. The key is to identify the different factors, principles or mechanisms, and then to specify how they work together. When formulating theories of such mechanisms, computer simulations, as well as facts about the brain, keep one honest. However, for present purposes, the key issue is whether a depictive representation is ever used during imagery, and on this point the theory has been unwavering.

Finally, Pylyshyn, at the close of his 2003 work, likens the current situation to trying to decide whether the sun goes around the earth or vice versa based purely on observation. In fact, astronomy is built on such observations. His point is that introspections about imagery are inherently misleading, but the assumption underlying this quip is misguided. Instead of watching only the sun, astronomers chart the motion of thousands of heavenly bodies and try to devise simple principles that underlie the regularities in their movements. Where would astronomy be today if researchers had restricted their range of data to one or few types of celestial bodies? Similarly, we are much better off trying to account for multiple sources of data—including those arising from facts about the brain.

Conclusions

One could claim that the early computer simulations of imagery that incorporated depictive representations (Kosslyn & Shwartz, 1977) were only a demonstration that in principle a system *can* be built without a homunculus, but that such a system bears no resemblance to the way our brains actually work. The current, neurally inspired, version of our theory should allow us once and for all to settle the concern that a homunculus is required to interpret mental images. This concern is neatly countered if depictive mental images are representations in the same system that processes visual information during perception. It is clear why we don't worry about a "little man" in perception; the depictive representations on the retina, in the lateral geniculate nucleus, and in early visual cortex send neural signals to later areas, and these signals are interpreted (i.e., they activate additional pieces of information stored in these areas). If imagery relies on the same system as visual perception, then it is also clear why we need not concern ourselves with the potential problem of the homunculus in imagery.

In addition to settling the issue of the homunculus and constraining theories, neural data have generated new questions and hypotheses. For example, neural considerations led to the idea that people can adopt specific alternative strategies (both implicitly and explicitly) to perform the same task (Kosslyn, Thompson, et al., 2001; Wraga et al., 2003). It is difficult to see how behavioral evidence could provide such strong support for the use of distinct processing strategies. In addition, neuroimaging has enlightened us on questions of the nature of individual differences in cognition (see Ganis, Thompson, & Kosslyn, 2005; Kosslyn, Thompson, Shephard, et al., 2004).

However, even though we have motivated our theory of imagery by first considering processing during perception and have not created the theory out of whole cloth simply to explain data, the theory is in fact a structured set of hypotheses. Its purpose is not simply to organize existing data but to direct research, to raise new questions. Thus, we examined crucial predictions of the theory. First, neural machinery used in visual perception was also expected to be invoked during imagery. We found strong evidence for this prediction, and the patterns of activation are largely consistent with those we predicted. Second, when we reviewed evidence and arguments that some have taken to counter our theory, we saw that none seriously undermine the central claims we have made.

Given the counterarguments and data that have been presented in the previous pages, one might wonder why the imagery debate is still a going concern. In the final chapter we turn to this and related issues.

Notes

1. Kosslyn (1980) theorized that "skeletal images" provide the spatial layout of an object; according to that early version of the theory, these images are produced at

the outset, and then details are added to flesh them out. We have replaced this concept with that of the object map, which is more general and closer to the neural substrate. The parietal lobes depict object maps (because of their spatial nature), whereas the occipital lobes depict high-resolution details and qualities (such as color) of the shapes of objects. Object maps differ from low-spatial-frequency versions of visual scenes (which convey certain global features of visual scenes) because they explicitly represent the spatial relationships among objects in visual scenes or parts of a single object.

2. Top-down processing can also be driven by beliefs and goals, which often rely on the results of on-going computation; such states may be represented in short-term associative memory. For present purposes (i.e., motivating the foundations for a theory of imagery), we need not address such cases.

3. We assume that all processes are running simultaneously. Thus, the processes involved in top-down search are not waiting for complete outputs from earlier systems before becoming active. Rather, as soon as any representations are activated in long-term associative memory, the information shunting system operates. However, if subsequent information encoded bottom-up is sufficient to identify the object, top-down processing may be interrupted.

4. As another example of the role of facts about the brain as constraints on theorizing, we note an important aspect of the neuroanatomy of the visual system: namely, the backward connections from the visual memory areas to topographically organized cortex are diffuse (Douglas & Rockland, 1992; Rockland, Saleem, & Tanaka, 1992; Salin & Bullier, 1995). They do not simply mirror the orderly connections coming from earlier areas to later areas. Thus, image generation is not like painting a picture on a screen, or simply replaying a stored memory. Rather, the process must be constructive. Kosslyn (1994) suggests that when one encodes a new object, part or characteristic, there is learning even in the early visual areas. This learning adjusts the strength of connections among neurons in these areas. These adjustments subsequently allow top-down input to function as an attractor in a neural net (or, by analogy, a catalyst in a saturated solution): the input leads the neurons to fire in a specific configuration, which reconstructs the local geometry of the shape.

5. It is worth stressing that an image is a state of the system as a whole. Although depictive representations rely on the visual buffer, they also rely on the subsystems downstream that process input from it. Thus, for example, input to the object-properties-processing subsystem confers meaning on the image (it depicts an object, not simply an arbitrary pattern); similarly, inputs to the spatial-properties-processing subsystem allow the three-dimensional structure to be ascertained. The various subsystems operate at the same time, and it is the state of the entire system that gives rise to imagery.

6. This was a problem that was discovered early in the process of developing the original Kosslyn and Shwartz (1977, 1978) computer model.

7. This is not to say that our theory specifies the only ways in which depictive representations can be used. For example, Grossberg (1999a, 1999b, 2000) proposes

a sophisticated model of how top-down and bottom-up processes may interact. In this model, topographically organized cortex plays a key role in forming the representations that underlie imagery (Grossberg, 1999a). This model appears to fall into the same class as our own, but is much more detailed and more narrowly focused than our theory.

8. Although the crucial comparisons are between the two conditions, imagery versus perception, we nevertheless needed a baseline against which to assess the degree of activation. We employed an event-related fMRI paradigm, which allows us to assess activation separately for each trial, and used activation during the interval between subsequent trials as a baseline. Because the purpose of this study was to compare the overall brain areas involved in imagery and perception, we wanted to minimize the chance of subtracting out activation of interest (cf. Friston, Frith, Fletcher, & Liddle, 1996; Stark & Squire, 2001), which may be more likely with more complex baselines. Note that this type of baseline is different from the resting baseline used in PET studies (Gusnard & Raichle, 2001), where participants spend several minutes "resting." We have no idea what participants actually do while resting (perhaps daydream, forming images?). In our paradigm, the baseline is embedded in the task and, from the participant's point of view, it feels like a natural pause between trials.

9. However, some researchers have reported differences in prefrontal cortex between activation elicited during visual imagery and visual perception (e.g., Ishai, Haxby, & Ungerleider, 2002; Ishai, Ungerleider, & Haxby, 2000). We suspect that such differences were due in large part to differences between the tasks used in the two conditions. Indeed, in these studies visual imagery was usually compared with passive viewing of visual stimuli. Our results suggest that, when appropriately matched, visual perception that relies on top-down processing and visual mental imagery activate the same subset of prefrontal and parietal regions.

10. Such details may be specified more precisely in the left cerebral hemisphere (Kosslyn, 1987; Marsolek, Nicholas, & Andersen, 2002), which would explain why a patient with a left-lateralized lesion could recognize the overall shape of the object (which appears to be represented preferentially in the right hemisphere) but not details.

6

Science and Mental Imagery

In the previous chapters we have shown that the conceptual arguments against depictive representations are easily countered, and we have illustrated the rich harvest of empirical findings that supports the depictive view. We have also shown that no empirical findings pose a serious challenge to the claim that depictive representations are used in visual mental imagery. Moreover, we showed that it is possible to formulate a neurologically plausible theory of imagery in which depictive representations play a central role. Given all of this, why has the imagery debate persisted for so long? For three overarching reasons, we believe. First, the two sides hold fundamentally different views of what a theory of imagery (and cognition in general) should look like; second, they disagree fundamentally about the role of the brain in theorizing about mental events; and third, there are sociological and personal reasons for the differences in views. We consider each class of reasons in turn.

The Nature and Purposes of Theories

Much of the reason the debate has persisted is that the different sides seek different forms of theory and expect theories to do different sorts of work, as summarized below. The different sorts of theories are at cross-purposes, which explains why the arguments often seem to slide past each other.

Nature of Theories

Part of the reason the debate has continued is that the two camps focus on different levels of theorizing. When considering theories of cognitive processing in general, and imagery in particular, we must emphasize a crucial distinction between two classes of theories. On the one hand, theories of *competence* specify principles that describe a system; the system itself does not actually follow those principles any more than a seal solves differential equations when it hunches its neck to catch a ball on its nose or the planets follow the laws of motion when they wheel around the sun. On the other hand, theories of *processing performance* specify principles of how information is represented and transformed in a system, in real time. The distinction between competence and performance emerged from the field of linguistics (Chomsky, 1965).[1]

The two sorts of theories can characterize the same sets of phenomena, but are designed to answer very different types of questions. For example, a theory of competence will not account for, nor make predictions about, response times—whereas this is the bread and butter of theories of processing performance.

The initial phases of the debate pitted depictive versus propositional theories against each other, which was appropriate—both are theories of processing performance. However, with the advent of tacit knowledge accounts, the debate shifted. The alternative to depictive theories was no longer another mechanistic theory, but—as far as we can tell—a theory of competence (e.g., of the sort that Pylyshyn [2002] believes has been successful in characterizing language).[2] That is, the theory merely describes what people know (attributing this to tacit knowledge) and ways in which that knowledge can be used—without characterizing the mechanisms that give rise to performance.

To our knowledge, there are no detailed competence-based theories of imagery, in large part because they do not address the sorts of data that have been collected. Instead, Pylyshyn and his colleagues urge us to consider the most general constraints or boundary conditions that have to be met by a system of imagistic reasoning. For example, Fodor and Pylyshyn (1988) have proposed such constraints as productivity, compositionality, and systematicity. In addition, Pylyshyn (1978) has also proposed some constraints on images; for example, they must represent token individuals and visual rather than abstract properties and must not encode properties of sets, such as cardinality, or represent negative statements. These proposals appear to be based purely on armchair considerations, and some are highly debatable. For example, Barsalou (1999) challenges the idea that images must represent only token individuals; instead, he offers arguments that perceptual representations can perform all the functions often assumed to require symbolic or amodal representations. But perhaps more important, these very general principles do not illuminate the empirical findings and say nothing about the format of the internal representations used during imagery.

Consistent with our sense that the debate has stalled because the two sides have different conceptions of the appropriate type of theory, Pylyshyn (2002, 2003) not only argues that the depictive theory is incorrect, but goes so far as to suggest that the entire issue at hand is irrelevant! According to this view, pursuing knowledge about the format of images tells us nothing truly interesting about imagery. If he is (implicitly) focusing on a theory of competence, we can make sense of this claim. In this case, he would seek an abstract characterization of what people know—not how information is represented and processed when one actually performs specific tasks. In contrast, if one seeks a mechanistic theory, then the claim is incomprehensible. In this case, we focus on a fundamental question about the nature of information processing: Is there a single "language of thought"? The answer to this question has wide-ranging implications for studies of many faculties. On the one hand, if it turns out that there really is only a single type of internal representation, this fact would place very strong constraints on theories of all forms of cognition. On the other hand, if it turns out that there are different types of representations, this opens the door to theories of specialized mechanisms for specialized tasks. To address the question of the format of representations in imagery, one needs to specify a theory of processing mechanisms.

As we have discussed in the previous chapters, at its core the imagery debate is about the *format* of the representations used in imagery: when we visualize shapes with high resolution, either a depictive representation is activated or it is not. If psychology is a science, we should be able to answer the question. Shifting to focus on theories of competence—which do not address properties of mechanisms, such as the format in which representations are stored—could be viewed as an attempt to sidestep this central issue.

Purpose of Theories

We also suspect that the debate has dragged on so long because of different perspectives on the work that should be accomplished by a theory. Specifically, Pylyshyn (taking him as the prototypical antidepictive theorist) considers it a major drawback if a theory is "speculative" and simply dismisses such theories out-of-hand; his view seems to be that a theory must be considered as "speculative" if any of its details are not motivated by irrefutable facts. In contrast, we (taking ourselves as typical prodepictive theorists) maintain that there is a sense in which *any* theory is "speculative." According to our view, theories organize the existing body of knowledge and project into the unknown. That's what they are for. Provided that theories lead to new discoveries, they are worth their salt. The antidepictive view seems to hold that a theory should be rock-solid from the start, but we know of no case in science in which an "adequate theory" (to use Pylyshyn's term) was in place before properties of the subject matter were fully characterized. In fact, it often goes the other way around; theories are constructed by an act of bootstrapping, with general principles being abstracted out of individual discoveries—which in turn were guided by earlier theories (e.g., see Fodor, 2003).

In addition, the two camps value different outcomes from theorizing. First, the prodepictive view assumes that neural mechanisms are worth understanding in part because of what one can do with that knowledge. For example, such knowledge is useful for those interested in building artificial systems that mimic human information processing as well as for those who want to learn how to cope with the effects of brain damage. (Indeed, some researchers are actively pursuing work at the intersection of these two concerns: namely, building chips that can compensate for damaged neural tissue.) Second, the antidepictive theorists place a greater emphasis on explaining previous findings with simple, overarching principles. Third, the prodepictive theorists stress the importance of generating and testing new predictions, whereas the antidepictive theorists are usually content to try to explain previous findings. (We note that depictive theories have led to an avalanche of new empirical discoveries [e.g., Kosslyn, 1980, 1994; Kosslyn, Ganis, & Thompson, 2001; Kosslyn & Thompson, 2003; Thompson & Kosslyn, 2000], whereas it is not clear that the tacit knowledge view has led to many new discoveries.)

Relevance of the Brain

Another reason for the extended nature of this debate hinges on its recent focus on neural evidence. The antidepiction view rejects the very idea that facts about the brain can be used to address the issue, whereas the prodepiction view has come increasingly to rely on such facts. For example, Pylyshyn points out that knowing about the projections from the retina to the brain has led to fruitless debates about why we don't see the world upside down. In sharp contrast, the depictive camp, as evident in the preceding pages, emphasizes that studying the wiring of the visual system has led to enormous progress in our understanding of how vision works (e.g., Desimone & Ungerleider, 1989; Felleman & Van Essen, 1991; Hubel, 1988). For example, the fact that object-properties processing and spatial-properties processing (see chapter 5) are accomplished by separate systems allows us to understand why we sometimes erroneously conflate shape and location information. Similarly, by observing the relative amount of cortex devoted to the foveal versus peripheral areas of the retina, we gain insight into the nature of visual acuity. Moreover, as already mentioned, facts about the brain allow us to escape from the slipperiness of structure/process tradeoffs. Why do the two camps make opposite assumptions on the potential utility of neuroscientific data? One reason may be that no hint of a mapping to neural mechanisms has been found for theories that posit only tacit knowledge or only propositional representations.

In addition, the two camps hold different assumptions about what sorts of data bear on the issues. According to some antidepictive theorists (e.g., Dennett, 2002; Pylyshyn, 2002), *only* behavioral evidence can reveal how the brain actually works. This view sharply contrasts with that of the prodepictive theorists, who note that we learn an enormous amount about the course of information processing by tracking the temporal course of activity in the brain itself (e.g., Chen, Yao, & Chen, 2003; Thierry, Ibarrola, Demonet, & Cardebat, 2003). From the perspective of depictive theories, the approach advocated by the opposing camp throws away most of the tools and evidence we have to understand the system that underlies all information processing. According to this view, it is as if during the early stages of research on the building blocks of life researchers had decided to throw away X-ray crystallography data by assuming it had nothing to do with understanding "life." (But without this tool, they would not have discovered DNA!)

Furthermore, the antidepictive theorists—perhaps as an outgrowth of their distrust of introspection—have discounted the value of studying internal events that do not lead to overt, observable behavior. Again in contrast, the prodepictive view is that by studying the brain we can discover the nature of processing that never leads to an overt response. To take a simple example, it has long been known that after extinction of a classically conditioned stimulus-response pair, animals later can be conditioned again more easily than they were at the outset. But why is this so? Is it because there is still some residual learning that was not affected by extinction, and thus not all neural connections need to be reestablished? Is it because extinction replaces the conditioned response with a new one, and relearning consists of removing the new response? As it happens, LeDoux and colleagues (reviewed in LeDoux, 1996) have shown that extinction of classically conditioned responses relies on the frontal lobe's suppressing reflexive connections (mediated by the amygdala). That is, extinction does not obliterate or overwrite the conditioned memory, it simply keeps it in check—but that memory is always there, lurking in the background. Observing behavior alone would never tell us this, because, by all overt appearances, even though the behavior has been eliminated, it can be relearned relatively easily—but without access to the neuroscientific data, we may never have learned why.

Another similar point of divergence is that some in the antidepictive camp assert that biological or neuroscience-based data do not have a special role in evaluating theories of information processing. As illustrated in previous chapters, the prodepictive theorists argue that if we want to discover whether tacit knowledge underlies all imagery phenomena, neuroanatomical and neurophysiological facts do play a special role: not only are they not easily affected (if at all) by one's tacit knowledge or beliefs, but also they introduce constraints on theorizing that prevent theories from being arbitrarily modified to fit data.

Sociological and Personal Considerations

The debate also may have persisted in part because researchers had varying intuitions. In this section, we consider two sources of intuitions, programming languages and introspections.

One source of intuitions may have come from models and research in artificial intelligence. At least in the early days, much of this work relied on the computer programming language LISP—and most of the models proposed showed the hallmarks of this language (e.g., Winston, 1977). This language is tailor-made to represent information in propositional data structures, such as hierarchically organized tree structures, and provides the means to process such representations efficiently. Although arrays could be implemented in such languages, they were not well suited to representing information. Thus, even the early models of computer vision were highly symbolic (e.g., Waltz, 1975). Psychologists, seeking inspiration from this exciting field, may have allowed their intuitions to be swayed by the nature of the models being developed.

A second possible source of intuitions is closer to home, namely one's own introspections. This notion was raised by Daniel Reisberg, a noted imagery researcher who has confessed that he himself has no experience of imagery. His idea was that one's phenomenology might shape one's scientific intuitions. If so, then researchers who do not have the experience of imagery might favor the descriptive view—whereas those who have the usual phenomenology might favor the depictive view. Reisberg invited

David Pearson and Stephen Kosslyn to collaborate on a study to investigate this possibility. Reisberg, Pearson, and Kosslyn (2003) sent a questionnaire to 188 psychologists, neuroscientists, and philosophers who had published widely cited papers on mental imagery and received responses from 150 of these individuals. The participants were asked to complete Marks's (1973) Vividness of Visual Imagery Questionnaire (VVIQ, which requires one to provide ratings of the vividness of one's imagery) and to respond to a number of questions, but we will focus here on only two: they were asked to indicate their attitude about the "imagery debate" in 1980 (when the propositional arguments were still lively), and then were asked to indicate their current attitude about the debate—based on current evidence.

The results were straightforward: of the ninety-four who indicated what their position was in 1980 (not all respondents were active during the 1980s, and so fewer provided answers to the initial question), only about 7 percent (seven individuals) chose the purely propositional view. Of the 143 who indicated their current view, only about 6 percent (nine individuals) adopted this extreme view (the responses could vary along a four-point scale). So, the first conclusion is that researchers who are familiar with the area overwhelmingly accept the claim that depictive representations play a role in mental imagery.

In addition, the VVIQ scores were correlated with the responses for the views in 1980: the results indicated that researchers who reported less vivid imagery were more inclined toward the propositional view. Thus, in the early stages of the debate, researchers' personal experiences were related to their theoretical stances. In contrast, when the VVIQ scores were correlated with their current views, the scores were found *not* to be correlated with their current attitudes. This finding suggests that scientists really do pay attention to data and let the data take precedence over their introspections or intuitions. As results from increasing numbers of imagery experiments were reported and the case for depictive representations grew stronger, even many of those with poor depictive imagery became convinced that depictive representations exist and are used in imagery. Nevertheless, some of the extreme cases—who reported no imagery—persisted in denying the existence of depictive representations.[3]

Closing Remarks

The imagery debate has focused on whether depictive representations are used in human cognition. We hope we have shown that facts about the neuroanatomy and function of the brain have played a decisive role in the most recent phase of this debate. We believe such facts have been incisive for five reasons.

1. They have helped us understand how representations can depict information and how such representations are used within the context of a processing system.
2. They have introduced constraints that prevent theorists from altering theories simply in order to account for data (thereby circumventing the possibility of structure/process tradeoffs, which is always possible when theorizing on the basis of purely behavioral data).
3. They provide a strong antidote to tacit knowledge accounts of imagery results. Task demands may lead participants to vary how much time they require to respond, but they won't lead participants to alter the amount or pattern of activation in specific brain areas.
4. They have invited new ways to test cognitive theories. By opening the door to neuroimaging, transcranial magnetic stimulation, and all of the other methods described in previous pages, bridging to the brain has vastly increased the scope and depth of empirical inquiry in the study of mental imagery.
5. Finally, this approach has led to new distinctions. For example, contrast the purely computational theory of Kosslyn (1980) with the neurally inspired version of Kosslyn (1994). By rooting processing in the brain, the latter theory posits a distinction between object versus spatial imagery, which we have seen is very useful. It also develops a more sophisticated view of the nature of the visual buffer, moving away from the simple analogy to an array in a computer. Moreover, it allows us to compare much more precisely the ways in which imagery and perception are similar and different than was previously possible.

Proponents of the tacit knowledge account suggest that we are simply barking up the wrong tree, that the very sort of theory we seek is misguided. We have focused on mechanistic accounts in part because they allow us to account for behavioral findings, such as response times in specific tasks. Mechanisms operate in real time, which provides a basis for understanding such effects. In addition, such theories lend themselves to being simulated on the computer, which forces one to be explicit. In fact, such theories have direct relevance to building devices that mimic human cognition, which are desirable for many reasons. Furthermore, such theories naturally map into the physical substrate, the brain. As we stated earlier, from our perspective, the mind is what the brain does. Theories of the sort we propose attempt to characterize what the brain does, and thus have the potential to illuminate the workings of that most complex of organs.

Even Pylyshyn concedes that tacit knowledge accounts falter when confronted with phenomena such as the oblique effect or even mental rotation (Pylyshyn, 2002, p. 224). As William James (1896) famously pointed out, all it takes is a single white crow to disprove the generalization that all crows are black. In this book we have spotted many white crows; in particular, tacit knowledge cannot explain away patterns of brain activation.

Pylyshyn (2003) says that experience from other sciences and other branches of cognition tells us that we may have to accept that there is no account for the phenomenology of imagery, just as (he says) physics has had to accept the fact that the mystery of action-at-a-distance does not have a reductive explanation. But this is not at all the situation in the study of imagery. We have proposed a mechanistic explanation and have tested it; we have considered alternatives and ruled them out at every turn. There comes a point where one must simply decide that the weight of the evidence is clear: the earth is not flat, it is round. And there comes a point when one must decide that imagery does rely in part on depictive representations, and build from there. We hope we have convinced the reader that the field has reached this point.

Notes

1. This distinction is similar to the organization/structure distinction of Maturana and Varela (1980):

> The organization of a machine (or system) does not specify the properties of the components which realize the machine as a concrete system, it only specifies the relations which these must generate to constitute the machine or system as a unity. Therefore, the organization of a machine is independent of the properties of its components which can be any, and a given machine can be realized in many different manners by many different kinds of components. In other words, although a given machine can be realized by many different structures, for it to constitute a concrete entity in a given space its actual components must be defined in that space, and have the properties which allow them to generate the relations which define it. (Maturana & Varela, 1980, p. 77)

In this sense our theory is one of structure (performance) rather than organization (competence).

2. Note that the domain of imagery is not the only one in which there has been tension between theories of competence and theories of performance. This distinction arose in linguistics (Chomsky, 1965), and similar debates have taken place in the study of language (e.g. Bates & Elman, 1993; Eckman, 1994).

3. Individual differences in imagery are not restricted to the phenomenology. As we have noted in earlier chapters, not only do people differ in how well they can perform specific imagery tasks but they also differ in how activated specific parts of their brains are when they perform such tasks (e.g., see Kosslyn, Thompson, Shephard, et al., 2004, as well as the references in Reisberg et al., 2003).

Appendix: Neuroimaging Studies of Visual Mental Imagery

What follows is a review of the neuroimaging studies of visual mental imagery that were included in the meta-analysis summarized in chapter 4. The inclusion criteria for this review were as follows: (a) Only studies of visual mental imagery were considered, and thus studies of auditory and motor imagery were excluded;[1] (b) only positron emission tomography (PET), functional magnetic resonance imaging (fMRI), or single photon emission computed tomography (SPECT) studies were included (the spatial resolution of electroencephalography is too low for present purposes; similarly, findings from studies of brain-damaged patients were not treated as primary data because the lesions typically are too large and diffuse to localize precisely their effects in the brain); (c) each study had to include at least one condition in which participants were specifically instructed to use visual mental imagery or were compelled to do so by the nature of the task; (d) studies had to include a baseline condition, whether rest, an "off condition," or an appropriately matched control condition, and the analysis technique contrasted the imagery condition with at least one baseline; (e) studies that did not require generating an imagined pattern on the basis of stored information were excluded; this criterion led to the exclusion of studies of mental rotation in which stimuli were presented purely perceptually (for a review of such studies, see Thompson & Kosslyn, 2000); and (f) only studies that were reported in enough detail to allow further analysis were included. Thus, the following review includes only findings that appeared in full reports, not those from abstracts or short descriptions that appeared as part of a larger review. Studies were located by searching PsycINFO and MEDLINE and reviewing all appropriate journals from 1987 through the end of 2002.[2]

When we coded the studies, each reported imagery condition was compared with one baseline condition. If only a resting baseline was reported, it was coded accordingly. If, in addition, one or more other baseline conditions were reported, the comparison between resting baseline and the imagery condition was not considered because Kosslyn, Thompson, Kim, et al. (1995) previously showed that this baseline leads to hypermetabolism in the early visual cortex; instead, the baseline condition judged most appropriate for isolating activation due to imagery per se was coded. If more than one imagery condition was reported in a given study, each condition was considered separately in the analysis. However, the same data (i.e., the same participants performing the same imagery condition) were not coded more than once.

The review is divided into two major parts. We first consider studies that reported activation of the early visual cortex during visual mental imagery; following this, we consider studies that did not report such activation. Early visual cortex is defined as areas 17 and 18, which were taken to include primary visual cortex, secondary visual cortex, and medial occipital cortex. In many studies, the Talairach coordinates were provided, which allowed verification of the location of the areas; when these coordinates were not provided, the authors' classification of the location of the activation was respected. In some cases in which the authors' classification was vague, the data were coded in accordance with figures (if they were provided), descriptions of the activated regions, or specifications of the regions of interest (typically provided in SPECT studies).

Within each of the two major parts of this appendix, we review first those studies that relied on PET (initially the most common neuroimaging method used to study imagery), then fMRI, and then SPECT. Within each of these subsections, we present the studies in chronological order. In what follows, we do not report lateralized results because the lateralized differences were typically very small in these medial brain structures (often well within the spatial resolution of the techniques); however, such information is provided in table A.1 for other reported regions of activation.

Studies Reporting Activation of the Early Visual Cortex

The following studies reported activation of the early visual cortex during visual mental imagery.

PET Studies

For the most part the PET studies were analyzed using parametric statistics, averaging over participants. The early visual cortex was treated as having been activated if there was statistically greater activation in this area during imagery than during a baseline condition.

(*text continues on p. 195*)

Table A.1
Summary of Key Variables and Results of the Studies

Study/Comparison	Talairach coordinates	IT	N	HR	NS	EI	NR	Other activated regions[a]
Charlot et al. (1992)		S	11	N	N	Y	N	
Chen et al. (1998), hometown walking task	—	4M	9	Y	N	Y	Y	18, 39
Chen et al. (1998), flashing light task	—	4M	12	Y	Y	Y	Y	—
D'Esposito et al. (1997)		1M	7	N	Y	N	Y	L-3d, L-10d, L-38b
Formisano et al. (2002)		1M	6	N	N	N	Y	B-5, B-9, B-23, B-34a, B-37c, 46b
Ghaëm et al. (1997), VIL Task		P	5	N	Y	Y	N	B-12b, L-12c, L-15d, L-22b, R-33b, L-35a
Goebel et al. (1998), contours task	—	1M	5	N	Y	Y	Y	B-14b, 24, B-44d, 50[b]
Goebel et al. (1998), dots task	—	1M	5	Y	Y	Y	Y	B-14b, 24, B-44d, 50[b]
Goebel et al. (1998), stripes task	—	1M	5	Y	Y	Y	Y	B-14b, 24, B-44d, 50[b]
Goldenberg, Podreka, Steiner, & Willmes (1987)		S	11	N	Y	N	Y	L-21a, B-42a, L-45a
Goldenberg, Podreka, Steiner, et al. (1989) experiment 1, high-imagery sentences	—	S	14	Y	Y	N	Y	B-49a
Goldenberg, Podreka, Steiner, et al. (1989) experiment 2, corner counting task		S	18	Y	N	Y	Y	—
Goldenberg, Podreka, Uhl, et al. (1989), colors		S	10	N	Y	Y	N	—
Goldenberg, Podreka, Uhl, et al. (1989), faces		S	10	N	Y	Y	N	L-12a, R-15a
Goldenberg, Podreka, Uhl, et al. (1989), map		S	10	N	N	Y	N	—
Goldenberg, Podreka, Steiner, Franzen, & Deecke (1991)		S	14	Y	Y	Y	Y	L-49a

(*continued*)

Table A.1

(*Continued*)

Study/Comparison	Talairach coordinates	IT	N	HR	NS	EI	NR	Other activated regions[a]
Goldenberg, Steiner, et al. (1992), high-imagery sentences	—	S	10	Y	Y	N	Y	—
Gulyás (2001), alphabet task		P	10	N	Y	N	N	B-17c, L-20a, L-25c, L-35c, R-42e
Gulyás (2001), anthem task		P	10	N	Y	N	N	R-8, L-13d, B-17c, L-20a
Handy et al. (2004), nouns	—	1M	14	N	Y	N	N	L-10d, R-13e, L-13f, L-14h, L-20a, L-21f, L-35c, L-36c
Handy et al. (2004), pictures	—	1M	14	Y	Y	Y	N	L-10d, L-13c, L-14h, L-16d, L- 21f, R-21g, L-21h, L-36c, R-42f
Ishai, Ungerleider, & Haxby (2000)		1M	9	N	Y	Y	Y	B-3f, B-7a, B-10e, B-10f, B-10g, B-13a, B-15d, B-17e, B-21d, B-25b, B-36a, B-42d, B-42h
Ishai, Haxby, & Ungerleider (2002), LTM	12, 61, 5	3M	9	Y	Y	N	Y	R-1, L-10c, B-13a, B-17a, B-36a, B-45d[c]
Ishai, Haxby, & Ungerleider (2002), LTM + attention	12, 61, 5	3M	9	Y	Y	N	Y	R-1, L-10c, B-13a, B-17a, L-36a, B-45d[c]
Ishai, Haxby, & Ungerleider (2002), STM	12, 61, 5	3M	9	Y	Y	Y	Y	R-1, L-10c, B-12a, B-13a, B-17a, B-36a, B-45d[c]
Ishai, Haxby, & Ungerleider (2002), STM + attention	12, 61, 5	3M	9	Y	Y	Y	Y	B-1, L-10c, B-13a, B-17a, B-36a, B-45d[c]
Klein, Paradis, et al. (2000), abstract event 1	—	3M	8	N	Y	N	Y	—
Klein, Paradis, et al. (2000), concrete event 1	—	3M	8	Y	Y	N	Y	—

(*continued*)

Table A.1
(*Continued*)

Study/Comparison	Talairach coordinates	IT	N	HR	NS	EI	NR	Other activated regions[a]
Klein, Paradis, et al. (2000), abstract event 2	—	3M	8	N	Y	N	Y	—
Klein, Paradis, et al. (2000), concrete event 2	—	3M	8	Y	Y	N	Y	—
Knauff et al. (2000)	—	1M	10	Y	N	Y	Y	L-14e, B-25d, B-44i
Kosslyn, Alpert, Thompson, Maljkovic, et al. (1993), experiment 1	−1, −65, 12	P	7	Y	N	Y	Y	M-3a, M-33a, B-37c, L-39
Kosslyn, Alpert, Thompson, Maljkovic, et al. (1993), experiment 2	24, −63, 8; −18, −63, 28	P	5	Y	N	Y	Y	B-2a, R-4a, M-9, L-10a, R-12a, L-14a, L-15a, B-22b, M-36a, B-37c, B-44a, R-49a
Kosslyn, Alpert, Thompson, Maljkovic, et al. (1993), experiment 3	15,−89, 0; 8, −69, 8	P	16	Y	Y	N	N	L-22a, L-35a, R-37c, L-45a
Kosslyn, Thompson, Kim, et al. (1995)	−13, −102, 8; 15, −102, −4; 6, −88 −8; 8, −79, 4; 2, −83, 0; −4, −83, −8; −2, −60, 16	P	12	Y	Y	Y	Y	—
Kosslyn, Shin, et al. (1996)	15, −74, 20; 22,−88, 8; −2, −76, −4	P	7	Y	Y	Y	Y	B-16e, L-21j
Kosslyn, Pascual-Leone, et al. (1999)	−2, −88, −12	P	8	Y	Y	Y	Y	L-4b
Lambert et al. (2002)	0, −92, 4; 0, −72, −4; 0, −84, −10; −12, −84, 0; −4, −102, 10; −14, −96, −10; 12, −76, 10; 18, −82, 8; 2, −84, 18	1M	6	Y	Y	N	Y	B-7a, L-14d, L-14h, L-43c, B-44f, R-44h, R-45c
Le Bihan et al. (1993)	—	1M	7	N	Y	Y	Y	—

(*continued*)

Table A.1
(*Continued*)

Study/Comparison	Talairach coordinates	IT	N	HR	NS	EI	NR	Other activated regions[a]
Mazard et al. (2002), no fMRI noise		P	6	N	N	Y	Y	B-7b, M-7d, R-13h, L-13i, L-14c, L-15e, R-22c, L-35f, B-36e, B-42h, L-42i, R-44e, M-49a
Mazard et al. (2002), with fMRI noise		P	6	N	N	Y	Y	R-3b, R-3e, L-7b, RM-7d, R-13h, L-13i, L-15e, B-16b, R-20c, R-21d, R-22c, M-30, L-35a, L-35f, B-36e, B-42h, M-49a
Mellet, Tzourio, Denis, & Mazoyer (1995)		P	8	Y	N	Y	N	7d, R-43b, 46a
Mellet, Tzourio, Crivello, et al. (1996)		P	9	N	N	Y	Y	R-13a, R-15d, R-36a, B-38c, B-43b, M-46a, R-47b
Mellet, Tzourio, Denis, & Mazoyer (1998)		P	8	N	Y	N	Y	L-10c, L-14f, B-15c, B-15d, L-35a, L-35e, L-38a
Mellet, Bricogne, et al. (2000), mental map		P	6	N	N	Y	N	R-12a, L-16b, L-17a, B-17d, B-19, R-21d, R-22d, B-35h, LM-42c, R-42h, B-45b, R-47b
Mellet, Bricogne, et al. (2000), mental navigation		P	5	N	N	Y	N	L-17d, R-21d, B-26, B-27, R-33b, B-35h, R-42c
Mellet, Tzourio-Mazoyer, et al. (2000), verbal encoding		P	7	N	N	Y	Y	B-7c, R-7d, R-13a, R-15d, L-16b, B-17a, R-21d, R-21k, RM-31, L-35e, B-41, R-42h, B-43b, L-49b

(*continued*)

Table A.1

(*Continued*)

Study/Comparison	Talairach coordinates	IT	N	HR	NS	EI	NR	Other activated regions[a]
Mellet, Tzourio-Mazoyer, et al. (2000), visual encoding		P	7	N	N	Y	Y	R-3b, B-7c, L-7d, R-13a, R-15d, L-16c, B-17a, R-21k, M-31, R-42d, B-43b, L-49b
O'Craven & Kanwisher (2000), places	9, −48, 6; −21, −60, 18	1M	8	N	Y	Y	Y	—
Roland, Eriksson, et al. (1987)		P	10	Y	N	Y	N	B-6a, B-6b, L-7a, B-9, R-13b, B-13g, B-15f, L-16a, L-17b, B-17f, R-21b, R-21l, L-21m, B-37b, B-37d, R-37e, B-37f, B-37g, R-40, B-43a, B-44b, B-44c, R-45a, B-47a, B-49a
Roland & Gulyás (1995)		P	11	N	Y	Y	N	L-2c, R-3c, B-13h, L-15b, L-16b, B-21d, R-36b, R-42b, R-42h, L-42j, R-43a, R-44j, R-45e, L-48
Sabbah et al. (1995)	—	1M	10	N	Y	Y	Y	—
Sack et al. (2002)		1M	6	N	N	N	Y	B-11a, L-14i, M-20b, B-21i, L-32, R-35b, L-35d, L-35g, BM-36d, L-43d, B-44h
Shin et al. (1999)	−8, −68, −12; −16, −100, 0	P	8	Y	Y	Y	Y	L-7a, R-10c, R-14f, R-21e, L-35a, B-44g
Suchan et al. (2002)		P	10	N	N	Y	Y	M-8, L-14h, M-42f
Thompson et al. (2001)	−2, −90, −12	P	8	Y	Y	Y	Y	L-2b, L-7a

(*continued*)

Table A.1
(*Continued*)

Study/Comparison	Talairach coordinates	IT	N	HR	NS	EI	NR	Other activated regions[a]
Trojano et al. (2000), experiment 1	1M	7	N	N	N	Y	L-14g, B-29, B-34b
Trojano et al. (2000), experiment 2	1M	4	N	N	N	Y	B-11b, L-14g, B-29, B-34b, L-35b, R-37a, R-42g
Wheeler et al. (2000)	1M	18	N	Y	Y	Y	L-10b, B-21c, B-25a, L-28a, R-28b, B-36d

Notes. A dash indicates that data were not reported. The Talairach coordinates specify only the location in area 17 or 18 when such activation occurred and coordinates were reported. IT = imaging technique; HR = high-resolution details; NS = nonspatial images; EI = exemplar images; NR = nonresting baseline; seconds = SPECT (single photon emission computed tomography); N = no; Y = yes; 4M = 4-Tesla (T) fMRI (functional magnetic resonance imaging); 1M = 1T fMRI; VIL = visual imagery of landmarks; P = PET (positron emission tomography); LTM = long-term memory; 3M = 3T fMRI; STM = short-term memory.
[a]Other activated brain regions are reported when they were reported in the original study. Each number corresponds to a brain region reported in at least one study. We were faithful to the terminology the authors used to report the regions, which are listed alphabetically with their corresponding numbers. Brain areas are organized hierarchically, with a broad category defined and then subregions within that category listed under the general heading. L, R, or M before the region number indicates the laterality of the reported region (left, right, or midline, respectively). B indicates bilateral activation. If a number is presented without an accompanying letter, the laterality of the brain region was not reported. Regions more than five millimeters from the midline were considered to be lateralized. Reported brain regions and corresponding numbers are shown below.
[b]The comparison of all three motion imagery conditions against fixation also revealed the following regions to be activated: dorsolateral prefrontal cortex (area 9/46), precentral sulcus/superior frontal gyrus (frontal eye field, area 6), anterior cingulate gyrus, and insular gyrus.
[c]Estimates of significance of other reported regions were based on effect size and error bars depicted in figures 3, 4, 5, and 6 of Ishai, Haxby, & Ungerleider (2002).

Reported brain regions and corresponding numbers:

1. Amygdala

2a. Angular gyrus
2b. Angular gyrus (occipito-temporo-parietal junction; areas 19/39/7)
2c. Anterior angular gyrus

3a. Anterior cingulate
3b. Anterior cingulate cortex
3c. Anterior cingulate gyrus

3d. Anterior cingulate gyrus (area 24)
3e. Anterior/median cingulate cortex
3f. Caudal anterior cingulate

4a. Area 19
4b. Area 19/18

5. Auditory cortex

6a. Caudate/putamen
6b. Head of caudate

(*continued*)

Table A.1
(*Continued*)

7a. Cerebellum	16c. Anterior insula/inferior frontal gyrus
7b. Cerebellar cortex	
7c. Cerebellar hemisphere	16d. Insula (area 13)
7d. Cerebellar vermis	16e. Insular cortex
8. Cingulate gyrus (area 24)	17a. Intraparietal sulcus
	17b. Anterior intraparietal
9. Frontal eye field	17c. Intraparietal sulcus, banks (area 40)
10a. Fusiform	17d. Intraparietal sulcus/precuneus
10b. Fusiform (area 19)	17e. Intraparietal sulcus/superior parietal
10c. Fusiform gyrus	17f. Posterior intraparietal
10d. Fusiform gyrus (area 37)	
10e. Lateral fusiform gyrus	18. Lateral geniculate nucleus
10f. Medial fusiform gyrus	
10g. Posterior fusiform gyrus	19. Lenticular nucleus
	20a. Medial frontal gyrus/medial frontal gyrus (area 6)
11a. Heschl's gyrus (area 41)	
11b. Heschl's gyrus (area 41/42)	20b. Medial frontal gyrus (supplementary motor area; area 6)
12a. Hippocampus	20c. Median frontal gyrus
12b. Middle hippocampal regions	
12c. Posterior hippocampal regions	21a. Middle frontal
	21b. Anterior midfrontal
13a. Inferior frontal gyrus	21c. Middle frontal (area 6)
13b. Anterior inferior frontal	21d. Middle frontal gyrus
13c. Inferior frontal gyrus (area 11)	21e. Middle frontal gyrus (area 10)
13d. Inferior frontal gyrus (area 44)	21f. Middle frontal gyrus (area 46)
13e. Inferior frontal gyrus (area 45)	21g. Middle frontal gyrus (area 46/9)
13f. Inferior frontal gyrus (area 47)	21h. Middle frontal gyrus (area 47)
13g. Inferior frontal pole	21i. Middle frontal gyrus (area 9)
13h. Inferior frontal sulcus	21j. Middle frontal gyrus (area 9/8)
13i. Inferior frontal sulcus/precentral sulcus	21k. Middle frontal sulcus
	21l. Middle midfrontal
14a. Inferior parietal	21m. Posterior midfrontal
14b. Inferior parietal cortex	
14c. Inferior parietal gyrus	22a. Middle temporal
14d. Inferior parietal gyrus (area 40)	22b. Middle temporal gyrus
14e. Inferior parietal lobe (area 40)	22c. Middle temporal/middle occipital gyrus
14f. Inferior parietal lobule	
14g. Inferior parietal lobule (area 39/40)	22d. Middle temporal sulcus
14h. Inferior parietal lobule (area 40)	
14i. Inferior parietal lobule (area 7)	23. Motor cortex
	24. Middle temporal/medial superior temporal visual motion area
15a. Inferior temporal	
15b. Inferior posterior temporal gyrus	
15c. Inferior temporal/fusiform gyrus	25a. Occipital gyrus (area 19)/middle occipital (area 19)
15d. Inferior temporal gyrus	
15e. Inferior temporal gyrus (posterior part)	25b. Dorsal occipital
15f. Posterior inferior temporal	25c. Lateral occipital gyrus (area 19)
	25d. Medial occipital gyrus/inferior temporal gyrus (area 19)
16a. Insula	
16b. Anterior insula	

(*continued*)

Table A.1
(*Continued*)

26. Occipitoparietal sulcus

27. Parahippocampal gyrus

28a. Parietal (area 7)
28b. Parietal (area 7/40)

29. Perisylvian cortex (area 45/insula)

30. Pons

31. Pontomesencephalic tegmentum

32. Postcentral gyrus (area 2)

33a. Posterior cingulate
33b. Posterior cingulate gyrus

34a. Posterior parietal cortex
34b. Posterior parietal cortex (area 7)

35a. Precentral gyrus
35b. Precentral gyrus (area 4)
35c. Precentral gyrus (area 6)
35d. Precentral gyrus (frontal eye field, area 6)
35e. Precentral/middle frontal sulcus
35f. Precentral sulcus
35g. Precentral sulcus (area 4)
35h. Precentral/superior frontal sulcus

36a. Precuneus
36b. Posterior precuneus
36c. Precuneus (area 19)
36d. Precuneus (area 7)
36e. Precuneus/parietooccipital sulcus

37a. Prefrontal cortex
37b. Anterior intermedial prefrontal
37c. Dorsolateral prefrontal
37d. Posterior intermedial prefrontal
37e. Superior anterior prefrontal
37f. Superior middle prefrontal
37g. Superior posterior prefrontal

38a. Premotor
38b. Premotor area (area 6)
38c. Premotor cortex

39. Pulvinar

40. Putamen/pallidum

41. Rectal gyrus

42a. Superior frontal
42b. Lateral superior frontal gyrus
42c. Median superior frontal gyrus
42d. Superior frontal gyrus
42e. Superior frontal gyrus (area 10)
42f. Superior frontal gyrus (area 6)
42g. Superior frontal gyrus (area 6/8)
42h. Superior frontal sulcus
42i. Superior frontal sulcus (anterior part)
42j. Superior medial frontal gyrus

43a. Superior occipital
43b. Superior occipital gyrus
43c. Superior occipital gyrus (area 19)
43d. Superior occipital gyrus/superior parietal lobule (areas 19/7)

44a. Superior parietal
44b. Posterior lateral superior parietal
44c. Posterior medial superior parietal
44d. Superior parietal cortex
44e. Superior parietal gyrus
44f. Superior parietal gyrus (area 19)
44g. Superior parietal lobule
44h. Superior parietal lobule (area 7)
44i. Superior parietal lobule/precuneus (area 7)
44j. Superior posterior parietal lobule

45a. Superior temporal
45b. Superior temporal gyrus
45c. Superior temporal gyrus (area 39)
45d. Superior temporal sulcus
45e. Superior temporal sulcus/posterior angular gyrus

46a. SMA
46b. Anterior SMA

47a. Supramarginal
47b. Supramarginal gyrus

48. Temporal pole

49a. Thalamus
49b. Medial thalamus

50. V3

Kosslyn, Alpert, Thompson, Maljkovic, Weise, Chabris, et al. (1993, experiment 1). This article reported three experiments, each of which was analyzed separately in this review. In experiment 1, two groups of seven participants were tested. One group completed an imagery condition and an analogous perception condition; the other group completed a sensorimotor control condition and the perception condition. The participants in the imagery condition visualized previously learned block letters as they had appeared in grids, and decided whether an X would fall on the letter if it were in fact present in the grid. The stimuli subtended 2.6 degrees horizontally by 3.4 degrees vertically, and hence relatively high resolution was required to resolve the X probe (which was one-quarter as wide and one-fifth as high as the overall stimulus). In the perception condition, the participants decided whether an X fell on a letter that was present in a grid. In the sensorimotor control condition (which also controlled for the effects of attention per se), participants simply alternated responses, making a response as soon as an X mark was removed from the grid. When activation during imagery was compared with that during perception, area 17 was found to be activated as well as a portion of the cuneus that is part of area 18; no such finding occurred in the sensorimotor control condition. The authors noted that the portion of area 17 that was activated was unexpectedly anterior; use of the perception baseline may have removed some of the activation in area 17. Patterns of response times validated that imagery was used.

Kosslyn et al. (1993, experiment 2). In experiment 2, the task was the same as in experiment 1, but the perceptual stimuli and X probe were visually degraded. Moreover, all stimuli were presented for only 200 milliseconds. The baseline condition required the five participants to view and respond to (alternating responses) the appearance of grid stimuli from the imagery condition; participants performed this baseline before learning the letters and without instructions to image. Distinctive patterns of error rates validated the use of imagery. For the imagery versus baseline comparison, area 17 and area 18 were activated.

Kosslyn et al. (1993, experiment 3). In experiment 3, sixteen participants were asked to visualize the appearance of all twenty-six letters of the alphabet in a standard block font. In one condition, the participants were to visualize the letters as small as possible while still being able to distinguish their parts. In the other condition, they were to visualize the letters as large as possible, without overflowing the imaginal visual field. Participants were told to visualize and retain the image until they heard a cue, which they received four seconds after hearing the name of the letter. The cues required the participants to judge the shape of the letters (e.g., whether any curved lines were present, whether a vertical line was on the left, or whether an enclosed space was present), and response times and errors were recorded. As found in previous imagery studies (e.g., Kosslyn, 1975), the participants required more time to judge letters imaged at a small size; indeed, when data from three participants who did not show this expected response time pattern were removed, a stronger pattern was evident in the PET blood flow data. Each condition (large and small imagery) served as a control for the other. When activation in the small-image condition was subtracted from that in the large-image condition, there was evidence of activation at a very posterior location in area 17; the reverse subtraction produced evidence of activation at a relatively anterior location in area 17. Thus, analogous to what has been found in perception (e.g., Fox et al., 1986), visualizing objects at larger sizes activated more anterior regions of early cortex.

Kosslyn, Thompson, Kim, and Alpert (1995). Twelve participants memorized the appearance of line drawings of objects and later were asked to visualize them at three different sizes, very small (subtending 0.25 degrees of visual angle), medium (4 degrees), or large (16 degrees). Each size was visualized during a separate condition, and both the order of conditions and assignment of stimuli to conditions were counterbalanced over participants. During neuroimaging, participants closed their eyes and heard the names of objects, one at a time. They were asked to form an image of the corresponding object at the appropriate size, and hold the image for four seconds after the cue was read. At this point they heard the name of a cue, which required the participants to evaluate the shapes of the particular drawings they had memorized (e.g., to determine whether the left side of the object in the drawing was higher than the right side). Two baselines were included: listening and resting. In the listening baseline, participants listened to the names of objects and cue words and alternated responses to the cue words. This baseline was administered before the participants knew the meaning of the cues; these stimuli had the same form as those in the imagery conditions. In the resting baseline, participants were simply told to rest and "have it black in front of your mind's eye" (p. 496). Response times and accuracy rates were recorded in the imagery conditions. As was found in experiment 3 of Kosslyn, Alpert, Thompson, Maljkovic, et al. (1993), larger mental images evoked activation at increasingly anterior locations along the calcarine sulcus (which defines area 17). In sharp contrast, no effects of imagery were observed when the resting baseline was used. Indeed, when regional cerebral blood flow (rCBF) in the two baselines was directly compared, it was clear that there was significantly more blood flow in area 17 in the resting baseline than in the listening baseline—and using the data from the resting baseline as the comparison cancelled out activation due to imagery. Note that the size-specific results eliminate the possibility that the imagery results are simply an artifact of hypometabolism in the listening baseline.

Kosslyn, Shin, Thompson, McNally, Rauch, Pitman, and Alpert (1996). After studying a set of neutral or aversive photographs, seven participants viewed or visualized the pictures (with each type of stimulus presented in a separate block of trials). After each stimulus was presented, the participants heard a statement (delivered by the computer) and determined whether it correctly described the stimulus. The statements described subtle visual or spatial aspects of the stimulus, of the sort that previous research has demonstrated typically are recalled through imagery (e.g., Kosslyn & Jolicoeur, 1980). Neutral pictures were used as the baseline for the aversive pictures. Participants had their eyes closed while they visualized the pictures. Response times and error rates were recorded. Visualizing aversive stimuli, relative to visualizing neutral stimuli, enhanced rCBF in areas 17 and 18.

Kosslyn, Pascual-Leone, Felician, Camposano, Keenan, Thompson, et al. (1999). Eight participants memorized the appearance of a pattern containing four quadrants, each of which was labeled by a number. Each quadrant contained a set of stripes, and the stripes varied in their length, width, spacing, and tilt. In the imagery condition, participants heard the numbers naming two of the quadrants followed by a cue word; the cue word directed them to compare the two sets of stripes along one of the four dimensions in which they differed. If the stripes in the quadrant named first had more of the property than those in the quadrant named second, the participants pressed one button; if the stripes in the quadrant named second had more of the property, they pressed another button. The participants maintained the image for at least three seconds. The baseline consisted of listening to similar words while alternating responses from side to side (and not visualizing). Areas 17 and 18/19 were activated. An important feature of this study was the demonstration that rTMS delivered to the medial occipital lobe prior to the task (performed outside the scanner) disrupted subsequent performance, which is evidence that activation in early visual cortex played a functional role in this task.

Shin, McNally, Kosslyn, Thompson, Rauch, Alpert, et al. (1999). In one condition, eight participants recalled a traumatic event from their past and imagined it vividly for the entire duration of the scan; in the other condition, they recalled a neutral event from their past and imagined it for the entire scan. The order of conditions was counterbalanced. Activation was compared between the two conditions. Areas 17 and 18 were activated during imagery for the neutral event compared with imagery of the traumatic event. Imagery vividness ratings were obtained and participants tended to have the highest ratings of visual imagery in the neutral condition, which is consistent with the brain activation results. In contrast, the participants reported that their imagery during the traumatic condition was "most prominent" in the tactile modality.

Thompson, Kosslyn, Sukel, and Alpert (2001). Thompson et al. designed a study to examine the effects of using high resolution to visualize a shape (not a spatial relationship such as relative heights, as examined by Mellet, Tzourio-Mazoyer, et al., 2000). Eight participants visualized sets of four stripes, just as did the participants in the study reported by Kosslyn, Pascual-Leone, et al. (1999). As in the earlier study, the participants were asked to compare the stripes in two named quadrants according to different dimensions, such as the spacing between the stripes or their length (both of which required focusing on only part of the overall pattern). In this study, different amounts of resolution were required to distinguish the sets of stripes; one set was composed of thin (high-spatial-frequency) stripes, whereas another was composed of relatively thick (low-spatial-frequency) stripes. The baseline consisted of listening to words that were similar to those used as cues in the experimental conditions and alternating yes and no responses. As expected, area 17 was activated in the imagery task. However, there was no difference in activation between the two types of striped patterns. The response times and error rates indicated that—although the stimuli differed in the resolution required to resolve the stripes—the discriminations needed for the two sets of stripes required comparable resolution.

fMRI Studies

In most of the fMRI studies, the data from individual participants were analyzed separately. In the analysis, area 17 or 18 was treated as activated if at least half of the participants showed such activation. It was not possible to compute the precise probability that the voxels in early visual cortex would be activated due to chance; this probability depends on many parameters that affect analyses, such as the total number of voxels, spatial normalization procedures, motion-correction algorithms, and corrections for multiple comparisons. However, by any measure the probability that chance alone could account for activation in this region in at least half the participants is very small, and thus it makes sense to try to discern the factors that led to such activation. The issue was whether the task *could* produce activation; viewed from the other perspective, if at least half the participants did have activation in early visual cortex, it would not be reasonable to classify that study as showing no activation in this region.

Le Bihan, Turner, Zeffiro, Cuénod, Jezzard, and Bonnerot (1993; 1.5T fMRI). Seven participants were asked to visualize red flashing lights that they had seen previously in a perceptual condition. The lights were diodes geometrically arranged as two square patterns, flashing at a rate of 16 Hz. The lights were visible for twenty-four seconds, followed by an equal period of darkness. During some "off" blocks, the participants were asked to recall the lights as they had seen them. During the baseline condition, the participants completed an off block but were not asked to form images. No behavior was measured. All participants had bilateral activation in area 17 in the perceptual condition; five of the seven participants also had area 17 activation in the imagery condition (this activation also extended to area 18).

Sabbah, Simond, Levrier, Habib, Trabaud, Murayama, Mazoyer, Briant, Raybaud, and Salamon (1995; 1.5T fMRI). Ten participants were asked to view or visualize a flashing white light. The light flashed at a rate of 8 Hz for twenty-eight seconds, followed by an equal period of darkness. During some of these periods of darkness, the participants were asked to visualize the light. During other periods of darkness, the participants were not asked to form images. No behavior was recorded. Area 17 was activated during imagery.

Goebel, Khorram-Sefat, Muckli, Hacker, and Singer (1998; 1.5T fMRI). Three conditions were administered. In one, the five participants were asked to visualize a rotating striped wheel. The diameter subtended 16.7 degrees of visual angle, and the wheel rotated at a rate of 170 degrees per second. The wheel was covered with thirty alternating black and white stripes, each subtending about 0.5 degrees of visual angle. In another condition, the participants were asked to visualize a field of rotating dots. In a third condition, the participants visualized shifting square contours that were created by opening notches in the sides of four filled circles (thus generating Pac-Man–type stimuli). To create the illusion of appearing and disappearing squares, the participants were to visualize the notches in the four circles as if they were opened or closed. Moreover, the stimulus alternated from right to left of the fixation point. In each condition, the images were formed for twenty-four seconds, and the baseline condition was fixation on a cross. No behavior was measured. In all three conditions, area 18 was activated bilaterally, but area 17 was not activated.

Chen, Kato, Zhu, Ogawa, Tank, and Ugurbil (1998; 4T fMRI). There were two tasks: First, nine participants were asked to imagine walking through their home-towns; they were instructed to focus on objects that they would see along the route, not on the walking component. The task was similar to that of Roland, Eriksson, Stone-Elander, & Widen (1987), except that no starting or ending point was given. The baseline was an "off" condition. All participants had robust activation in area 17. Indeed, eight participants also showed activation in the lateral geniculate nucleus (a subcortical structure that receives input directly from the eyes). Second, twelve participants were asked to visualize a flashing pattern of lights (that they previously had seen). Seven of these participants had activation in area 17.

Klein, Paradis, Poline, Kosslyn, and Le Bihan (2000; 3T fMRI). On each trial, participants heard the name of an animal, which cued them to visualize that animal; fourteen seconds later they heard the name of a characteristic, which could either be concrete (e.g., "has pointy ears") or abstract (e.g., "is affectionate"). When they heard the characteristic, participants decided, as quickly and accurately as possible, whether the named animal has the characteristic. Concrete and abstract characteristics were presented in separate blocks of trials, and participants were told in advance what sorts of characteristics would be queried. This was an event-related fMRI study, with the blood oxygen level–dependent response being monitored relative to the initial cue to form the image and, separately, relative to presentation of the name of a characteristic. For all eight participants, area 17 was activated whenever an image was formed, regardless of whether it was in anticipation of a concrete or an abstract characteristic. Moreover, area 17 was activated when both sorts of characteristics were evaluated. Most participants (seven of eight) had greater activation when they were evaluating a characteristic than when they initially were generating the image.

Handy, Miller, Schott, Shroff, Janata, Van Horn, et al. (2004; 1.5T fMRI). In a separate perceptual condition, the fourteen participants heard the name of each of a set of common objects and studied the corresponding pictures. They were warned that they would soon be asked to recall these objects. Participants took part in two imagery conditions. In the pictures imagery condition, the participants were asked to visualize the pictures that they studied during the perceptual condition; in contrast, in the nouns condition, they were asked to visualize a general version of the object, on the basis of their semantic knowledge, instead of visualizing a specific instance. During neuroimaging, the names of objects were presented every 3.5 seconds; participants passively listened to abstract words during the baseline condition. Although a group analysis did not reveal activation in early visual cortex in either imagery condition, an analysis of the data from individual participants revealed that in the pictures condition, nine of the fourteen participants had activation in the early visual cortex, whereas in the nouns condition ten of the participants had such activation. These results underscore the importance of examining data from individual participants, and they illustrate how a group analysis may mask significant activation, in part because of small differences in the location of activation from one participant to another.

O'Craven and Kanwisher (2000; 1.5 T fMRI.) Only experiment 1 is discussed here (the other two experiments did not examine activation in the early visual cortex). In the perception condition, eight participants viewed faces of famous people or buildings. In the imagery condition, the participants were asked to form vivid, detailed visual mental images of both faces and places. Participants were given two seconds between stimuli, and an "off" condition (lasting twelve seconds) was interleaved with the experimental conditions. The authors reported activation in anterior calcarine cortex (part of area 17) and area 18 when the participants visualized places compared with activation when they visualized faces (the activation overlapped in imagery and perception). The authors suggested that this activation may occur in peripheral retinotopic cortex when it processes larger images (because the place scenes were larger than the faces in this study). The comparisons between the face and place imagery conditions and the off baseline were not reported.

Ishai, Haxby, and Ungerleider (2002; 3T fMRI). In this study, nine participants either perceived or visualized famous faces. The study was conducted with a block design. In the perception condition, famous faces were presented at a rate of one every four seconds. The perception control consisted of viewing images of scrambled faces that were presented at this same rate. The study was designed to examine the differences in imagery processing when images are retrieved from short-term memory (STM) versus when they are retrieved from long-term memory (LTM). Participants were instructed to visualize vivid images of famous faces in all of the following four imagery conditions: (1) imagery from STM, in which participants were asked to visualize specific pictures of famous faces that they had seen and memorized a short time before; (2) imagery from LTM, in which participants were asked to visualize famous faces without having seen them previously during the experiment; (3) imagery from STM plus attention, which was the same as in the STM condition except that the participants were also asked to focus on a facial feature and answer a question about the face (e.g., "small nose?"); and (4) imagery from LTM plus attention, which was the same as the LTM condition except that the participants were asked to focus on and answer a question about a facial feature. In the imagery control condition, the participants passively viewed letter strings at the same rate that the images were to be visualized during the imagery conditions (0.5 seconds to see the stimulus, followed by 3.5 seconds during which the screen was black). In the imagery plus attention conditions, behavioral data (response times and error rates) were collected. Participants achieved 96 percent accuracy, which indicates that they were in fact performing the tasks. Imagery of faces generated from STM generated more activation than imagery from LTM. Compared with the imagery control condition, activation of area 17 during imagery was found in all four imagery conditions. This activation was generally bilateral. However, there was no additional activation in this area when participants were asked to answer a question about a particular facial feature (which suggests that imagery-based activation cannot be ascribed solely to the effects of attention).

Lambert, Sampaio, Scheiber, and Mauss (2002; 1.5 T fMRI). Six participants listened to names of familiar animals and were asked to visualize each one in color, in its environment, and in a dynamic situation. In the baseline condition, the participants simply listened to abstract words. The participants were given two seconds between cue words, and the entire set of stimuli was presented twice. Four of the six participants reported during debriefing that they could not form elaborate mental images within the allotted time, but that their images were more detailed during the second set of trials. After testing, the participants were asked to recall the stimulus words, and they did so far better than chance (which is indirect evidence that the participants did in fact perform the task). Activation of calcarine cortex was found during mental imagery for five out of six participants.

Finally, case studies that examined a single participant were not included in this analysis, simply because it seemed unreasonable to allow them to have the same weight as group studies. Nevertheless, it is worth noting two published case studies briefly. Pütz et al. (1996; 1.5T fMRI) tested an expert user of a soroban (Japanese abacus) while she visualized the device to make calculations. The researchers found bilateral activation of area 17 near the region that registers the center of the visual field (where the participant was asked to visualize the soroban). In addition, Tootell, Hadjikani, et al. (1998; 3T fMRI) essentially conducted a variant of experiment 3 of Kosslyn, Alpert, Thompson, Maljkovic, et al. (1993), asking a participant to visualize letters at the smallest "visible" size or visualize a field of letters (sparing a small central region). A cortical unfolding algorithm was used to show definitively that areas 17 and 18 were activated during both conditions, although—as reported by Kosslyn, Alpert, Thompson, Maljkovic, et al., (1993) and Kosslyn, Thompson, et al. (1995)—there was greater activation in the foveal region when images were formed at a small size than when they covered the field.

SPECT Studies

SPECT has both lower spatial and temporal resolution than either PET or fMRI, but Goldenberg and colleagues have reported that the spatial resolution is 12 millimeters full width half-maximum in the axial plane. Although this resolution may not be sufficient to distinguish activation in area 17 versus area 18, it should be sufficient to document activation in one of the two areas as distinct from other nearby regions.

Goldenberg, Podreka, Steiner, Willmes, Suess, and Deecke (1989, experiment 1). In experiment 1, twenty-eight participants were divided into two equal-sized groups. One group performed two tasks. In one task, they verified statements that required imagery to evaluate, such as "Elephants have little eyes with many wrinkles around them," flashing a light each time they disagreed. In the other task, these participants evaluated statements requiring motor imagery, such as "One can touch the left ear with the right index and the nose with the right thumb at the same time." The other group also performed two tasks. In one, they verified statements that did not require imagery to evaluate, and in the other they simply pressed a button when they heard "no." The results from the different conditions were compared with each other. No behavior was reported. Inferior area 17 or 18 was activated during the visual imagery condition (compared with activation engendered when participants evaluated low-imagery sentences, the baseline of interest here).

Goldenberg, Steiner, Podreka, and Deecke (1992). Ten participants were asked to evaluate the truth of twenty-five statements about shape that required imagery to verify, such as "The ears of a bear are pointed." Ten additional participants evaluated twenty-five sentences about color that required imagery to verify, such as "The interior of a watermelon is violet," and both groups also evaluated twenty-five sentences that did not require imagery, such as "Leap years have 366 days." Statements were presented auditorily every fifteen seconds. For a baseline, rCBF for high-imagery statements was compared with that for low-imagery statements. Participants had to evaluate the statements, and comparable numbers of errors were committed in the two imagery conditions. The SPECT results were comparable in the shape and color imagery tasks: area 17 or 18 had higher rCBF in the high-imagery conditions than in the low-imagery condition.

Studies Not Reporting Activation of the Early Visual Cortex

No evidence of area 17 or 18 activation during visual mental imagery was reported in the following studies, again organized by technique and chronologically within each technique. Note that various other areas were activated in these studies, as summarized in table A.1.[3]

PET Studies

The following studies were analyzed using parametric statistics. No activation in early visual cortex was assumed if the comparison to the baseline condition did not reach statistical significance.

Roland, Eriksson, Stone-Elander, and Widen (1987). Ten participants were asked to close their eyes and imagine walking through their hometowns. They were instructed to imagine going out the door and taking the first left turn, then alternating right and left turns while paying attention to their surroundings. The participants were to imagine their surroundings vividly and in full color, and they were not to pay attention to their own movements. Imagery was monitored continuously for 180–200 seconds. The baseline was rest; participants were instructed to avoid thinking about anything in particular and especially to avoid mental images. All participants reported that during rest, it had been "dark in their mind's eye" (p. 2376). After participants finished the task, they indicated the location where they had arrived, and this location was looked up on a map. The authors did not report whether the participants made the appropriate left and right alternations, but did claim that the participants were never lost and always able to recall images of their surroundings. There was no activation of area 17 or 18, but there was activation of bilateral superior occipital cortex (probably precuneus or area 19) as well as other areas.

Mellet, Tzourio, Denis, and Mazoyer (1995). Eight participants were selected for good imagery abilities, as determined by spatial abilities tests. These participants were asked to scan continuously over an image of a previously memorized map of a fictional island, shifting their focus from one object to another in a clockwise, then counterclockwise, direction around the island. The task was performed in total darkness. The baseline was rest. After the study, they were to point to landmarks on a visualized map to ensure that they knew where each of the landmarks had been. Although neither area 17 nor area 18 was activated, there was increased activation in the superior occipital lobe in the imagery versus rest comparison (as well as in other areas) and a moderate but insignificant increase in activation in the precuneus during imagery. The participants also performed a perceptual task in which they explored the same map visually, as seen through a mirror.

Roland and Gulyás (1995). Eleven participants first memorized the appearance of a series of ten colored, geometric patterns. Following this, they were scanned as they recalled the patterns in sequence, visualizing each until it began to fade and then moving on to the next pattern. The participants were scanned while performing this task after studying the patterns twice, and were scanned again after studying them twenty to twenty-four times (the number of exposures varied for different participants). Participants were told not to use verbal strategies to memorize the patterns. Judging from the example provided in the article, the figures included complex patterns and small dots and subtended 33 degrees (the entire visual field of participants in the scanner). In the recognition phase, the memorized patterns were randomly intermixed with new patterns. The patterns were exposed for 100 milliseconds, followed by 900 milliseconds of darkness, during which the participants indicated recognizing a pattern by slight extension of the right thumb. All participants were able to learn and recall the patterns satisfactorily. The baseline was rest; participants were blindfolded and asked to "have it black in front of your mind's eye" (p. 80). PET results from each participant were examined to determine whether they were truly visualizing; the brain patterns were similar across participants, leading the authors to infer that the participants were engaged in the same process (whatever it may have been). The recall (imagery) condition was compared with the rest condition and also with the learning and recognition conditions. The left inferior posterior temporal lobe was more strongly activated during recall (imagery) than during rest. No occipital regions were activated more during recall (imagery) than during learning or recognition.

Roland, Gulyás, Seitz, Bohm, and Stone-Elander (1990) published a preliminary report of these data, using a different statistical analysis. For present purposes, the results from that report did not differ from those reported here, and in any case we cannot justify treating an earlier analysis of the same data as if it were a separate study.

Mellet, Tzourio, Crivello, Joliot, Denis, and Mazoyer (1996). Nine participants constructed images of three-dimensional objects. Each figure was composed of twelve cubes, and participants mentally built up the figures as they heard eleven directional words. These words were presented at the rate of one every two seconds; twenty-two seconds were required to complete the description of an object, and another five seconds were provided for the participants to visualize the completed object. Each participant mentally constructed four objects in the imagery condition. In one of the baseline conditions, the participants listened to four lists of abstract words, presented at the rate of one word every two seconds; these words were phonetically matched to the direction words used in the test condition. There was also a resting baseline. After scanning, the participants were presented with the four objects they had just mentally built and were asked to identify the correct order of construction. In only 5.5 percent of cases they chose the order where all the cubes were out of sequence (this was taken as evidence that the participants did pay attention to the task); the authors did not report the percentage of time that the participants were actually correct. There was no area 17 or 18 activation; however, the imagery versus rest comparison revealed activation in a large portion of bilateral occipitoparietal cortex, with local maxima in the inferior parietal lobule. The imagery versus listening baseline comparison revealed bilateral activation of the superior occipital cortex (the border of precuneus and area 19), as well as other areas.

Ghaëm, Mellet, Crivello, Tzourio, Mazoyer, Berthoz, and Denis (1997). Five participants were taken to an unfamiliar suburban area and asked to walk an 800-meter route and memorize what they saw, including seven landmarks pointed out by the investigator. The participants walked the route three times. The following day, a few hours prior to PET scanning, the participants were trained to perform a task requiring visual imagery of landmarks. In this task, the participants were to visualize the named landmark and hold the image for ten seconds until the name of another landmark was presented, which then was to be visualized. The study also included a resting baseline. Both the imagery and baseline were replicated, but no behavior was required.

Participants also performed a mental simulation of routes task, which was interspersed in a random order with the landmarks visual imagery task and the resting baseline. That task and its results were reported in a subsequent article, Mellet, Bricogne, et al. (2000), as the "mental navigation" task, summarized below.

Mellet, Tzourio, Denis, and Mazoyer (1998). Eight participants listened to dictionary definitions of concrete versus abstract words. Each word and its definition were presented for a total of six seconds, followed by two seconds of silence before the next word and definition were presented. In the concrete condition, participants heard common words that referred to objects or animals that were easy to visualize, such as a bottle, lion, or guitar. In this condition, the participants were explicitly encouraged to form a mental image and perfect it according to the definition. In the abstract condition, the words referred to concepts that were unlikely to produce mental imagery; moreover, participants were instructed not to produce any mental images during this condition. After the PET scanning session was over, the participants were able to recall more concrete words than abstract words and could retrieve more concrete words from their definitions. There was also a resting baseline.

Mellet, Bricogne, Tzourio-Mazoyer, Ghaëm, Petit, Zago, et al. (2000). Two groups were tested. The five participants in one group learned the spatial layout of a park with various landmarks by physically navigating through it; the six participants in the other group learned a spatial layout by studying a map. Both groups were then scanned while they performed two different tasks: In the "mental navigation task," the participants first were trained on the task a few hours before the PET session. They heard the names of two landmarks, and they were asked to visualize the path between them. In the PET session, they pressed a key when the second landmark was reached. A total of five segments were presented. In the mental scanning task the participants first learned a map of the park, using slides projected onto a blank screen. The map was presented for study for a total of three minutes at the beginning and end of the training sessions; in the middle, each of seven land-marks was presented individually on its own map for five seconds. During the training session, participants learned the task, which was to visualize a laser dot moving between two landmarks (colored dots), the names of which they heard presented through earphones. Participants pressed a button when they reached the second landmark. The time to press the button increased with distance traversed, which provided evidence that participants did in fact perform the task. There was a resting baseline. Area 18/19 was activated in common in the two tasks (using a "conjunction analysis"). In the mental navigation task, another part of area 18/19 was activated more than in mental scanning; however, given the Talairach coor-dinates provided in the article, these regions are most likely within area 19, not medial, and not part of early visual cortex.

Results from the mental navigation task were also reported in Ghaëm et al., (1997), referred to there as the "mental simulation of routes" task. Ghaëm et al. (1997) used an alternative method of data analysis in that report. The results were essentially unchanged; again, as in the 1997 report, there was evidence of occipital activation on the border of areas 18 and 19. Mellet et al. did not consider this activation to fall within the scope of the early visual cortex (E. Mellet, personal communication, October 8, 2001). The region was not medial and in this later report, the analyses indicated to these authors that it is clearly within area 19, rather than area 18.

Mellet, Tzourio-Mazoyer, Bricogne, Mazoyer, Kosslyn, and Denis (2000). Seven participants took part in two conditions. In one, they studied and learned a series of simple colored geometric forms arranged in order by seeing the scenes (visual encoding condition); in the other, they listened to a series of verbal de-scriptions that specified how the geometric forms were arranged (verbal encoding condition). In the verbal encoding condition they were asked to form a visual mental image of the scenes that had been described. In both conditions, geometric forms were visualized on a bar that was divided into regular units, each labeled by a letter. Two scenes were memorized prior to scanning in each condition; the scenes were named by numbers. During scanning, participants formed an image of a named scene and then decided whether the portion of the scene over a named letter was higher than the portion over another named letter. During the baseline, the participants heard similar cues and simply alternated between the two responses. Although at this point they had gone through the training phase, participants reported being able to refrain from forming visual mental images during the baseline task. Response times and error rates were recorded.

Gulyás (2001). This report described results from two visual imagery tasks, as compared with a resting baseline. In one task, ten participants visualized capital letters of the Hungarian alphabet. In this self-paced task, the participants were asked to inspect each imaged letter for straight or curved lines. If they arrived at the end of the alphabet, they were to start over at the beginning, and continue the task until the end of the PET scan. After the session was completed, participants were asked how many times they went through the alphabet and at which letter they stopped. This report was used to calculate the number of letters they imaged during the scan. The participants were not told to visualize the letters at any particular size, and thus probably visualized them at the large "default size" assessed by Kosslyn (1978). In the second imagery task, the same participants visualized capital letters from the Hungarian national anthem at their own pace. They were instructed to visualize each letter in the Hungarian national anthem in sequence until they reached the end of the anthem. They were to inspect each imaged letter's straight or curved lines. At the end of the task, the participants again indicated where they were focusing, and the author computed the rate of visualizing the letters on the basis of these data.

Mazard, Mazoyer, Etard, Tzourio-Mazoyer, Kosslyn, and Mellet (2002). Prior to scanning, six participants memorized the appearance of a set of simple geometric stimuli as well as two orders in which the stimuli were lined up on a surface. During scanning, the participants were cued to visualize the objects in one order and then to compare the shapes in terms of their relative height at specific points along the surface. During imagery, the participants either did or did not hear a recording of fMRI scanner-like noise. The participants had four seconds to visualize a cued arrangement. Two baselines were included; in one, the participants heard the probes and alternated responses without visualizing, whereas in the other they simply rested. Response times and error rates were collected. The participants performed far better than chance, but had greater difficulty forming a clear and vivid image when auditory noise was presented—which was also reflected in the higher error rates in the noise imagery condition.

Suchan, Yágüez, Wunderlich, Canavan, Herzog, Tellman, et al. (2002). Ten participants visualized lines connecting six visible circles, each of which contained a number. The numbers ranged from 1 to 6, and the participants visualized the lines connecting the numbered circles in ascending order (i.e., a line going from circle 1 to circle 2 to circle 3, and so on). The participants then decided whether three or more lines crossed; if so, they were to press one button, if not, the other. Response times and error rates were recorded. During the baseline task, the participants fixated their gaze on the circled numbers in ascending order until they reached the final number. At this point, they were to press a button and to fixate on the circles in descending order until they reached the lowest number, indicating this with a button press, and so on. The participants probably made more eye movements during this baseline task than during the experimental task, but no measures were taken.

fMRI Studies

The fMRI studies were sometimes analyzed by group and sometimes in terms of individual participants. For group designs, if the comparison to baseline (typically an "off" state) did not reach statistical significance, early visual cortex was assumed not to have been activated. For individual designs, if fewer than half the participants exhibited activation in the early visual cortex, relative to baseline, the early visual cortex was assumed not to have been reliably activated.

D'Esposito, Detre, Aguirre, Stallcup, Alsop, Tippet, et al. (1997; 1.5T fMRI). Seven participants were asked to listen to words in two conditions. The words in the imagery condition were judged by the authors to be concrete, whereas the words in the baseline condition were judged to be abstract. A new word was presented every second. In the imagery condition, the participants were instructed to visualize the appearance of each named object; the appearance of the object necessarily was recalled from LTM. In the abstract word condition, the participants were instructed to listen passively to the words. Data analyses were performed for individual participants. No behavior was required. The authors note that if they had used a more complex task requiring a behavioral response, this might have increased the number of neural systems involved and rendered it more difficult to interpret the data. They also noted that results from their previous event-related potential studies were correlated with individual differences in imagery, which suggests that participants were in fact performing the tasks.

Ishai, Ungerleider, and Haxby (2000; 1.5 T fMRI). Nine participants visualized specific examples of houses, faces, or chairs that they recalled from LTM. At the same time, they viewed a gray square. In a corresponding perception condition, stimuli were presented every second; the timing was not provided for the imagery condition, but it seems safe to assume that it was the same. The control condition for the perception task consisted of viewing scrambled pictures. In the baseline condition for the imagery task, the participants simply viewed a gray square. No behavior was required. One of the major goals of this study was to demonstrate that the network of brain areas activated during visual mental imagery differs depending on whether one visualizes chairs, houses or faces. Here, the focus is on the comparison between imagery (the combination of the houses, faces and chairs imagery conditions) and the imagery control condition, as reported in the text and in tables 1, 3, and 4 of Ishai, Ungerleider, & Haxby (2000). Although there was no evidence that the early visual cortex was activated during imagery, regions in the ventral temporal cortex responded differently depending on whether participants visualized houses, faces, or chairs.

Knauff, Kassubek, Mulack, and Greenlee (2000; 1.5T fMRI). In the perception condition, ten participants, who were first trained on a computer outside the scanner, looked at a grid and decided whether a highlighted cell fell on or off an abstract figure filling half the cells of the grid. In the imagery condition, the participants visualized the abstract figure in the grid and decided whether a highlighted cell would have fallen on the figure if it were actually present. In both conditions, the highlighted cell fell on the figure half the time, and half the time it fell off the figure. In the baseline condition, participants saw blank grids with one highlighted cell and pressed a button when they saw it. Finally the investigators included a standard fMRI off condition. Stimuli were presented once every 4.1 seconds, and each condition was repeated twice for each participant. Response times and error rates were measured. Participants achieved an accuracy rate of 85 percent inside the scanner.

Trojano, Grossi, Linden, Formisano, Hacker, Zanella, et al. (2000; 1.5T fMRI). Two visual imagery experiments were reported in this article. For present purposes, they differed primarily in the baseline condition; the imagery task was the same in both experiments. In experiment 1, the researchers asked the seven participants to listen to pairs of times (e.g., 5:30 and 8:00) and to visualize the corresponding clock faces; the participants then decided on which clock face the angle between the two hands would be larger. In the control task for experiment 1, the participants decided which of two times was numerically greater. In experiment 2, a perception condition was also included, as well as a control condition that consisted of an off period between imagery sessions. The four participants were also asked, in another task that the authors used for comparison, to count the number of syllables in each pair of times as it was presented verbally and to decide whether that number was odd or even. In experiment 1, participants closed their eyes, whereas in experiment 2, they kept them open and fixated on a point in order to avoid eye movements. In all tasks, the participants responded by pressing a key under the left or right hand, as appropriate to indicate their judgments. Responses were collected during fMRI scanning and were analyzed for accuracy. The accuracy rate was greater than 90 percent in both experiments 1 and 2.

Wheeler, Petersen, and Buckner (2000; 1.5T fMRI). Eighteen participants included in the final analysis studied pictures and sounds over two days. Each of the stimuli was paired with an appropriate label. Participants were scanned on the third day. During the imagery (recall) task, the participants were presented with visual labels of the previously studied stimuli and were asked to retrieve each stimulus from LTM. After they had completely retrieved the stimulus, the participants were to indicate with a button press whether "their memory was of a picture or sound" (Wheeler et al., 2000, p. 11126). The participants achieved an accuracy rate of almost 99 percent. This event-related fMRI study featured two sets of perception trials and two sets of imagery trials. The visual, auditory, and baseline (fixation) trials were randomly intermixed. The participants were given the perception task during the first two sets of trials, and the recall (imagery) trials during the next two. The results from the picture and sound imagery tasks were contrasted with each other.

Formisano, Linden, Di Salle, Trojano, Esposito, Sack, et al. (2002; 1.5T fMRI). In this event-related fMRI study, twelve participants heard pairs of words, each of which specified a specific time of day, and visualized the corresponding analog clock faces; they then decided on which face the hands would form a larger angle. All stimuli specified full hours or half-hours (e.g., 8:00 or 9:30). The imaged clock hands were either in the right or left hemifield, and stimuli were balanced for this factor. The group analysis was based on results from a first group of participants (n = 6). A second group of six participants, which performed twenty-three trials at a higher sampling rate (higher temporal resolution) but with fewer brain slices, essentially confirmed the finding of sequential activation in the left, then right, posterior parietal cortex. Data from this second group also served in an fMRI and TMS study of mental imagery, reported by Sack et al., (2002; see below). Here, data only from the first group of six participants is considered. The participants completed a total of sixty-four trials, presented in four fMRI blocks of 256 seconds.

Sack, Sperling, Prvulovic, Formisano, Goebel, Di Salle, et al. (2002; 1.5T fMRI). In this event-related fMRI study, six participants performed the same task used by Formisano et al. (2002). They were asked to form a mental image of two analog clock faces, each cued by an auditory probe, and to report on which clock face the hands formed a larger angle. The temporal resolution was higher in Sack et al.'s study than in Formisano et al.'s study, although fewer slices of the brain were imaged. The results revealed a bilateral posterior parietal activation in imagery and no activation of early visual cortex. An additional group of sixty participants received rTMS prior to the task. The rTMS results suggest that the right parietal lobule may play a critical functional role in this spatially based task.

SPECT Studies

The SPECT studies were all analyzed using parametric statistics in group designs. In all cases, activation in early visual cortex was not statistically greater than activation in a baseline condition.

Goldenberg, Podreka, Steiner, and Willmes (1987). Participants were asked to listen to and memorize a series of words, one every five seconds; thirty seconds later they decided whether a probe word was in the memorized set. There were three different types of words, with different participants receiving each type: meaningless (seven participants), concrete (eighteen participants), and abstract (eight participants); eighteen additional participants performed a resting baseline. The participants assigned to learn concrete words, and only these participants, were divided into two groups—eleven were instructed to use imagery to remember the words whereas seven were given no explicit strategy (participants in this group were asked to memorize a list of words during a pilot test and were questioned about which technique they used to memorize them—one participant was excluded because of having used imagery). After the task, the participants were questioned again, and one participant who had switched to an imagery strategy after the first list was reassigned to the imagery instruction group. The participants were scanned as they memorized the words. Although no behavior was recorded during scanning, afterwards the participants recognized 84.4 percent of the meaningless words, 73.1 percent of the abstract words, 73.1 percent of the concrete words when imagery was not used, and 96.9 percent of the concrete words when imagery was used. Although no area 17 or 18 activation was observed, some participants who used imagery to learn concrete words had strong activation in inferior occipital regions. From the diagrams of the regions of interest, it appears that this region is perhaps within twenty-five millimeters of midline.

Goldenberg, Podreka, Uhl, Steiner, Willmes, and Deecke (1989). Ten participants visualized a previously studied color, another ten visualized a previously studied face, and another ten visualized a previously studied set of geometric figures arranged to symbolize a map. In the first two conditions, the participants were to form a vivid image and retain it until the name of the next stimulus was presented. The investigators did not tell the participants to visualize the stimuli exactly as they had actually appeared, but instead told them to modify each face or color to make it easier to visualize. In the face condition, participants were told not to visualize the actual living person's face, but rather a static, achromatic rendition. In the map condition, participants visualized a path connecting two points on the map. Participants were blindfolded, with eyes closed, and received an auditory cue as to which color, face, or route to visualize; they visualized a stimulus for fifteen seconds before the next one was presented. The baseline condition was rest, but twelve of thirty participants reported spontaneously forming visual images during the resting state (seven in the color group, two in the face group, and three in the map group). No behavior was recorded.

Goldenberg, Podreka, Steiner, Willmes, Suess, and Deecke (1989, experiment 2). In experiment 2, eighteen participants memorized the appearance of twenty-three letters in Helvetica font. Following this, they were scanned while they were auditorily cued to visualize each letter and count its corners, flashing a light for each corner. (Two participants later reported either that they had not experienced any imagery, or only vague imagery, during this task.) For each letter, participants had an image for eight to fifteen seconds, depending on the number of corners. Participants were 93.1 percent accurate in the corner counting task. In the baseline condition, participants were given the names of two letters and counted the number of letters in the alphabet between those two. Eight participants reported having had visual images of the letters during this baseline task, but all denied using imagery as a strategy to perform it. No brain area was activated more strongly in the imagery condition than in the control condition. It is possible that the control condition not only involved imagery (and hence removed it in the comparison) but also was more challenging than the imagery task.

Goldenberg, Podreka, Steiner, Franzen, and Deecke (1991). Fourteen participants first memorized color photos of five different objects. They subsequently heard the names of these objects in pseudo-random order, one every fifteen seconds, while their brains were being scanned. Participants were asked to form vivid mental images of each object. In the baseline condition, participants listened to five low-imagery words, which were presented at the same rate as the words in the imagery condition. No behavior was recorded. There was no significant increase in occipital cortex during the visual imagery task; the authors attributed this failure to find significant activation to inter-participant variability.

Charlot, Tzourio, Zilbovicius, Mazoyer, and Denis (1992). Eleven participants were assigned to a high-imagery group, and another eleven were assigned to a low-imagery group. Scores on the Minnesota Paper Form Board and the Mental Rotations Test (both of which assess spatial imagery) were used to determine group membership; the highest-scoring third were considered to be high imagers (the group of interest here) whereas the lowest-scoring third were considered low imagers. Participants were asked to imagine landmarks on a fictional island and then to explore the visualized island from point to point. Participants continuously explored the island for 4.5 minutes, which is the time it takes to obtain an image with SPECT, but they started from a new landmark every forty-five seconds. The baseline was rest, and no behavior was assessed. (Although activation in area 17 or 18 was found in low-imagers, this activation is likely to be an artifact of general whole-brain increases for low imagers.) There was very little increase in any location for high imagers, and no hint of an increase in activation in early visual cortex.

At first glance, this review would seem to paint a very muddy picture. Thus, it is impressive that the analyses described in chapter 4 brought order to this seemingly complex set of results.

Notes

1. Studies in which area 17 or 18 was not monitored were also excluded. For example, Roland and Friberg (1985) used Xe-133 in a route-finding task, but the recording sites would not allow them to detect area 17 or 18 activation. In addition, studies with special populations were excluded. For example, Rauch et al. (1996) used a script-driven imagery task with PTSD patients and found area 17 or 18 activation when participants visualized traumatic scripts compared to neutral ones. Kosslyn and Thompson also examined but did not include in the analysis nine additional studies that did not meet the inclusion criteria. In three of the studies (Decety, Kawashima, Gulyás, & Roland, 1992; Goldberg, Berman, Randolph, Gold, & Weinberger, 1996; Kawashima, Roland, & O'Sullivan, 1995), imagery instructions were not used, and we had no firm grounds for inferring that the tasks actually required the use of imagery; in two of the studies (Menon et al., 1993) the lack of details in a short report prevented us from coding the results; two of the papers reported case studies (Pütz et al., 1996; Tootell, Hadjikani, et al., 1998); and two of the reports were one-page abstracts (Damasio et al., 1993; Kuo, Chen, Humg, Tzeng, & Hsieh, 2000). Of these, seven studies reported activation in early visual cortex and two did not.

2. The journals were *American Journal of Psychiatry, Behavioural Brain Research, Brain, Brain and Cognition, Brain Research, Brain Research Bulletin, Cerebral Cortex,*

Cortex, European Journal of Cognitive Psychology, European Journal of Neuroscience, European Neurology, Human Brain Mapping, Journal of Cognitive Neuroscience, Journal of Neuroscience, Nature, Nature Neuroscience, NeuroImage, Neuron, Neuropsychologia, Neuropsychology, NeuroReport, Proceedings of the National Academy of Sciences (USA), Proceedings of the Royal Society, Science, Trends in Cognitive Sciences, Trends in Neuroscience.

3. In three of the results reported as not finding activation in the early visual cortex, the researchers actually found more activation in the baselines than in the imagery condition: Goldenberg, Podreka, Uhl, et al. (1989), when color imagery was compared to rest, and Mazard, Mazoyer, et al. (2002), for both imagery conditions (noise and no noise).

References

Aleman, A., van Lee, L., Mantione, M. H. M., Verkoijen, I. G., & de Haan, E. H. F. (2001). Visual imagery without visual experience: Evidence from congenitally totally blind people. *Neuroreport: For Rapid Communication of Neuroscience Research, 12,* 2601–2604.

Andersen, R. A., Essick, G. K., & Siegel, R. M. (1985). Encoding of spatial location by posterior parietal neurons. *Science, 230,* 456–458.

Anderson, J. R. (1978). Arguments concerning representations for mental imagery. *Psychological Review, 85,* 249–277.

Anderson, J. R., & Bower, G. H. (1973). *Human associative memory.* New York: V. H. Winston & Sons.

Anderson, R. E., & Balsom, E. W. (1997, November). *Visual imagery, discovery, and creativity.* Paper presented at the 38th annual meeting of the Psychonomic Society, Philadelphia, PA.

Appelle, S. (1972). Perception and discrimination as a function of stimulus orientation: The "oblique effect" in man and animals. *Psychological Bulletin, 78,* 266–278.

Arditi, A., Holtzman, J. D., & Kosslyn, S. M. (1988). Mental imagery and sensory experience in congenital blindness. *Neuropsychologia, 26,* 1–12.

Armstrong, J. (1996) *Looking at pictures—an introduction to the appreciation of art.* London: Duckworth.

Baddeley, A. (1986). *Working memory.* Oxford: Clarendon Press.

Barone, P., Batardiere, A., Knoblauch, K., & Kennedy, H. (2000). Laminar distribution of neurons in extrastriate areas projecting to visual areas V1 and

V4 correlates with the hierarchical rank and indicates the operation of a distance rule. *Journal of Neuroscience, 20,* 3263–3281.

Barsalou, L. W. (1999). Perceptual symbol systems. *Behavioral and Brain Sciences, 22,* 577–660.

Bartolomeo, P. (2002). The relationship between visual perception and visual mental imagery: A reappraisal of the neuropsychological evidence. *Cortex, 38,* 357–378.

Bartolomeo, P., Bachoud-Levi, A.-C., De Gelder, B., Denes, G., Barba, G. D., Brugieres, P., et al. (1998). Multiple-domain dissociation between impaired visual perception and preserved mental imagery in a patient with bilateral extrastriate lesions. *Neuropsychologia, 36,* 239–249.

Bartolomeo, P., Bachoud-Levi, A.-C., & Denes, G. (1997). Preserved imagery for colours in a patient with cerebral achromatopsia. *Cortex, 33,* 369–378.

Bartolomeo, P., & Chokron, S. (2002). Can we change our vantage point to explore imaginal neglect? *Behavioral and Brain Sciences, 25,* 184–185.

Bates, E. A., & Elman, J. L. (1993). Connectionism and the study of change. In Mark Johnson (Ed.), *Brain Development and Cognition: A Reader* (pp. 623–642). Oxford: Blackwell.

Baylor, G. W. (1971). A treatise on the mind's eye: An empirical investigation of visual mental imagery. *Dissertation Abstracts International, 32* (10-B), 6024.

Beckers, G., & Zeki, S. (1995) The consequences of inactivating areas V1 and V5 on visual motion perception. *Brain, 118,* 49–60.

Behrmann, M., Winocur, G., & Moscovitch, M. (1992). Dissociation between mental imagery and object recognition in a brain-damaged patient. *Nature, 359,* 636–637.

Biederman, I. (1987). Recognition-by-components: A theory of human image understanding. *Psychological Review, 94,* 115–147.

Bisiach, E., & Luzzatti, C. (1978). Unilateral neglect of representational space. *Cortex, 14,* 129–133.

Bisiach, E., Luzzatti, C., & Perani, D. (1979). Unilateral neglect, representational schema, and consciousness. *Brain, 102,* 609–618.

Blanco, F., & Travieso, D. (2003). Haptic exploration and mental estimation of distances on a fictitious island: From mind's eye to mind's hand. *Journal of Visual Impairment & Blindness, 97,* 298–300.

Boden, M. (1977). *Artificial intelligence and natural man.* New York: Basic Books.

Boring, E. G. (1950). *A history of experimental psychology* (2nd ed.) New York: Appleton-Century-Crofts.

Brandimonte, M. A., Hitch, G. J., & Bishop, D. V. (1992). Verbal recoding of visual stimuli impairs mental image transformations. *Memory & Cognition, 20,* 449–455.

Brefczynski, J. A., & DeYoe, E. A. (1999). A physiological correlate of the spotlight of visual attention. *Nature Neuroscience, 2,* 370–374.

Britten, K., Shadlen, M. N., Newsome, W. T., & Movshon, J. A. (1992). The analysis of visual motion: a comparison of neuronal and psychophysical performance. *Journal of Neuroscience, 12,* 4745–4767.

Britten, K. H., Newsome, W. T., Shadlen, M. N., Celebrini, S., & Movshon, J. A. (1996). A relationship between behavioral choice and the visual responses of neurons in macaque MT. *Visual Neuroscience, 13,* 87–100.

Bundesen, C., & Larsen, A. (1975). Visual transformation of size. *Journal of Experimental Psychology: Human Perception and Performance, 1,* 214–220.

Caramazza, A., & Hillis, A. E. (1990). Spatial representation of words in the brain implied by studies of a unilateral neglect patient. *Nature, 346,* 267–269.

Cave, K. R., & Kosslyn, S. M. (1989). Varieties of size-specific visual selection. *Journal of Experimental Psychology: General, 118,* 148–164.

Chabris, C. F., & Kosslyn, S. M. (1998). How do the cerebral hemispheres contribute to encoding spatial relations? *Current Directions in Psychological Science, 7,* 8–14.

Chambers, D., & Reisberg, D. (1992). What an image depicts depends on what an image means. *Cognitive Psychology, 24,* 145–174.

Charlot, V., Tzourio, N., Zilbovicius, M., Mazoyer, B., & Denis, M. (1992). Different mental imagery abilities result in different regional cerebral blood flow activation patterns during cognitive tests. *Neuropsychologia, 30,* 565–580.

Chatterjee, A., & Southwood, M. H. (1995). Cortical blindness and visual imagery. *Neurology, 45,* 2189–2195.

Chen, H., Yao, D. & Chen, L. (2003). Analysis of fMRI data by blind separation of data in a tiny spatial domain into independent temporal component. *Brain Topography 15,* 223–232.

Chen, W., Kato, T., Zhu, X.-H., Ogawa, S., Tank, D. W., & Ugurbil, K. (1998). Human primary visual cortex and lateral geniculate nucleus activation during visual imagery. *NeuroReport, 9,* 3669–3674.

Chklovskii, D. B., & Koulakov, A. A. (2004). Maps in the brain: what can we learn from them? *Annual Review of Neuroscience, 27,* 369–392.

Chomsky, N. (1965). *Aspects of the theory of syntax.* Cambridge, MA: MIT Press.

Clark, H. H., & Chase, W. G. (1972). On the process of comparing sentences against pictures. *Cognitive Psychology, 3,* 472–517.

Clavagnier, S., Falchier, A., & Kennedy, H. (2004). Long-distance feedback projections to area V1: implications for multisensory integration, spatial awareness, and visual consciousness. *Cognitive and Affective Behavioral Neuroscience, 4,* 117–126.

Cohen, J., Cohen, P., West, S. G., & Aiken, L. S. (2003). *Applied Multiple Regression/ Correlation Analysis for the Behavioral Sciences.* Mahwah, New Jersey: Lawrence Erlbaum.

Cohen, M. S., & Bookheimer, S. Y. (1994). Location of brain function using magnetic resonance imaging. *Trends in Neurosciences, 17,* 268–277.

Cohen, M. S., Kosslyn, S. M., Breiter, H. C., DiGirolamo, G. J., Thompson, W. L., Anderson, et al. (1996). Changes in cortical activity during mental rotation. A mapping study using functional MRI. *Brain, 119,* 89–100.

Cooper, A. N., & Shepard, R. N. (1973). The time required to prepare for a rotated stimulus. *Memory & Cognition, 1,* 246–250.

Corbetta, M., Miezen, F. M., Schulman, G. L., & Petersen, S. E. (1993). A PET study of visuo-spatial attention. *Journal of Neuroscience, 13,* 1202–1226.

Craver-Lemley, C., Arterberry, M. E., & Reeves, A. (1999). "Illusory" illusory conjunctions: The conjoining of features of visual and imagined stimuli. *Journal of Experimental Psychology: Human Perception & Performance, 25,* 1036–1049.

Craver-Lemley, C., & Reeves, A. (1992). How visual imagery interferes with vision. *Psychological Review, 99,* 633–649.

Crick, F., & Koch, C. (1995). Are we aware of neural activity in primary visual cortex? *Nature, 375,* 121–123.

Dalla Barba, G., Rosenthal, V., & Visetti, Y.-M. (2002). The nature of mental imagery: How null is the "null hypothesis"? *Behavioral and Brain Sciences, 25,* 187–188.

Damasio, A. R. (1985). The frontal lobes. In K. M. Heilman & E. Valenstein (Eds.), *Clinical neuropsychology* (pp. 339–402). New York: Oxford University Press.

Damasio, H., Grabowski, T. J., Damasio, A., Tranel, D., Boles-Ponto, L., Watkins, G. L., et al. (1993). Visual recall with eyes closed and covered activates early visual cortices. *Society for Neuroscience Abstracts, 19,* 1603.

D'Angiulli, A. (2002). Mental image generation and the contrast sensitivity function. *Cognition, 85,* B11-B19.

Davis, K. D., Kwan, C. L., Crawley, A. P., & Mikulis, D. J. (1998). Functional MRI study of thalamic and cortical activations evoked by cutaneous heat, cold, and tactile stimuli. *Journal of Neurophysiology, 80,* 1533–1546.

Decety, J., Kawashima, R., Gulyás, B., & Roland, P. E. (1992). Preparation for reaching: A PET study of the participating structures in the human brain. *NeuroReport, 3,* 761–764.

Decety, J., & Jeannerod, M. (1995). Mentally simulated movements in virtual reality: Does Fitts's law hold in motor imagery? *Behavioural Brain Research, 72,* 127–134.

Denis, M., & Carfantan, M. (1985). People's knowledge about images. *Cognition, 20,* 49–60.

Denis, M., & Kosslyn, S. M. (1999). Scanning visual images: A window on the mind. *Cahiers de Psychologie Cognitive/Current Psychology of Cognition, 18,* 409–465.

Dennett, D. C. (1969). *Content and consciousness.* New York: Humanities Press.

Dennett, D. C. (1991). *Consciousness explained.* Boston: Little, Brown.

Dennett, D. C. (2002). Does your brain use the images in it, and if so, how? *Behavioral and Brain Sciences, 25,* 189–190.

Desimone, R., & Ungerleider, L. G. (1989). Neural mechanisms of visual processing in monkeys. In F. Boller & J. Grafman (Eds.), *Handbook of neuropsychology* (pp. 267–299). Amsterdam: Elsevier.

D'Esposito, M., Detre, J. A., Aguirre, G. K., Stallcup, M., Alsop, D. C., Tippet, L. J., et al. (1997). A functional MRI study of mental image generation. *Neuropsychologia, 35,* 725–730.

DeYoe, E. A., Bandettini, P., Neitz, J., Miller, D., & Winans, P. (1994). Functional magnetic resonance imaging (FMRI) of the human brain. *Journal of Neuroscience Methods, 54,* 171–187.

Douglas, K. L., & Rockland, K. S. (1992). Extensive visual feedback connections from ventral inferotemporal cortex. *Society of Neuroscience Abstracts, 18,* 390.

Dror, I., & Kosslyn, S. M. (1993). Mental imagery and aging. *Psychology and Aging, 9,* 90–102.

Eckman, F. R. (1994). The competence-performance issue in second language acquisition theory: A debate. In E. Tarone, S. Gass, & A. Cohen (Eds.), *Research methodology in second language acquisition* (pp. 3–15). Hillsdale, NJ: Lawrence Erlbaum.

Edelman, G. M., Reeke, G. N., Jr., Gall, W. E., Tononi, G., Williams, D., & Sporns, O. (1992). Synthetic neural modeling applied to a real-world artifact. *Proceedings of the National Academy of Sciences, USA, 89,* 7267–7271.

Edelman, S. (1998). Representation is representation of similarities. *Behavioral and Brain Sciences, 21,* 449–498.

Egly, R., Driver, R., & Rafal, R. D. (1994). Voluntary and reflexive saccades after lesions of the human frontal eye fields. *Journal of Cognitive Neuroscience, 6,* 400–411.

Einstein, A. (1945). A testimonial from Professor Einstein (Appendix II). In J. Hadamard (Ed.), *An essay on the psychology of invention in the mathematical field* (pp. 142–143). Princeton, NJ: Princeton University Press.

Engel, S. A., Rumelhart, D. E., Wandell, B. A., Lee, A. T., Glover, G. H., Chichilnisky, E. J., et al. (1994). fMRI of human visual cortex. *Nature, 369,* 525.

Farah, M. J. (1988). Is visual imagery really visual? Overlooked evidence from neuropsychology. *Psychological Review, 95,* 307–317.

Farah, M. J. (1995). Current issues in the neuropsychology of image generation. *Neuropsychologia, 23,* 1455–1472.

Farah, M. J., Soso, M. J., & Dasheiff, R. M. (1992). Visual angle of the mind's eye before and after unilateral occipital lobectomy. *Journal of Experimental Psychology: Human Perception and Performance, 18,* 241–246.

Felleman, D. J., & Van Essen, D. C. (1991). Distributed hierarchical processing in primate cerebral cortex. *Cerebral Cortex, 1,* 1–47.

Finke, R. A. (1989). *Principles of mental imagery.* Cambridge, MA: MIT Press.

Finke, R. A. (1990). *Creative imagery: Discoveries and inventions in visualization.* Hillsdale, NJ: Erlbaum.

Finke, R. A., Johnson, M. K., & Shyi, G. C.-W. (1988). Memory confusions for real and imagined completions of symmetrical visual patterns. *Memory and Cognition, 16,* 133–137.

Finke, R. A., & Pinker, S. (1982). Spontaneous imagery scanning in mental extrapolation. *Journal of Experimental Psychology: Learning, Memory, and Cognition, 8,* 142–147.

Finke, R. A., & Pinker, S. (1983). Directional scanning of remembered visual patterns. *Journal of Experimental Psychology: Learning, Memory, and Cognition, 9,* 398–410.

Finke, R. A., & Shepard, R. N. (1986). Visual functions of mental imagery. In K. R. Boff, L. Kaufman, & J. P. Thomas (Eds.), *Handbook of perception and human performance* (pp. 37-1–37-55). New York: Wiley-Interscience.

Fisher, R. P. (1995). Interviewing victims and witnesses of crime. *Psychology, Public Policy, & Law, 1*, 732–764.

Fisher, R. P., Geiselman, R. E., & Amador, M. (1989). Field test of the cognitive interview: Enhancing the recollection of the actual victims and witnesses of crime. *Journal of Applied Psychology, 74*, 722–727.

Fodor, J. (1968). Psychological explanation: An introduction to the philosophy of psychology. New York: Random House.

Fodor, J. A. (2003). *Hume variations.* Oxford: Clarendon Press.

Fodor J. A., & Pylyshyn, Z. W. (1988). Connectionism and cognitive architecture: A critical analysis. *Cognition, 28*, 3–71.

Formisano, E., Linden, D. J., Di Salle, F., Trojano, L., Esposito, F., Sack, A. T., et al. (2002). Tracking the mind's image in the brain I: Time-resolved fMRI during visuospatial mental imagery. *Neuron, 35*, 185–194.

Fox, P. T., Mintun, M. A., Raichle, M. E., Meizen, F. M., Allman, J. M., & Van Essen, D. C. (1986). Mapping human visual cortex with positron emission tomography. *Nature, 323*, 806–809.

Fox, P. T., Mintun, M. A., Reiman, E. M., & Raichle, M. E. (1988). Enhanced detection of focal brain responses using intersubject averaging and change-distribution analysis of subtracted PET images. *Journal of Cerebral Blood Flow and Metabolism, 8*, 642–653.

Fox, P. T., & Pardo, J. V. (1991). Does inter-subject variability in cortical functional organization increase with neural distance from the periphery? *CIBA Foundation Symposium, 163*, 125–140.

Frahm, J., Merboldt, K., & Hnicke, W. (1993). Functional MRI of human brain activation at high spatial resolution. *Magnetic Resonance in Medicine, 29*, 139–144.

Friston, K. J., Frith, C. D., Fletcher, P., & Liddle, P. F. (1996). Functional topography: Multidimensional scaling and functional connectivity in the brain. *Cerebral Cortex, 6*, 156–164.

Fujita, I., Tanaka, K., Ito, M., & Cheng, K. (1992). Columns for visual features of objects in monkey inferotemporal cortex. *Nature, 360*, 343–346.

Galton, F. (1883). *Inquiries into human faculty and its development.* Bristol, UK: Thoemmes Press.

Ganis, G., Thompson, W. L., & Kosslyn, S. M. (2004). Brain areas underlying visual mental imagery and visual perception: An fMRI study. *Cognitive Brain Research, 20*, 226–241.

Ganis, G., Thompson, W. L., & Kosslyn, S. M. (2005). Understanding the effects of task-specific practice in the brain: Insights from individual differences analyses. *Cognitive, Affective and Behavioral Neuroscience, 5*(2), 235–245.

Ganis, G., Thompson, W. L., Mast, F. W., & Kosslyn, S. M. (2003). Visual imagery in cerebral visual dysfunction. *Neurologic Clinics, 21*, 631–646.

Garner, W. R., Hake, H. W., & Eriksen, C. W. (1956). Operationism and the concept of perception. *Psychological Review, 63*, 149–159.

Ghaëm, O., Mellet, E., Crivello, F., Tzourio, N., Mazoyer, B., Berthoz, A., & Denis, M. (1997). Mental navigation along memorized routes activates the hippocampus, precuneus, and insula. *NeuroReport, 8,* 739–744.

Gilden, D., Blake, R., & Hurst, G. (1995). Neural adaptation of imaginary visual motion. *Cognitive Psychology, 28,* 1–16.

Goebel, R., Khorram-Sefat, D., Muckli, L., Hacker, H., & Singer, W. (1998). The constructive nature of vision: Direct evidence from fMRI studies of apparent motion and motion imagery. *European Journal of Neuroscience, 10,* 1563–1573.

Gold, I. (2002). Interpreting the neuroscience of imagery. *Behavioral and Brain Sciences, 25,* 190–191.

Goldberg, T. E., Berman, K. F., Randolph, C., Gold, J. M., & Weinberger, D. R. (1996). Isolating the mnemonic component in spatial delayed response: A controlled PET ^{15}O-labelled water regional cerebral blood flow study in normal humans. *NeuroImage, 3,* 69–78.

Goldenberg, G. (1992). Loss of visual imagery and loss of visual knowledge—a case study. *Neuropsychologia, 30*(12), 1081–1099.

Goldenberg, G. (1993). The neural basis of mental imagery. *Balliere's Clinical Neurology, 2,* 265–286.

Goldenberg, G. (1998). Is there a common substrate for visual recognition and visual imagery? *Neurocase, 4,* 141–147.

Goldenberg, G. (2002). Loss of visual imagery: Neuropsychological evidence in search of a theory. *Behavioral and Brain Sciences, 25,* 191.

Goldenberg, G., & Artner, C. (1991). Visual imagery and knowledge about the visual appearance of objects in patients with posterior cerebral artery lesions. *Brain and Cognition, 15,* 160–186.

Goldenberg, G., Müllbacher, W., & Nowak, A. (1995). Imagery without perception—a case study of anosagnosia for cortical blindness. *Neuropsychologia, 33,* 1159–1178.

Goldenberg, G., Podreka, I., Steiner, M., Franzen, P., & Deecke, L. (1991). Contributions of occipital and temporal brain regions to visual and acoustic imagery—A SPECT study. *Neuropsychologia, 29,* 695–702.

Goldenberg, G., Podreka, I., Steiner, M., & Willmes, K. (1987). Patterns of regional cerebral blood flow related to memorizing of high and low imagery words: An emission computer tomography study. *Neuropsychologia, 25,* 473–485.

Goldenberg, G., Podreka, I., Steiner, M., Willmes, K., Suess, E., & Deecke, L. (1989). Regional cerebral blood flow patterns in visual imagery. *Neuropsychologia, 27,* 641–664.

Goldenberg, G., Podreka, L., Uhl, F., Steiner, M., Willmes, K., & Deecke, L. (1989). Cerebral correlates of imagining colours, faces and a map. *Neuropsychologia, 27,* 1315–1328.

Goldenberg, G., Steiner, M., Podreka, I., & Deecke, L. (1992). Regional cerebral blood flow patterns related to verification of low- and high-imagery sentences. *Neuropsychologia, 30,* 581–586.

Goldston, D. B., Hinrichs, J. V., & Richman, C. L. (1985). Subjects' expectations, individual variability, and the scanning of mental images. *Memory and Cognition, 13,* 365–370.

Gould, S. J., & Lewontin, R. C. (1979). The spandrels of San Marco and the Panglossian paradigm: A critique of the adaptationist programme. *Proceedings of the Royal Society of London, 205,* 281–288.

Grawert, F., Kobras, S., Burr, G. W., Hanssen, H., Riedel, M., Jefferson, C. M., et al. (2000). *Content-addressable holographic databases.* Paper presented at SPIE Conference on Critical Technologies for the Future of Computing, paper 4109-3, San Diego, CA, August 2, 2000.

Gregory, R. L. (1970). *The intelligent eye.* London: Weidenfeld and Nicholson.

Gross, C. G., & Mishkin, M. (1977). The neural basis of stimulus equivalence across retinal translation. In S. Harnad, R. Doty, J. Jaynes, L. Goldstein, & G. Krauthamer (Eds.), *Lateralization in the nervous system* (pp. 109–122). New York: Academic Press.

Grossberg, S. (1999a). How does the cerebral cortex work? Learning, attention, and grouping by the laminar circuits of visual cortex. *Spatial Vision, 12,* 163–185.

Grossberg, S. (1999b). The link between brain learning, attention, and consciousness. *Consciousness and Cognition, 8,* 1–44.

Grossberg, S. (2000). How hallucinations may arise from brain mechanisms of learning, attention, and volition. *Journal of the International Neuropsychological Society, 6,* 583–592.

Grüsser, O.-J., & Landis, T. (1991). Non-existent visual worlds: Afterimages, illusions, hallucinations and related phenomena. In O.-J. Grüsser & T. Landis. (Eds.), *Visual agnosias and other disturbances of visual perception and cognition: Vision and visual dysfunction,* Vol. 12, (pp. 467–476). London: Macmillan.

Gulyás, B. (2001). Neural networks for internal reading and visual imagery of reading: A PET study. *Brain Research Bulletin, 54,* 319–328.

Gusnard, D. A., & Raichle, M. E. (2001). Searching for a baseline: Functional imaging and the resting brain. *Nature Reviews Neuroscience, 2,* 685–694.

Handy, T. C., Miller, M. B., Schott, B., Schroff, N. M., Janata, P., Van Horn, J. D., et al. (2004). Visual imagery and memory—Do retrieval strategies affect what the mind's eye sees? *European Journal of Cognitive Psychology, 16*(5), 631–652.

Harman, G. (1990). The intrinsic quality of experience. In J. E. Tomberlin (Ed.), *Philosophical perspectives: Vol. 4. Action theory and philosophy of mind* (pp. 31–52). Atascadero, CA: Ridgeview.

Hasnain, M. K., Fox, P. T., & Woldorff, M. G. (1998). Intersubject variability of functional areas in the human visual cortex. *Human Brain Mapping, 6,* 301–315.

Haxby, J. V., Grady, C. L., Horwitz, B., Ungerleider, L. G., Mishkin, M., Carson, R. E., et al. (1991). Dissociation of object and spatial visual processing pathways in human extrastriate cortex. *Proceedings of the National Academy of Sciences, USA, 88,* 1621–1625.

Hedera, P., Wu, D., Collins, S., Lewin, J. S., Miller, D., Lerner, A. J., et al. (1998). Sex and electroencephalographic synchronization after photic stimulation predict signal changes in the visual cortex on functional MR images. *American Journal of Neuroradiology, 19,* 853–857.

Heeger, D. J. (1999). Linking visual perception with human brain activity. *Current Opinion in Neurobiology, 9,* 474–479.

Helstrup, T., & Anderson, R. E. (1991). Imagery in mental construction and decomposition tasks. In R. H. Logie & M. Denis (Eds). *Mental images in human cognition* (pp. 229–240). Oxford, England: North-Holland.

Helstrup, T., & Anderson, R. E. (1996). On the generality of mental construction in imagery: When bananas become smiles. *European Journal of Cognitive Psychology, 8,* 275–293.

Hong, J. H., McMichael, I., Chang, T. Y., Christian, W., & Paek, E. G. (1995). Volume holographic memory systems: Techniques and architectures. *Optical Engineering, 34,* 2193–2203.

Howard, R. J., ffytche, D. H., Barnes, J., McKeefry, D., Ha, Y., Woodruff, P. W., et al. (1998). The functional anatomy of imagining and perceiving colour. *Neuroreport, 9,* 1019–1023.

Hubel, D. H. (1988). *Eye, brain and vision.* New York: W.H. Freeman.

Ingle, D. (2002). Problems with a "cortical screen" for visual imagery. *Behavioral and Brain Sciences, 25,* 195–196.

Intons-Peterson, M. J. (1983). Imagery paradigms: How vulnerable are they to experimenters' expectations? *Journal of Experimental Psychology: Human Perception and Performance, 9,* 394–412.

Intraub, H., & Hoffman, J. E. (1992). Reading and visual memory: Remembering scenes that were never seen. *American Journal of Psychology, 105,* 101–114.

Intriligator, J., & Cavanagh, P. (2001). The spatial resolution of visual attention. *Cognitive Psychology, 43,* 171–216.

Ishai, A., Haxby, J. V., & Ungerleider, L. G. (2002). Visual imagery of famous faces: Effects of memory and attention revealed by fMRI. *NeuroImage, 17,* 1729–1741.

Ishai, A., Ungerleider, L. G., & Haxby, J. V. (2000). Distributed neural systems for the generation of visual images. *Neuron, 28,* 979–990.

James, W. (1892/1962). *Psychology, briefer course.* New York: Collier.

James, W. (1896). Address of the president before the Society for Psychical Research. *Science, New Series, 3,* 881–888.

Jankowiak, J., Kinsbourne, M., Shalev, R. S., & Bachman, D. L. (1992). Preserved visual imagery and categorization in a case of associative visual agnosia. *Journal of Cognitive Neuroscience, 4,* 119–131.

Johnson, M. K., & Raye, C. L. (1981). Reality monitoring. *Psychological Review, 88,* 67–85.

Jolicoeur, P., & Kosslyn, S. M. (1985). Is time to scan visual images due to demand characteristics? *Memory and Cognition, 13,* 320–332.

Julesz, B. (1971). *Foundations of cyclopean perception.* Chicago: University of Chicago Press.

Just, M. A., & Carpenter, P. A. (1976). Eye fixations and cognitive processes. *Cognitive Psychology, 8,* 441–480.

Kastner, S., Demmer, I., & Ziemann, U. (1998). Transient visual field defects induced by transcranial magnetic stimulation over human occipital pole. *Experimental Brain Research, 118,* 19–26.

Kaufman, L., & Richards, W. (1969). Spontaneous fixation tendencies for visual forms. *Perception and Psychophysics, 5,* 85–88.

Kawashima, R., Roland, P. E., & O'Sullivan, B. T. (1995). Functional anatomy of reaching and visuomotor learning: A positron emission tomography study. *Cerebral Cortex, 5,* 111–122.

Kerr, N. H. (1983). The role of vision in "visual imagery" experiments: Evidence from the congenitally blind. *Journal of Experimental Psychology: General, 112,* 265–277.

Klein, I., Dubois, J., Mangin, J. M., Kherif, F., Flandin, G., Poline, et al. (2004). Retinotopic organization of visual mental images as revealed by functional magnetic resonance imaging. *Cognitive Brain Research, 22*(1), 26–31.

Klein, I., Paradis, A.-L., Poline, J.-B., Kosslyn, S. M., & Le Bihan, D. (2000). Transient activity in human calcarine cortex during visual imagery: An event-related fMRI study. *Journal of Cognitive Neuroscience, 12,* 15S-23S.

Knauff, M., Kassubek, J., Mulack, T., & Greenlee, M. W. (2000). Cortical activation evoked by visual mental imagery as measured by fMRI. *NeuroReport, 11,* 3957–3962.

Koechlin, E., Basso, G., Pietrini, P., Panzer, S., & Grafman, J. (1999). The role of the anterior prefrontal cortex in human cognition. *Nature, 399,* 148–151.

Kosslyn, S. M. (1973). Scanning visual images: Some structural implications. *Perception and Psychophysics, 14,* 90–94.

Kosslyn, S. M. (1975). Information representation in visual images. *Cognitive Psychology, 7,* 341–370.

Kosslyn, S. M. (1976). Can imagery be distinguished from other forms of internal representation? Evidence from studies of information retrieval times. *Memory and Cognition, 4,* 291–297.

Kosslyn, S. M. (1978). Measuring the visual angle of the mind's eye. *Cognitive Psychology, 10,* 356–389.

Kosslyn, S. M. (1980). *Image and mind.* Cambridge, MA: Harvard University Press.

Kosslyn, S. M. (1981). The medium and the message in mental imagery: A theory. *Psychological Review, 8,* 46–66.

Kosslyn, S. M. (1983). *Ghosts in the mind's machine.* New York: W. W. Norton.

Kosslyn, S. M. (1987). Seeing and imagining in the cerebral hemispheres: A computational approach. *Psychological Review, 94,* 148–175.

Kosslyn, S. M. (1994). *Image and brain: The resolution of the imagery debate.* Cambridge, MA: MIT Press.

Kosslyn, S. M. (in preparation). *Imagining mind.* New York: Oxford University Press.

Kosslyn, S. M., & Alpert, S. N. (1977). On the pictorial properties of visual images: Effects of image size on memory for words. *Canadian Journal of Psychology, 31*, 32–40.

Kosslyn, S. M., Alpert, N. M., Thompson, W. L., Chabris, C. F., Rauch, S. L., & Anderson, A. K. (1994). Identifying objects seen from different viewpoints: A PET investigation. *Brain, 117*, 1055–1071.

Kosslyn, S. M., Alpert, N. M., Thompson, W. L., Maljkovic, V., Weise, S. B., Chabris, C. F., et al. (1993). Visual mental imagery activates topographically organized visual cortex: PET investigations. *Journal of Cognitive Neuroscience, 5*, 263–287.

Kosslyn, S. M., Ball, T. M., & Reiser, B. J. (1978). Visual images preserve metric spatial information: Evidence from studies of image scanning. *Journal of Experimental Psychology: Human Perception and Performance, 4*, 47–60.

Kosslyn, S. M., & Cave, C. B. (1984). *Dissociation between reduced perceptual and imagery fields.* Unpublished raw data.

Kosslyn, S. M., Cave, C. B., Provost, D., & Von Gierke, S. (1988). Sequential processes in image generation. *Cognitive Psychology, 20*, 319–343.

Kosslyn, S. M., Flynn, R. A., Amsterdam, J. B., & Wang, G. (1990). Components of high-level vision: A cognitive neuroscience analysis and accounts of neurological syndromes. *Cognition, 34*, 203–277.

Kosslyn, S. M., Ganis, G., & Thompson, W. L. (2001). Neural foundations of imagery. *Nature Reviews Neuroscience, 2*, 635–642.

Kosslyn, S. M., Ganis, G., & Thompson, W. L. (2003). Mental imagery: Against the nihilistic hypothesis. *Trends in Cognitive Sciences, 7*, 109–111.

Kosslyn, S. M., & Jolicoeur, P. (1980). A theory-based approach to the study of individual differences in mental imagery. In R. E. Snow, P-A. Fredrico, & W. E. Montague (Eds.), *Aptitude, learning, and instruction: Cognitive processes analyses.* Hillsdale, NJ: Erlbaum.

Kosslyn, S. M., & Koenig, O. (1992). *Wet mind: The new cognitive neuroscience.* New York: The Free Press.

Kosslyn, S. M., Pascual-Leone, A., Felician, O., Camposano, S., Keenan, J. P., Thompson, W. L., et al. (1999). The role of area 17 in visual imagery: Convergent evidence from PET and rTMS. *Science, 284*, 167–170.

Kosslyn, S. M., & Pomerantz, J. R. (1977). Imagery, propositions, and the form of internal representations. *Cognitive Psychology, 9*, 52–76.

Kosslyn, S. M., Reiser, B. J., Farah, M. J., & Fliegel, S. J. (1983). Generating visual images: Units and relations. *Journal of Experimental Psychology: General 112*, 278–303.

Kosslyn, S. M., Shin, L. M., Thompson, W. L., McNally, R. J., Rauch, S. L., Pitman, R. K., et al. (1996). Neural effects of visualizing and perceiving aversive stimuli: A PET investigation. *NeuroReport, 7*, 1569–1576.

Kosslyn, S. M., & Shwartz, S. P. (1977). A simulation of visual imagery. *Cognitive Science, 1*, 265–295.

Kosslyn, S. M., & Shwartz, S. P. (1978). Visual images as spatial representations in active memory. In E. M. Riseman & A. R. Hanson (Eds.), *Computer vision systems.* New York: Academic Press.

Kosslyn, S. M., Sukel, K. E., & Bly, B. M. (1999). Squinting with the mind's eye: Effects of stimulus resolution on imaginal and perceptual comparisons. *Memory and Cognition, 27,* 276–287.

Kosslyn, S. M., & Thompson, W. L. (2003). When is early visual cortex activated during visual mental imagery? *Psychological Bulletin, 129,* 723–746.

Kosslyn, S. M., Thompson, W. L., & Alpert, N. M. (1995). Identifying objects at different levels of hierarchy: A positron emission tomography study. *Human Brain Mapping, 3,* 107–132.

Kosslyn, S. M., Thompson, W. L., & Alpert, N. M. (1997). Neural systems shared by visual imagery and visual perception: A positron emission tomography study. *NeuroImage, 6,* 320–334.

Kosslyn, S. M., Thompson, W. L., Costantini-Ferrando, M. F., Alpert, N. M., & Spiegel, D. (2000). Hypnotic visual illusion alters color processing in the brain. *American Journal of Psychiatry, 157,* 1279–1284.

Kosslyn, S. M., Thompson, W. L., Gitelman, D. R., & Alpert, N. M. (1998). Neural systems that encode categorical vs. coordinate spatial relations: PET investigations. *Psychobiology, 26,* 333–347.

Kosslyn, S. M., Thompson, W. L., Kim, I. J., & Alpert, N. M. (1995). Topographical representations of mental images in primary visual cortex. *Nature, 378,* 496–498.

Kosslyn, S. M., Thompson, W. L., Kim, I. J., Rauch, S. L., & Alpert, N. M. (1996). Individual differences in cerebral blood flow in area 17 predict the time to evaluate visualized letters. *Journal of Cognitive Neuroscience, 8,* 78–82.

Kosslyn, S. M., Thompson, W. L., Shephard, J. M., Ganis, G., Bell, D., Danovitch, J., et al. (2004). Brain rCBF and performance in visual imagery tasks: Common and distinct processes. *European Journal of Cognitive Psychology, 16,* 696–716.

Kosslyn, S. M., Thompson, W. L., Sukel, K. E., & Alpert, N. M. (2005). Two types of image generation: Evidence from PET. *Cognitive, Affective and Behavioral Neuroscience, 5*(1), 41–53.

Kosslyn, S. M., Thompson, W. L., Wraga, M., & Alpert, N. M. (2001). Imagining rotation by endogenous and exogenous forces: Distinct neural mechanisms for different strategies. *Neuroreport, 12,* 2519–2525.

Koulakov, A. A., & Chklovskii, D. B. (2001). Orientation preference patterns in mammalian visual cortex: A wire length minimization approach. *Neuron, 29,* 519–527.

Kowler, E. (1990). The role of visual and cognitive processes in the control of eye movement. In E. Kowler (Ed.), *Reviews of oculomotor research: Vol. 4. Eye movements and their role in visual and cognitive processes* (pp. 1–70). Amsterdam: Elsevier.

Kowler, E., Benson, G. E., & Steinman, R. M. (1975). *The role of small saccades in small decisions.* Paper presented at the 16th annual meeting of the Psychonomic Society, Denver, Colorado, November.

Kozhevnikov, M., Hegarty, M., & Mayer, R. E. (2002). Revisiting the visualizer-verbalizer dimension: Evidence for two types of visualizers. *Cognition & Instruction, 20,* 47–78.

Kozhevnikov, M., & Kosslyn, S. M. (2000). *Revising the visualizer/verbalizer cognitive style: Two orthogonal types of visualizers.* Paper presented at 41st Annual Meeting of the Psychonomic Society, New Orleans, November 19–22.

Kozhevnikov, M., Kosslyn, S. M., & Shephard, J. M. (2005). Spatial versus object visualizers: A new characterization of visual cognitive style. *Memory and Cognition, 33*(4), 710–726.

Kuhn, T. S. (1962). *The structure of scientific revolutions.* Chicago: University of Chicago Press.

Kuo, W.-J., Chen, C.-F., Hung, D., Tzeng, O., & Hsieh, J.-C. (2000). A fMRI study on mental imagery with Chinese character generation. *NeuroImage, 11,* S108.

Kwong, K. K., Belliveau, J. W., Chesler, D. A., Goldberg, I. E., Weisskoff, R. M., Poncelet, B. P., et al. (1992). Dynamic magnetic resonance imaging of human brain activity during primary sensory stimulation. *Proceedings of the National Academy of Sciences, USA, 89,* 5675–5679.

LaBerge, D., & Buchsbaum, M. S. (1990). Positron emission tomography measurements of pulvinar activity during an attention task. *Journal of Neuroscience, 10,* 613–619.

Laeng, B., Chabris, C. F., & Kosslyn, S. M. (2002). Spatial relations and the brain: Review and meta-analysis. In K. Hugdahl & R. J. Davidson (Eds.), *Brain asymmetry* (2nd ed.). Cambridge, MA: MIT Press.

Laeng, B., & Teodorescu, D.-S. (2002). Eye scanpaths during visual imagery reenact those of perception of the same visual scene. *Cognitive Science, 26,* 207–231.

Lambert, S., Sampaio, E., Scheiber, C., & Mauss, Y. (2002). Neural substrates of animal mental imagery: Calcarine sulcus and dorsal pathway involvement— An fMRI study. *Brain Research, 924,* 176–183.

Lea, G. (1975). Chronometric analysis of the method of loci. *Journal of Experimental Psychology: Human Perception & Performance, 1,* 95–104.

Le Bihan, D., Turner, R., Zeffiro, T. A., Cuénod, C. A., Jezzard, P., & Bonnerot, V. (1993). Activation of human primary visual cortex during visual recall: A magnetic resonance imaging study. *Proceedings of the National Academy of Sciences, USA, 90,* 11802–11805.

LeDoux, J. (1996). *The emotional brain.* New York: Simon and Schuster.

Lee, C. C., Jack, C. R., & Riederer, S. J. (1998). Mapping of the central sulcus with functional MR: Active versus passive activation tasks. *American Journal of Neuroradiology, 19,* 847–852.

Levin, D. T., & Simons, D. J. (1997). Failure to detect changes to attended objects in motion pictures. *Psychonomic Bulletin & Review, 4*(4), 501–506.

Levine, D. N., Warach, J., & Farah, M. J. (1985). Two visual systems in mental imagery: Dissociation of "what" and "where" in imagery disorders due to bilateral posterior cerebral lesions. *Neurology, 35,* 1010–1018.

Li, B., Peterson, M. R., & Freeman, R. D. (2003). Oblique effect: A neural basis in the visual cortex. *Journal of Neurophysiology, 90*(1), 204–217.

Luria, A. R. (1980). *Higher cortical functions in man.* New York: Basic Books.

Malach, R., Levy, I., & Hasson, U. (2002). The topography of high-order human object areas. *Trends in Cognitive Sciences, 6,* 176–184.

Marks, D. F. (1973). Visual imagery differences in the recall of pictures. *British Journal of Psychology, 64,* 17–24.

Marmor, G. S. (1978). Age at onset of blindness and the development of the semantics of color names. *Journal of Experimental Child Psychology, 25,* 267–278.

Marmor, G. S., & Zaback, L. A. (1976). Mental rotation by the blind: Does mental rotation depend on visual imagery? *Journal of Experimental Psychology: Human Perception & Performance, 2,* 515–521.

Marr, D. (1982). *Vision: A computational investigation into the human representation and processing of visual information.* New York: W. H. Freeman.

Marsolek, C. J., Nicholas, C. D., & Andersen, D. R. (2002). Interhemispheric communication of abstract and specific visual-form information. *Neuropsychologia, 40,* 1983–1999.

Mast, F., Berthoz, A., & Kosslyn, S. M. (2001). Mental imagery of visual motion modifies the perception of roll-vection stimulation. *Perception, 30,* 945–957.

Mast, F. W., & Kosslyn, S. M. (2002). Visual mental images can be ambiguous: Insights from individual differences in spatial transformation abilities. *Cognition, 86,* 57–70.

Mast, F., Kosslyn, S. M., & Berthoz, A. (1999). Visual mental imagery interferes with allocentric orientation judgments. *Neuroreport, 10,* 3549–3553.

Maturana, H. R., & Varela, F. J. (1980). Autopoiesis and cognition: The realization of the living, Vol. 42, *Boston Studies in the Philosophy of Science.* Dordrecht, The Netherlands: D. Reidel Publishing Company.

Mazard, A., Mazoyer, B., Etard, O., Tzourio-Mazoyer, N., Kosslyn, S. M., & Mellet, E. (2002). Impact of fMRI acoustic noise on the functional anatomy of visual mental imagery. *Journal of Cognitive Neuroscience, 14,* 172–186.

Mazard, A., Tzourio-Mazoyer, N., Crivello, F., Mazoyer, B., & Mellet, E. (2004). A PET meta-analysis of object and spatial mental imagery. *European Journal of Cognitive Psychology, 16*(5), 673–695.

McAuliffe, S. P., & Knowlton, B. J. (2000). Long-term retinotopic priming in object identification. *Perception and Psychophysics, 62,* 953–959.

McCrone, J. (2001). *Going inside: A tour round a single moment of consciousness.* New York: International Publishing Corp.

McDermott, K. B., & Roediger, H. L. (1994). Effects of imagery on perceptual implicit memory tests. *Journal of Experimental Psychology: Learning, Memory and Cognition, 20,* 1379–1390.

Meador, K. J., Loring, D. W., Bowers, D., & Heilman, K. M. (1987). Remote memory and neglect syndrome. *Neurology, 37,* 522–526.

Mellet, E., Bricogne, S., Tzourio-Mazoyer, N., Ghaëm, O., Petit, L., Zago, L., et al. (2000). Neural correlates of topographic mental exploration: The impact of route *versus* survey perspective learning. *NeuroImage, 12,* 588–600.

Mellet, E., Tzourio, N., Crivello, F., Joliot, M., Denis, M., & Mazoyer, B. (1996). Functional anatomy of spatial mental imagery generated from verbal instructions. *Journal of Neuroscience, 16,* 6504–6512.

Mellet, E., Tzourio, N., Denis, M., & Mazoyer, B. (1995). A positron emission tomography study of visual and mental spatial exploration. *Journal of Cognitive Neuroscience, 4,* 433–445.

Mellet, E., Tzourio N., Denis, M., & Mazoyer, B. (1998). Cortical anatomy of mental imagery of concrete nouns based on their dictionary definition. *Neuroreport, 9,* 803–808.

Mellet, E., Tzourio-Mazoyer, N., Bricogne, S., Mazoyer, B., Kosslyn, S. M., & Denis, M. (2000). Functional anatomy of high-resolution visual mental imagery. *Journal of Cognitive Neuroscience, 12,* 98–109.

Menard, S. (2002). *Applied logistic regression analysis* (2nd ed.). Thousand Oaks, CA: Sage Publications.

Menon, R., Ogawa, S., Tank, D. W., Ellermann, J. M., Merkele, H., & Ugurbil, K. (1993). Visual mental imagery by functional brain MRI. In D. Le Bihan, R. Turner, M. Mosley, & J. Hyde (Eds.), *Functional MRI of the brain: A workshop.* Arlington, VA: Society for Magnetic Resonance in Medicine.

Mesulam, M.-M. (1981). A cortical network for directed attention and unilateral neglect. *Annals of Neurology, 10,* 309–325.

Mesulam, M.-M. (1990). Large-scale neurocognitive networks and distributed processing for attention, language, and memory. *Annals of Neurology, 28,* 597–613.

Metzler, J., & Shepard, R. (1974). Transformational studies of the internal representation of three-dimensional objects. In R. Solso (Ed.), *Theories in cognitive psychology: The Loyola Symposium.* Potomac, MD: Lawrence Erlbaum.

Millar, S. (2002). Imagery and blindness. *Behavioral and Brain Sciences, 25,* 201–202.

Miller, A. I. (2000). *Insights of genius: Imagery and creativity in science and art.* Cambridge, MA: MIT Press.

Milner, A. D., & Goodale, M. A. (1995). *The visual brain in action.* Oxford: Oxford University Press.

Mishkin, M., Ungerleider, L. G., & Macko, K. A. (1983). Object vision and spatial vision: Two cortical pathways. *Trends in Neurosciences, 6,* 414–417.

Miyashita, Y. (1995). How the brain creates imagery: Projection to primary visual cortex. *Science, 268,* 1719–1720.

Miyashita, Y., & Chang, H. S. (1988). Neuronal correlate of pictorial short-term memory in the primate temporal cortex. *Nature, 331,* 68–70.

Miyashita, Y., & Hayashi, T. (2000). Neural representation of visual objects: Encoding and top-down activation. *Current Opinion in Neurobiology, 10,* 187–194.

Moran, T. P. (1973). The symbolic imagery hypothesis: An empirical investigation via a production system simulation of human behavior in a visualization task: I & II. *Dissertation Abstracts International, 35* (1-B), 551–552.

Moscovitch, M. (1973). Language and the cerebral hemispheres: Reaction time studies and their implications for models of cerebral dominance. In P. Pliner,

L. Krames, & T. Alloway (Eds.), *Communication and affect: Language and thought.* New York: Academic Press.

Mumford, D. (1991). On the computational architecture of the neocortex II: The role of cortico-cortical loops. *Biological Cybernetics, 65,* 241–251.

Munchau, A., Bloem, B. R., Irlbacher, K., Trimble, M. R., & Rothwell, J. C. (2002). Functional connectivity of human premotor and motor cortex explored with repetitive transcranial magnetic stimulation. *Journal of Neuroscience, 22,* 554–561.

Nakayama, K., & Mackeben, M. (1989). Sustained and transient components of focal visual attention. *Vision Research, 29,* 1631–1647.

Neisser, U. (1967). *Cognitive psychology.* New York: Appleton-Century-Crofts.

Neisser, U. (1976). *Cognition and reality.* San Francisco: W. H. Freeman.

Newell, A., Shaw, J. C., & Simon, H. A. (1957). Empirical explorations of the logic theory machine: A case study in heuristics. In *Proceedings of the 1957 Western Joint Computer Conference.* Western Joint Computer Conference.

Nielsen, G. D., & Smith, E. E. (1973). Imaginal and verbal representations in short-term recognition of visual forms. *Journal of Experimental Psychology, 101,* 375–378.

Oakley, D. A., Whitman, L. G., & Halligan, P. W. (2002). Hypnotic imagery as a treatment for phantom limb pain: Two case reports and a review. *Clinical Rehabilitation, 16,* 368–377.

O'Craven, K. M., & Kanwisher, N. (2000). Mental imagery of faces and places activates corresponding stimulus-specific brain regions. *Journal of Cognitive Neuroscience, 12,* 1013–1023.

Ogawa, S., Tank, D. W., Menon, R., Ellermann, J. M., Kim, S. G., Merkle, H., et al. (1992). Intrinsic signal changes accompanying sensory stimulation: Functional brain mapping with magnetic resonance imaging. *Proceedings of the National Academy of Sciences, USA, 89,* 5951–5955.

O'Regan, J. K. (1992). Solving the real mysteries of visual perception: The world as an outside memory. *Canadian Journal of Psychology, 46,* 461–488.

O'Regan, J. K., & Noë, A. (2001). A sensorimotor account of vision and visual consciousness. *Behavioral and Brain Sciences, 24,* 939–1011.

O'Regan, J. K., Rensink, R. A., & Clark, J. J. (1999). Change-blindness as a result of "mudsplashes." *Nature, 398*(6722), 34.

Osborne, L. C., Bialek, W., & Lisberger, S. G. (2004). Time course of information about motion direction in visual area MT of macaque monkeys. *Journal of Neuroscience, 24,* 3210–3222.

Paivio, A. (1971). *Imagery and verbal processes.* New York: Holt, Rinehart and Winston.

Palmer, S. E. (1978). Fundamental aspects of cognitive representation. In E. Rosch & B. Lloyd (Eds.), *Cognition and categorization.* Hillsdale, NJ: Erlbaum.

Paus, T., Marrett, S., Worsley, K. J., & Evans, A. C. (1995). Extraretinal modulation of cerebral blood flow in the human visual cortex: Implications for saccadic suppression. *Journal of Neurophysiology, 74,* 2179–2183.

Peterson, M. A. (1993). The ambiguity of mental images: Insights regarding the structure of shape memory and its function in creativity. In B. Roskos-

Ewoldsen, M. J. Intons-Peterson, & R. Anderson (Eds.), *Imagery, creativity, and discovery: A cognitive perspective.* Amsterdam: North Holland.

Peterson, M. A., Kihlstrom, J. F., Rose, P. M., & Glisky, M. L. (1992). Mental images can be ambiguous: Reconstruals and reference-frame reversals. *Memory & Cognition, 20,* 107–123.

Pinker, S. (1980). Mental imagery and the third dimension. *Journal of Experimental Psychology: General, 109*(3), 354–371.

Pinker, S., Choate, P., & Finke, R. A. (1984). Mental extrapolation in patterns constructed from memory. *Memory and Cognition, 12,* 207–218.

Pinker, S., & Kosslyn, S. M. (1983). Theories of mental imagery. In A. A. Sheikh (Ed.), *Imagery: Current theory, research, and application.* New York: Wiley.

Podgorny, P., & Shepard, R. N. (1978). Functional representations common to visual perception and imagination. *Journal of Experimental Psychology: Human Perception and Performance, 4,* 21–35.

Podzebenko, K., Egan, G. F., & Watson, J. D. (2005). Real and imaginary rotary motion processing: functional parcellation of the human parietal lobe revealed by fMRI. *Journal of Cognitive Neuroscience, 17,* 24–36.

Popper, K. (1959). *The logic of scientific discovery.* London: Hutchinson.

Posner, M. I., & Petersen, S. E. (1990). The attention system of the human brain. In W. M. Cowan, E. M. Shooter, C. F. Stevens, & R. F. Thompson (Eds.), *Annual review of neuroscience* (pp. 25–42). Palo Alto, CA: Annual Reviews.

Posner, M. I., Snyder, C. R., & Davidson, B. J. (1980). Attention and the detection of signals. *Journal of Experimental Psychology, 109,* 160–174.

Psaltis, D., & Mok, F. (1995). Holographic memories. *Scientific American, 273,* 70–76.

Putnam, H. (1973). Reductionism and the nature of psychology. *Cognition, 2,* 131–146.

Pütz, B., Miyauchi, S., Sasaki, Y., Takino, R., Ohki, M., & Okamoto, J. (1996). Activation of the visual cortex by imagery used in mental calculations. *NeuroImage 3,* S215.

Pylyshyn, Z. W. (1973). What the mind's eye tells the mind's brain: A critique of mental imagery. *Psychological Bulletin, 80,* 1–24.

Pylyshyn, Z. W. (1975). *Do we need images and analogues?* Paper presented at the Conference on Theoretical Issues in Natural Language Processing, June 10–13, Cambridge, MA.

Pylyshyn, Z. W. (1981). The imagery debate: Analogue media versus tacit knowledge. *Psychological Review, 87,* 16–45.

Pylyshyn, Z. W. (1984). *Computation and cognition: Toward a foundation for cognitive science.* Cambridge, MA: MIT Press.

Pylyshyn, Z. W. (1991a). Rules and representation: Chomsky and representational realism. In A. Kashir (Ed.), *The Chomskian turn* (pp. 231–251). Oxford: Basil Blackwell.

Pylyshyn, Z. W. (1991b). The role of cognitive architectures in theories of cognition. In K. VanLehn (Ed.), *Architectures for intelligence* (pp. 189–223). Hillsdale, NJ: Erlbaum.

Pylyshyn, Z. W. (2002). Mental imagery: In search of a theory. *Behavioral and Brain Sciences, 25,* 157–238.

Pylyshyn, Z. W. (2003). Return of the mental image: Are there pictures in the brain? *Trends in Cognitive Sciences, 7,* 113–118.

Raab, M., & Boschker, M. (2002). Time matters! Implications from mentally imaged motor actions. *Behavioral and Brain Sciences, 25,* 208–209.

Rao, S. C., Rainer, G., & Miller, E. K. (1997). Integration of what and where in the primate prefrontal cortex. *Science, 276,* 821–824.

Rauch, S. L., van der Kolk, B. A., Fisler, R. E., Alpert, N. M., Orr, S. P., Savage, C., et al. (1996). A symptom provocation study of posttraumatic stress disorder using positron emission tomography and script-driven imagery. *Archives of General Psychiatry, 53,* 380–387.

Reed, S. K. (1974). Structural descriptions and the limitations of visual images. *Memory & Cognition, 2,* 319–336.

Reed, S. K., & Johnsen, J. A. (1975). Detection of parts in patterns and images. *Memory & Cognition, 3,* 569–575.

Reid, L. S. (1974). Toward a grammar of the image. *Psychological Bulletin, 81,* 319–334.

Reisberg, D. (1996). The non-ambiguity of mental images. In C. Cornoldi, R. Logie, M. Brandimonte, G. Kaufmann, & D. Reisberg (Eds.), *Stretching the imagination: Representation and transformation in mental imagery* (pp. 119–172). New York: Oxford University Press.

Reisberg, D. (1998). Constraints on image-based discovery: A comment on Rouw et al. (1997). *Cognition, 66,* 95–102.

Reisberg, D. & Chambers, D. (1991). Neither pictures nor propositions: What can we learn from a mental image? *Canadian Journal of Psychology, 45,* 336–352.

Reisberg, D., Pearson, D. G., & Kosslyn, S. M. (2003). Intuitions and introspections about imagery: The role of imagery experience in shaping an investigator's theoretical views. *Applied Cognitive Psychology, 17,* 147–160.

Rensink, R. A. (2002). Change detection. *Annual Review of Psychology, 53,* 245–277.

Rensink, R. A., O'Regan, J. K., & Clark, J. J. (2000). On the failure to detect changes in scenes across brief interruptions. *Visual Cognition, 7,* 127–145.

Rensink, R. A., O'Regan, J. K., & Clark, J. J. (1997). To see or not to see: The need for attention to perceive changes in scenes. *Psychological Science, 8*(5), 368–373.

Rockland, K. S., & Drash, G. W. (1996). Collateralized divergent feedback connections that target multiple cortical areas. *Journal of Comparative Neurology, 373*(4), 529–548.

Rockland, K. S., Saleem, K. S., & Tanaka, K. (1992). Widespread feedback connections from areas V4 and TEO. *Society for Neuroscience Abstracts, 18,* 390.

Roeder, B., & Roesler, F. (1998). Visual input does not facilitate the scanning of spatial images. *Journal of Mental Imagery, 22,* 165–182.

Roelfsema, P. R., & Spekreijse, H. (2001). The representation of erroneously perceived stimuli in the primary visual cortex. *Neuron, 31,* 853–863.

Roland, P., Eriksson, L., Stone-Elander, S., & Widen, L. (1987). Does mental activity change the oxidative metabolism of the brain? *Journal of Neuroscience, 7,* 2373–2389.

Roland, P. E., & Friberg, L. (1985). Localization of cortical areas activated by thinking. *Journal of Neurophysiology, 53,* 1219–1243.

Roland, P. E., & Gulyás, B. (1995). Visual memory, visual imagery and visual recognition of large field patterns by human brain: Functional anatomy by positron emission tomography. *Cerebral Cortex, 1,* 79–93.

Roland, P. E., Gulyás, B., Seitz, R. J., Bohm, C., & Stone-Elander, S. (1990). Functional anatomy of storage, recall, and recognition of a visual pattern in man. *NeuroReport, 1,* 53–56.

Rollins, M. (2001). The strategic eye: Kosslyn's theory of perception and imagery. *Minds and Machines, 11,* 267–286.

Rorty, R. (1979). *Philosophy and the mirror of nature.* Princeton, NJ: Princeton University Press.

Rouw, R., Kosslyn, S. M., & Hamel, R. (1997). Detecting high-level and low-level properties in visual images and visual percepts. *Cognition, 63,* 209–226.

Rouw, R., Kosslyn, S. M., & Hamel, R. (1998). Aspects of mental images: Is it possible to get the picture? *Cognition, 66,* 103–107.

Rubin, N., Nakayama, K., & Shapley, R. (1996). Enhanced perception of illusory contours in the lower versus upper visual hemifields. *Science, 271,* 651–653.

Rumelhart, D. E., McClelland, J. L., & the PDP Research Group (1986). *Parallel distributed processing: Explorations in the microstructure of cognition, Vols. 1 and 2.* Cambridge, MA: MIT Press.

Sabbah, P., Simond, G., Levrier, O., Habib, M., Trabaud, V., Murayama, N., et al. (1995). Functional magnetic resonance imaging at 1.5 T during sensorimotor and cognitive tasks. *European Neurology, 35,* 131–136.

Sack, A. T., Sperling, J. M., Prvulovic, D., Formisano, E., Goebel, R., Di Salle, F., et al. (2002). Tracking the mind's image in the brain II: Transcranial magnetic stimulation reveals parietal asymmetry in visuospatial imagery. *Neuron, 35,* 195–204.

Saenz, M., Buracas, G. T., & Boynton, G. M. (2002). Global effects of feature-based attention in human visual cortex. *Nature Neuroscience, 5,* 631–632.

Salin, P.-A., & Bullier, J. (1995). Corticocortical connections in the visual system: Structure and function. *Physiological Reviews, 75,* 107–154.

Sartre, J-P. (1948). *The psychology of imagination.* New York: Citadel Press. (Original work published 1940).

Schacter, D. L. (1987). Implicit memory: History and current status. *Journal of Experimental Psychology: Learning, Memory, and Cognition, 13,* 501–518.

Schacter, D. L. (1996). *Searching for memory.* New York: Basic Books.

Schlack, A., Hoffmann, K.-P., & Bremmer, F. (2003). Selectivity of macaque ventral intraparietal area (area VIP) for smooth pursuit eye movements. *Journal of Physiology, 551*(2), 551–561.

Schlaegel, T. F. (1953). The dominant method of imagery in blind compared to sighted adolescents. *Journal of Genetic Psychology, 83,* 265–277.

Sekuler, R., & Nash, D. (1972). Speed of size scaling in human vision. *Psychonomic Science, 27,* 93–94.

Sengpiel, F., & Huebener, M. (1999). Spotlight on the primary visual cortex. *Current Biology, 9,* R318-R321.

Sereno, M. I., Dale, A. M., Reppas, J. B., Kwong, K. K., Belliveau, J. W., Brady, T. J., et al. (1995). Borders of multiple visual areas in humans revealed by functional magnetic resonance imaging. *Science, 268,* 889–893.

Sereno, M. I., Pitzalis, S., & Martinez, A. (2001). Mapping of contralateral space in retinotopic coordinates by a parietal cortical area in humans. *Science, 294,* 1350–1354.

Shadlen, M. N., & Newsome, W. T. (1996). Motion perception: seeing and deciding. *Proceedings of the National Academy of Sciences, USA, 93,* 628–633.

Shenefelt, P. D. (2003). Hypnosis-facilitated relaxation using self-guided imagery during dermatologic procedures. *American Journal of Clinical Hypnosis, 45,* 225–232.

Shepard, R. N., & Cooper, L. A. (1982). *Mental images and their transformations.* Cambridge, MA: MIT Press.

Shepard, R. N., & Cooper, L. A. (1992). Representation of colors in the blind, color-blind, and normally sighted. *Psychological Science, 3,* 97–104.

Shepard, R. N., & Feng, C. (1972). A chronometric study of mental paper folding. *Cognitive Psychology, 3,* 228–243.

Shepard, R. N., & Metzler, J. (1971). Mental rotation of three-dimensional objects. *Science, 171,* 701–703.

Shin, L. M., McNally, R. J., Kosslyn, S. M., Thompson, W. L., Rauch, S. L., Alpert, N. M., et al. (1999). Regional cerebral blood flow during script-driven imagery in childhood sexual abuse-related PTSD: A PET investigation. *American Journal of Psychiatry, 156,* 575–584.

Shuttleworth, E. C., Syring, V., & Allen, N. (1982). Further observations on the nature of prosopagnosia. *Brain and Cognition, 1,* 302–332.

Simons, D. J., & Levin, D. T. (1997). Change blindness. *Trends in Cognitive Science, 1,* 261–267.

Skinner, B. F. (1974). *About behaviorism.* New York: Knopf.

Skinner, B. F. (1977). Why I am not a cognitive psychologist. *Behaviorism, 5,* 1–10.

Slezak, P. P. (2002). The imagery debate: *Déjà-vu* all over again? *Behavioral and Brain Sciences, 25,* 209–210.

Slotnick, S. D., Thompson, W. L., & Kosslyn, S. M. (2005). Visual mental imagery induces retinotopically organized activation of early visual areas. *Cerebral Cortex, 15*(10), 1570–1583.

Smith, E. E., & Jonides, J. (1997). Working memory: A view from neuroimaging. *Cognitive Psychology, 33,* 5–42.

Smith, E. E., & Jonides, J. (1999). Storage and executive processes in the frontal lobes. *Science, 283,* 1657–1661.

Sperling, G. (1960). The information available in brief visual presentations. *Psychological Monographs, 74,* 1–29.

Squire, L. R. (1987). *Memory and brain.* New York: Oxford University Press.

Stark, C. E., & Squire, L. R. (2001). When zero is not zero: The problem of ambiguous baseline conditions in fMRI. *Proceedings of the National Academy of Sciences, USA, 98,* 12760–12766.

Suchan, B., Yáguez, L., Wunderlich, G., Canavan, A. G. M., Herzog, H., Tellmann, L., et al. (2002). Neural correlates of visuospatial imagery. *Behavioral Brain Research 131,* 163–168.

Suzuki, W., Saleem, K. S., & Tanaka, K. (2000). Divergent backward projections from the anterior part of the inferotemporal cortex (area TE) in the macaque. *Journal of Comparative Neurology, 422,* 206–228.

Tabachnick, B. G., & Fidell, L. S. (1996). *Using multivariate statistics* (3rd ed.). New York: Harper Collins.

Tanaka, K. (1996). Inferotemporal cortex and object vision. *Annual Review of Neuroscience, 19,* 109–139.

Tanaka, K., Saito, H., Fukada, Y., & Moriya, M. (1991). Coding visual images of objects in the inferotemporal cortex of the macaque monkey. *Journal of Neurophysiology, 66,* 170–189.

Thierry, G., Ibarrola, D., Demonet, J. F., & Cardebat, D. (2003). Demand on verbal working memory delays haemodynamic response in the inferior prefrontal cortex. *Human Brain Mapping, 19,* 37–46.

Thomas, N. J. T. (1999). Are theories of imagery theories of imagination? An active perception approach to conscious mental content. *Cognitive Science, 23,* 207–245.

Thomas, N. J. T. (2002). The false dichotomy of imagery. *Behavioral and Brain Sciences, 25,* 211.

Thompson, W. L., & Kosslyn, S. M. (2000). Neural systems activated during visual mental imagery: A review and meta-analyses. In A. W. Toga & J. C. Mazziotta (Eds.), *Brain mapping: The systems* (pp. 535–560). San Diego, CA: Academic Press.

Thompson, W. L., Kosslyn, S. M., Sukel, K. E., & Alpert, N. M. (2001). Mental imagery of high- and low-resolution gratings activates Area 17. *NeuroImage, 14,* 454–464.

Thulborn, K. R., Waterton, J. C., Matthews, P. M., & Radda, G. K. (1982). Oxygenation dependence of the transverse relaxation time of water protons in whole blood at high field. *Biochimica et Biophysica Acta, 714,* 265–270.

Tippett, L. (1992). The generation of visual images: A review of neuropsychological research and theory. *Psychological Bulletin, 112,* 415–432.

Tolman, E. (1948). Cognitive maps in rats and men. *Psychological Review, 55,* 189–208.

Tootell, R. B. H., Hadjikani, N. K., Mendola, J. D., Marrett, S., & Dale, A. M. (1998). From retinotopy to recognition: fMRI in human visual cortex. *Trends in Cognitive Sciences, 2,* 174–183.

Tootell, R. B. H., Silverman, M. S., Switkes, E., & De Valois, R. L. (1982). Deoxyglucose analysis of retinotopic organization in primate striate cortex. *Science, 218,* 902–904.

Treisman, A. M., & Gelade, G. (1980). A feature integration theory of attention. *Cognitive Psychology, 12,* 97–136.

Trojano, L., Grossi, D., Linden, D. E. J., Formisano, E., Hacker, H., Zanella, F. E., et al. (2000). Matching two imagined clocks: The functional anatomy of spatial analysis in the absence of visual stimulation. *Cerebral Cortex, 10,* 473–481.

Tsao, D. Y., Vanduffel, W., Sasaki, Y., Fize, D., Knutsen, T. A., Mandeville, J. B., et al. (2003). Stereopsis activates V3A and caudal intraparietal areas in macaques and humans. *Neuron, 39,* 555–568.

Tye, M. (1991). *The imagery debate.* Cambridge, MA: MIT Press.

Ullman, S. (1995). Sequence of seeking and counter streams: A computational model for bidirectional information flow in the visual cortex. *Cerebral Cortex, 2,* 310–335.

Ungerleider, L. G., & Mishkin, M. (1982). Two cortical visual systems. In D. J. Ingle, M. A. Goodale, & R. J. W. Mansfield (Eds.), *Analysis of visual behavior* (pp. 549–586). Cambridge, MA: MIT Press.

Vandenberg, S. G., & Kuse, A. R. (1978). Mental rotations, a group test of three-dimensional spatial visualization. *Perceptual & Motor Skills, 47,* 599–604.

van der Kooij, K., Thompson, W. L., & Kosslyn, S. M. (2005). *The relative ease of "seeing" two types of properties in images.* Manuscript in preparation.

Van Essen, D. C. (1985). Functional organization of primate visual cortex. In A. Peters & E. G. Jones (Eds.), *Cerebral cortex, Vol. 3* (pp. 259–329). New York: Plenum Press.

Van Essen, D. C., Lewis, J. W., Drury, H. A., Hadjikhani, N., Tootell, R. B., Bakircioglu, M., et al. (2001). Mapping visual cortex in monkeys and humans using surface-based atlases. *Vision Research, 41,* 1359–1378.

Vecera, S. P., & Gilds, K. S. (1998). What processing is impaired in apperceptive agnosia? Evidence from normal subjects. *Journal of Cognitive Neuroscience, 10,* 568–580.

Vezzoli, J., Falchier, A., Jouve, B., Knoblauch, K., Young, M., & Kennedy, H. (2004). Quantitative analysis of connectivity in the visual cortex: extracting function from structure. *Neuroscientist, 10,* 476–482.

Waltz, D. L. (1975). Understanding line drawings of scenes with shadows. In P. H. Winston (Ed.), *Psychology of computer vision* (pp. 19–91). New York: McGraw-Hill.

Watson, J., Myers, R., Frackowiak, R., Hajnal, J., Woods, R., Mazziotta, J., et al. (1993). Area V5 of the human brain: Evidence from a combined study using positron emission tomography and magnetic resonance imaging. *Cerebral Cortex, 3,* 79–94.

Watson, J. B. (1913). Psychology as the behaviorist views it. *Psychological Review, 20,* 158–177.

Watson, J. B. (1928). *The ways of behaviorism.* New York: Harper & Brothers.

Wheeler, M. E., Petersen, S. E., & Buckner, R. L. (2000). Memory's echo: Vivid remembering reactivates sensory-specific cortex. *Proceedings of the National Academy of Sciences, USA, 97,* 11125–11129.

Williamson, A. (2002). Chronic psychosomatic pain alleviated by brief therapy. *Contemporary Hypnosis, 19,* 118–124.

Wilson, F. A. W., O'Scalaidhe, S. P., & Goldman-Rakic, P. S. (1993). Dissociation of object and spatial processing domains in primate prefrontal cortex. *Science, 260,* 1955–1958.

Winawer, J., Witthoft, N., Huk, A., & Boroditsky, L. (2005). Common mechanisms for processing of perceived, inferred, and imagined visual motion. *Journal of Vision, 5*(8), 491a.

Winston, P. H. (Ed.). (1975). *The psychology of computer vision.* New York: McGraw-Hill.

Winston, P. H. (1977). *Artificial intelligence.* Reading, MA: Addison-Wesley.

Wittgenstein, L. (1958). *Philosophical investigations.* New York: Macmillan.

Wraga, M., Thompson, W. L., Alpert, N. M., & Kosslyn, S. M. (2003). Implicit transfer of motor strategies in mental rotation. *Brain and Cognition, 52,* 135–143.

Zeki, S., & ffytche, D. H. (1998). The Riddoch Syndrome: insights into the neurobiology of conscious vision. *Brain, 121,* 25–45.

Author Index

Subject Index